D1592142

Norton Priory

Sandstone grave slab, found in the nave of the priory church, where it covered a wooden coffin. A tree of life, with oak leaves and acorns, grows from a cherubic face and is transformed into a cross.

The archaeology of a medieval
religious house

Norton
Priory

J. PATRICK GREENE

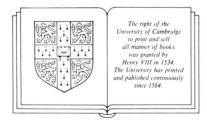

The right of the
University of Cambridge
to print and sell
all manner of books
was granted by
Henry VIII in 1534.
The University has printed
and published continuously
since 1584.

Cambridge University Press

Cambridge

New York   New Rochelle

Melbourne   Sydney

Published by the Press Syndicate of the University of Cambridge
The Pitt Building, Trumpington Street, Cambridge CB2 1RP
32 East 57th Street, New York, NY 10022, USA
10 Stamford Road, Oakleigh, Melbourne 3166, Australia

First published 1989

Printed in Great Britain by BAS Printers Ltd., Over Wallop

British Library cataloguing in publication data
Greene, J. Patrick
Norton Priory: the archaeology of a medieval religious house.
1. Norton Priory (Cheshire) 2. Christian antiquities–England–Norton
(Cheshire) 3. Excavation (Archaeology)–England–Norton (Cheshire)
I. Title
942.7'18   BR133.G73N/

Library of Congress cataloguing in publication data
Greene, J. Patrick
Norton Priory: the archaeology of a medieval religious house/
J. Patrick Greene.
        p.   cm.
Bibliography
Includes index.
ISBN   0-521-33054-8
1. Norton Priory (Norton, Cheshire) 2. Priories—England—Runcorn
(Cheshire)—History. 3. Augustinians—England—Runcorn (Cheshire)–
History. 4. Excavations (Archaeology)–England–Runcorn (Cheshire) 5.
Runcorn (Cheshire)–Church history. 6. Runcorn (Cheshire)–Antiqui-
ties. 7. England–Antiquities. 8. Christian antiquities–England–Runcorn
(Cheshire)   I. Title.
DA690. N878G74 1988
936.2'715–dc19   87-27637

ISBN 0 521 33054 8

Contents

To my wife Gill, with love

Illustrations

Fig. 1. Remains of the Georgian country house before excavation and restoration had started in 1971. This rusticated basement of the west front hid the medieval undercroft.

Fig. 2. Interior of the twelfth-century undercroft, before restoration, looking from the southern, rib vaulted bays to a dividing wall built in the thirteenth century, the door through which is blocked by nineteenth-century masonry.

Preface and acknowledgements

When I arrived at Norton Priory on 13 April 1971, it was to carry out a six-month excavation for Runcorn Development Corporation. The Development Corporation, engaged in the construction of a New Town, were keen to have a feature in the Town Park that would counteract the newness of their houses, factories, shops and roads. My expectation of the Town Park was very different from the reality. My preconception of neat municipal flower beds and carefully mown lawns through which elegant archaeological trenches might be sliced was shattered immediately. The parkland in fact consisted of some 200 hectares of fields and woods, with a canal. Norton Priory was concealed within these woods. The only structure that provided any reassurance that this might be an archaeological site was the sad remnant of a Georgian country house – just part of the basement, to which a Victorian porch had been added (fig. 1). Inside however, in the windowless gloom and decay, the heart beat faster. There was a magnificent, highly decorated, Norman doorway. Beyond that were three simple and attractive stone vaulted rooms – undoubtedly medieval (fig. 2).

The condition of the structure would have dismayed even the most ruin-hungry romantic artist. No tasteful wisps of ivy trailing over medieval tracery here – instead a battered Georgian shell around an eight hundred year old building that was now supporting (just) semi-mature trees that had become established on the 'roof', their roots infiltrating deeply the medieval lime mortar for their sustenance. The rich soil of what had once been gardens and pleasure grounds had now become a dense jungle of sycamore and *Rhododendron ponticum*.

During the previous summer Hugh Thompson, of the Society of Antiquaries, had penetrated the jungle with a dozen inmates from a local prison to cut a series of strategically placed trenches. These had revealed sufficient remains of walls to encourage the Development Corporation to go ahead with a larger investigation in 1971. That led to my six-month contract.

In fact, it was twelve years before I left Norton. That first season produced such exciting and rewarding results that the Development Corporation decided to press ahead with a large-scale excavation. The discovery of fine masonry walls, superb carved sandstone coffin lids, a remarkable mosaic tile floor, and a wealth of archaeological information generated widespread enthusiasm – not least in the prison workforce that carried out much of the work, with individuals who proved as adept at the intricacies of excavating human skeletons as they were at shifting huge quantities of garden soil and tree stumps.

The excavation eventually became the largest in area to be carried out by modern methods on any monastic site in Europe. As it proceeded, so too did accompanying historical and scientific research. To look into the past of such a little known archaeological site was, at first, to peer into a particularly dark and cloudy glass. As each season progressed, as the monastic buildings were gradually revealed, as each layer of soil was examined and removed, as each find was cleaned, identified and catalogued, as each historical reference to Norton was traced . . . so the image in the glass developed, at first faint and blurred, but then increasingly distinct and vivid. The image is of buildings being erected, embellished, enlarged, burning down, being repaired, being demolished and then replaced. It is of a landscape being shaped by the activities of its inhabitants, as subject to change as the buildings. Individuals also come into focus with all the variety, strengths and failings of humanity – pious, ambitious, corrupt, efficient, lax, violent, caring. In the pages that follow, some of these people will be introduced. Sometimes, through documents, we know their names, but others, although anonymous, are recognised by their craftsmanship and artistry with stone or clay.

Mortimer Wheeler was fond of saying that 'archaeology is nothing if it's not about people'. In the case of Norton, those people are not only the ones who are revealed by the archaeological and historical process. They are also people who, today, have contributed their labour to reveal the achievements of the past.

In the first season I was assisted in the direction of the excavation by Jan Roberts and in the second by Jennifer Laing. Subsequently Bevis Sale worked as assistant director throughout. His skills as surveyor and draughtsman were of particular value. Beryl Noake took responsibility for the finds, first as a volunteer, then as a full-time member of the team. Her role grew in importance as the quantity of finds and the amount of data accumulated.

From the beginning local volunteers were encouraged to participate and a skilled pool of helpers gradually developed (fig. 3). This group eventually became the

Norton Priory Society, a body which has given enormous assistance to the project in very many ways. In 1976 the first of a series of annual teaching excavations took place. They were open to all, organised in conjunction with the Institute of Extension Studies of Liverpool University. Peter Davey was instrumental in setting up the courses; he also provided assistance in a variety of other ways.

Runcorn Development Corporation, having initiated the project, backed it fully throughout. Roger Harrison, Chief Architect and Planning Officer, Derek Banwell and Ken Enderby, successive General Managers, took personal interest. Vere Arnold, the Development Corporation's Board Chairman, became Chairman of the Norton Priory Museum Trust when it was established in 1975. Other support came from a variety of educational establishments, research bodies and commercial companies whose contributions are acknowledged in the text. In the writing of this account my particular thanks are due to Dr Lawrence Butler of Leeds University for advice, criticism, and encouragement.

Fig. 3. Excavation in progress on the north east chapel in 1977. Visitors are watching the work from the site of the church; beyond is the west range undercroft.

Historical and archaeological research

Apart from a useful if idiosyncratic account of the history of Norton by William Beamont published in 1873, little historical research had been carried out prior to 1971. This can be explained partly by the absence of any surviving documentation for the priory. No cartulary (volume of charters) exists. From the outset it was clear that historical research had to complement archaeological excavations; both have been pursued by the writer. The research has consisted of spreading the net as widely as possible for references to Norton in documents and published sources. As a result, the many small pieces of information that have been amassed have gone some way to redressing the lack of Norton's own archive. The extent to which the evidence of documents and of archaeology have complemented one another has been particularly satisfying.

In the chapters which follow, the role of archaeology in investigating and elucidating the history of a little known monastic house will be described. Archaeology is here used in the sense of the broadly based discipline which it has become. Thus excavation and the evidence of artefacts provide only part of the material for study. Examination of structures and architectural details; scientific analysis of artefacts, plant and animal remains and soils;

xi

study of landscape from the air and on the ground – all these and many other techniques are part of the investigative process. There is no artificial divide between these and what might be conventionally considered as 'historical' sources of information such as written documents, maps and plans. The collection and correlation of evidence from as wide a spectrum of sources as possible provide the best means of investigating Norton Priory.

Fig. 4. The development sequence of the medieval priory.

The rediscovery of Norton Priory

The product of so many people's hard physical labour, methodical recording and analysis, and intellectual detective work, is a series of images of Norton Priory and its inhabitants. In the pages that follow the evidence will be set out, and interpreted. The story starts with the foundation of a priory at Runcorn in 1115 by a wealthy, powerful Norman, William fitz Nigel, baron of Halton. His son moved the Augustinian canons to Norton – a much more suitable location – in 1134. A dramatic growth in

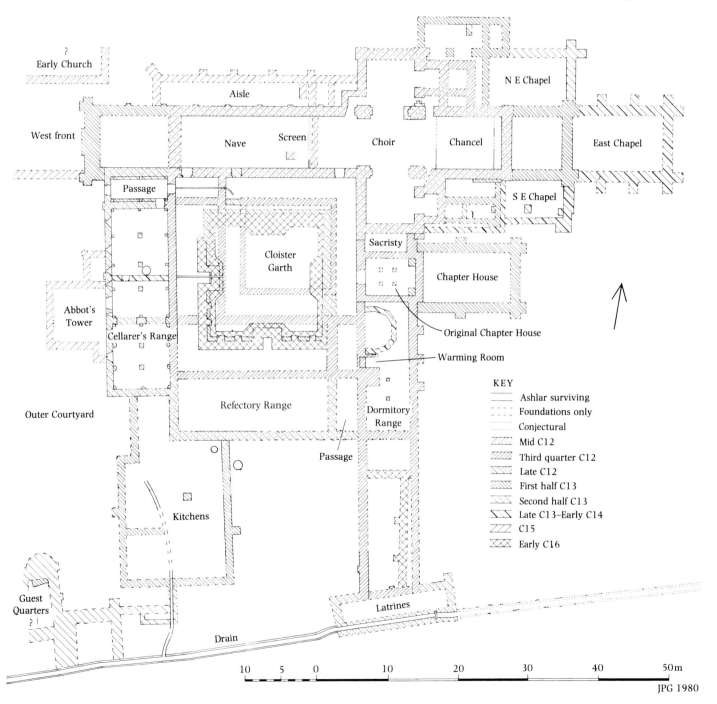

KEY
- Ashlar surviving
- Foundations only
- Conjectural
- Mid C12
- Third quarter C12
- Late C12
- First half C13
- Second half C13
- Late C13–Early C14
- C15
- Early C16

JPG 1980

the priory's possessions followed, fuelled by the piety and spiritual self-interest of the barons and their principal feudal lieutenants, the knights of the Dutton family. The priory became not only a place for prayers for the souls of deceased benefactors, but also the resting place of their mortal remains. The creation of a wonderful mosaic tile floor for the church can be linked with the Duttons' desire for embellishment of their burial chapel.

The landscape of Norton was profoundly affected by the ownership of the entire, extensive manor by the priory. The impact on the marshland of the Mersey, the woodland, villages, fields and roads was considerable. A picture of its appearance in the late medieval period begins to emerge. Equally fascinating is the way in which the products and resources of the manor were exploited – stone for the buildings, animals and crops to feed the canons, water for the kitchen and drains, for example.

The possession of large, productive land holdings gave the priory wealth and prestige. Mismanagement could nonetheless cause considerable problems, and the fortunes of the house fluctuated. Priors played an important role beyond the cloister. A high point was achieved in the late fourteenth century, when the priory was elevated to the status of an abbey, with the abbot entitled to wear a mitre. The credit for this unusual distinction for an Augustinian house can be found in the character and ambition of Prior Richard Wyche. By the time of the Dissolution, however, the activities of some of the canons, acting as vicars in neighbouring parish churches, was causing scandal. This provided one of the pretexts for closing the abbey – an event which itself was accompanied by circumstances that are lurid in their detail.

Discussion of the buildings of the priory (fig. 4) forms a substantial part of this book. This is the sort of information that archaeology is so good at revealing. It is possible to see how the very first buildings at Norton were erected – and to work out how the master mason set out the plan on the ground. Temporary wooden quarters for the canons were found. The dramatic expansion of the buildings is documented. The wonderful carved stone-work is described – and the origins of the master masons are investigated. A disastrous fire, the drama of casting a bell for the church, the creation of the mosaic tile floor – all these were revealed by the excavation. The opportunity to excavate a site such as Norton on a large scale over the dozen years that the project took reveals so much. How fortunate it was that this site was not the victim of a hurried rescue excavation in the face of an advancing bulldozer. Instead, the foresight of Runcorn Development Corporation enabled the remains to be restored, the site to be landscaped, and the surrounding woodland gardens to be re-established for the benefit of the public. The creation of a site museum by the Norton Priory Museum Trust ensured the preservation of the information derived from the excavation, and its presentation to the public in attractive exhibitions. Today, tens of thousands of people are drawn to visit Norton Priory every year. How the twelfth-century founders would have appreciated such pilgrimage.

1

Foundation and growth

The foundation at Runcorn

The Augustinian priory was originally founded at Runcorn in 1115 by the second baron of Halton, William fitz Nigel. Following the Norman conquest the earldom of Chester had been created, encompassing an area as large as the later county of Chester, but also controlling an area to the west of the Dee as far as the River Clwyd, and another area north of the Mersey as far as the River Ribble. Within his domain, the earl of Chester created eight barons whose principal manors were at Halton (Nigel), Malpas (Robert fitz Hugh), Mold (Robert of Montalt), Rhuddlan (Robert of Rhuddlan), Malbank or Nantwich (William Malbank), Kinderton Shipbrook (Richard Vernon), Dunham Massey (Hamon de Mascy) and Stockport (Gilbert de Venables) (Husain 1973, 112). Nigel and his successors were styled constable of Chester. As such they were second in command to the earl, and were charged with the duty of assembling his army when occasion demanded – usually for warfare in Wales.

The first earl of Chester, Hugh of Avranches, who was a nephew of King William, was responsible for the foundation of the first religious house within the earldom. A college of secular canons dedicated to St Werburgh had been established by Queen Aethelflaed in Chester in 907. Hugh refounded it as a Benedictine monastery. Anselm, abbot of Bec in Normandy, advised Hugh on the foundation and appointed one of his monks as the first abbot. The existing canons continued to hold their offices (Tait 1920, xxiv and 38). Hugh's monastery was therefore the successor of an existing institution, and he had a simple task in providing an endowment by granting the extensive possessions of the college, such as the valuable manors of Saighton, Ince and Sutton, to the new abbey (listed in Burne 1962, 196). To this were added various lesser grants from Hugh and others in the earldom,

including William fitz Nigel (*ibid.*, 197–201).

Hugh's motive in founding a monastery seems to have been the usual concern of a medieval magnate for his soul. The opportunity of founding a religious house whose inmates would be bound to pray for the eternal salvation of the founder's soul, and the souls of his family, was taken by many men of Hugh's rank. According to Eadmer's *Life of St Anselm*, the reason for the bishop's visit to Chester in 1092 was that Hugh was seriously ill (Burne 1962, 4). In the following year the abbey was founded, although in fact Hugh continued to live until 1101.

Twenty-one years later Runcorn Priory was founded, the second religious house in the earldom. The foundation charter (Tait 1939) makes it clear that once again a prominent churchman (Robert de Limesey, bishop of Chester) played an important part in persuading the founder. Again, the principal motive was one of spiritual survival, although appropriately William fitz Nigel included a charity obligation to the earl as well as himself and his family in the charter: 'for the salvation of the soul of Earl Hugh and of Earl Richard and of myself and my wife, and of my father and mother, my sons and daughters, my brothers and sisters, and all my ancestors and posterity' (Tait 1939, 22).

Another similarity between the two foundations is that, as at Chester, where an existing church formed the basis of a new monastery dedicated to a Saxon saint, Runcorn Priory was dedicated to the Saxon St Bertelin and in all probability was based on an existing church. Runcorn had been established as a burgh (a fortified stronghold) by Aethelflaed, Queen of the Mercians, in 915 according to the Mercian Register (Whitelock 1965, 64). Bertelin is a rather obscure saint, but he seems to have had connections in the Mercian heartland of Staffordshire. The only other known dedication to Bertelin is the church of Barthomley on the Cheshire–Staffordshire border. The reputed chapel of St Bertelin was excavated in 1954 to the west of the parish church of St Mary, Stafford – the town he is said to have founded.

In adapting an existing church as the basis for an Augustinian priory, Runcorn was by no means unique. Twenty Augustinian houses were based on previous collegiate establishments (Robinson 1980, 35–6). Robinson, following Dickinson 1950, considered the number founded at pre-existing parish churches as considerable (Robinson, 41). However, most of the evidence presented for this is circumstantial. The view that post-Dissolution use of a monastic church indicates that there was a church there when the monastery was founded is questionable. The case of Runcorn seems, on the basis of the dedication, a much more likely candidate than most.

Augustinian canons

It is interesting that William fitz Nigel chose the Augustinian order for his religious house, unlike the earl of

Chester who had chosen the Benedictines. The choice available to Hugh d'Avranches was limited to the Benedictines and the order which comprised the community of Cluny (introduced at Lewes in 1077). By the time that William fitz Nigel was contemplating the foundation of a religious house, the choice had been widened by the introduction into England of the canons regular of St Augustine. The development of the Rule, and its adoption by colleges of secular canons, was encouraged by the Gregorian reform movement. During the eleventh century it spread across much of Europe. It has been established that the first house of regular canons in England to adopt the Rule in the full Augustinian sense was Colchester, in 1104 or shortly afterwards (Dickinson 1950, 108). However, even during the medieval period, there was no certainty as to which Augustinian house had the distinction of being able to assert that it was 'first of the places of its order founded in England' – those words were used by Holy Trinity Aldgate (London) in a petition of 1451–2 to be granted Mitred Abbey status (*Cal. Papal Reg.* 10, 106, discussed in Greene 1979, 105). The foundation of Aldgate has in fact been dated to 1107, and another house that might have disputed Aldgate's claim is Huntingdon (Cambs.), founded shortly before 1108 (Dickinson 1950). Other early houses were Llanthony (Powys), founded soon after 1108, Barnwell (Cambs.), founded in 1112, Hexham (Northumberland) and Bridlington (Yorks.), both founded in 1113, and Merton (Surrey) and Nostell (Yorks.), 1114. Runcorn's foundation in 1115 therefore places it in the pioneer class of Augustinian priories. Eventually there were about two hundred Augustinian foundations in England – more than those of any other order (fig. 5).

William fitz Nigel's selection of the Augustinian order a little over a decade after its introduction, when there were still only ten or so Augustinian priories in England, shows that he was well informed as to developments in this field. The influence of two people can be detected in his choice. One was Robert de Limesey, bishop of Chester, whom the foundation charter specifically mentions as advising William fitz Nigel. Robert may have seen the Augustinian order as being particularly worthy of his support in that the inmates of Runcorn Priory, as canons, were subject to episcopal supervision (as the status of priory itself implied). Other bishops also encouraged the adoption of the Augustinian Rule, most notably Bishop Malachy who introduced it to Ireland as a means of bringing within reformed Latin practice clerks in holy orders and married priests.

The other person who may have influenced William fitz Nigel's choice was his cousin Walter de Gant. He had founded Bridlington Priory in 1113 (Farrer 1915, 2, 445) and of particular significance is the fact that William fitz Nigel was one of the benefactors of Bridlington, having given to it the church of Flamborough (Farrer 1915, 2, 193). Both Tait and Dickinson have suggested that the

first canons to occupy Runcorn Priory came from Bridlington (Tait 1939, 22; Dickinson 1950, 124) though the number that moved to Cheshire must have been small as Bridlington itself had so recently been established.

The status of William fitz Nigel – baron of Halton, and constable of Chester – accords well with the pattern of foundation of other Augustinian houses before 1135. Dickinson has shown that over seventy-five per cent of foundations in the early period were established by Henry I, officials of his court, or members of the royal entourage (Dickinson 1950, 129). William was not a member of that group, but as an important figure in the earldom of Chester, with extensive land holdings in many parts of England, he was certainly well able to provide his priory with an adequate endowment.

The move from Runcorn and foundation at Norton

The foundation charter of Norton Priory (Beamont 1873, 148–9; Ormerod 1882, 1, 691; both drawing on Leycester 1666) makes no mention of why, after nineteen years at Runcorn, the canons were transferred to Norton. The charter simply states that the move was made 'at the request and at the advice of Roger, bishop of Chester, and by the advice of my own people'. Two explanations can be

Fig. 5. Augustinian foundations in England and Wales. The location of Norton Priory is indicated by the cross symbol in north west England – a region with relatively few other Augustinian houses.

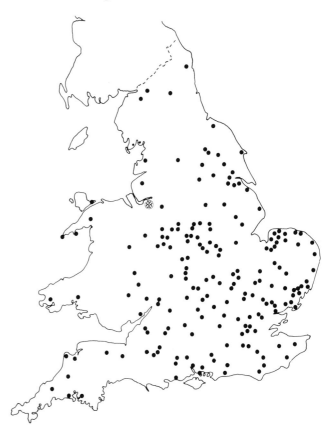

suggested. The first is that William fitz William, the founder's son and successor as baron of Halton, may have considered his father's alienation of the township of Runcorn a mistake for strategic reasons (Tait 1939, 14). The township was situated on the south bank of the River Mersey, where outcrops of sandstone on both banks narrow the river to form the Runcorn Gap. This was the only practical crossing point between Birkenhead at the mouth of the river, and Warrington further upriver, because elsewhere the Mersey was not only very wide, but it was also flanked by extensive marshland. Use of the Gap to control shipping on the Mersey was probably the reason for Aethelflaed's choice of the southern side for her burgh. The activities of the duke of Bridgewater, who removed the end of the promontory, the London Midland Railway Company, which used the promontory for constructing their railway bridge support, and finally the Manchester Ship Canal Company, which cut through the remainder of the promontory, have destroyed the remains of the burgh. Nonetheless, it is certain from various descriptions (such as Beamont 1873, 4) that this is where the burgh was situated. William fitz William may have considered it advisable to have this important point under his direct control.

The second explanation for the move to Norton is that the canons may have been influenced by the ascetic ideal of the Cistercian order. The similarly inclined Order of Savigny (amalgamated with the Cistercians in 1147) had founded their first English house at Tulketh near Preston (Lancs.) in 1123, moving to become the important abbey of Furness in 1127. Waverley, the first Cistercian house in England, was founded in 1128 (Brakspear 1905, 3) and the order spread rapidly – both Rievaulx and Fountains were established in 1132. By the time of Norton's foundation in 1134, the Cistercian emphasis on solitude of their communities for the greater sanctification of their members was becoming well known and admired. There was in any case an element within the Augustinian order that sought seclusion, exemplified most notably by Llanthony, which was established in a remote valley on the edge of the Black Mountains on the basis of an existing group of hermits (Craster 1963). When the canons of Runcorn moved, they left an established settlement for a part of Norton township that was one kilometre from the village of Norton and which archaeology and the evidence of plant remains have shown was a virgin site. A parallel can be drawn with the canons of Portchester, who moved away from their church so uncomfortably near a castle to the more tranquil setting of Southwick.

Twenty-one Augustinian houses changed sites, for a variety of reasons (Robinson 1980, 365). The moves usually involved only a modest distance, averaging 6 kilometres (3.7 miles) compared to the much larger average move for a Cistercian house of 29 kilometres (18 miles) (*ibid.*, 78). The move from Runcorn to Norton was only 4 kilometres.

The endowment of Runcorn (and subsequently Norton) Priory

In endowing a monastic house at its foundation, the intention of the donor was to provide capital assets and forms of income that would be sufficient to pay for the construction of the buildings, and to cover the running expenses. In the period before 1135 fifty-four Augustinian houses were established. Most had prominent founders who were able to provide substantial endowments. It is usually assumed, although direct evidence is in most cases lacking, that the minimum complement was twelve canons and a prior. In the case of the Cistercian order the minimum of thirteen undoubtedly applied, for it was specified in the Rule.

The endowment can be divided into two classes of assets, spiritual and temporal. Spiritualities included income derived from churches, which might provide pensions, gifts at shrines, burial gifts etc., and if the church was appropriated the rectorial tithes and often income from glebeland as well. The endowment also frequently included the gift of tithes, or a portion of the tithes, of manors held by the founder. Temporalities included gifts of land, ranging from small parcels to complete manors; mills or a proportion of the proceeds of manorial mills; urban properties; miscellaneous other income-producing properties such as fisheries, salt works and coalmines; and rights of various kinds, such as avoidance of tolls, rights of common, right to hold fairs, etc.

The foundation charter of Runcorn Priory listed the gifts that formed the canons' original endowment. For the sake of clarity these and subsequent gifts will be numbered consecutively (their location is shown in fig. 6). In the order in which they were listed in the 1115 charter, the original properties and privileges were:

1. All of Runcorn
2. The mill of Halton
3. Half the fisheries of Halton
4. Rights of common in woods, pastures and waters belonging to Halton
5. Half the baron's fishery at Thelwall, plus a bovate of land (about fifteen acres) and the fisherman
6. Two bovates of land in Widnes
7. Rights of common in the woods and pastures belonging to Appleton
8. Rights of common in the woods and pastures of Cuerdley
9. Two bovates of land in Halton and a house there
10. The mill of Barrow
11. Two thirds of the demesne tithes of Barrow
12. Two thirds of the demesne tithes of Guilden Sutton
13. Two thirds of the demesne tithes of Staining
14. Half the township of Staining (three ploughlands)
15. Two thirds of the demesne tithes of Stanney
16. Two thirds of the demesne tithes of Raby
17. A house in Chester

18. The church of Great Budworth
19. The church of Castle Donnington
20. The tithe of the mill of Castle Donnington
21. A ploughland in Castle Donnington, and half a ploughland called Wavertoft in the same township
22. The church of Ratcliffe on Soar
23. The church of Kneesall
24. The tithe of the mills of Kneesall which are near Southwell
25. The tithe of the mill of 'Alreton'
26. The church of Burton upon Stather
27. The church of Pirton
28. One and a half ploughlands in Clifton (i.e. half the township)

It was not only the baron who provided the endowment. His retainers were also encouraged to contribute from their holdings. Hugh, son of Odard, was one of the benefactors. He was a member of the family that was later to adopt the name Dutton. The Duttons became major landowners in the area and eventually the principal benefactors of the Priory. Hugh granted the canons a mill

jointly with his brother Gilbert, and Hugh alone gave a piece of land:

29. The mill of Walton
30. A furlong of land between Runcorn and Weston

Someone named Thurston (presumably the holder of one of the knight's fees in the barony) gave:

31. Two thirds of tithes of Sutton beyond the Mersey

The document states that the alms were given free of all services, customs, pleas and plaints.

Of the places mentioned, Runcorn, Halton, Thelwall, Clifton, Walton and Weston are all in north Cheshire along the south bank of the Mersey. Widnes, Appleton, Cuerdley and Sutton beyond the Mersey are all in south Lancashire. Barrow and Guilden Sutton are both near Chester, and Stanney and Raby are on the Wirral. Staining is in north Lancashire, Great Budworth is a large parish to the east of Runcorn, Castle Donnington is in Leicestershire, Ratcliffe on Soar and Kneesall are in Nottinghamshire. Burton on Stather is in Lincolnshire and Pirton is in Oxfordshire.

The total area of land comprised six ploughlands and five bovates in addition to Runcorn, which on the evidence of the Norton charter probably consisted of three ploughlands (a total in the region of 500 hectares or about

Fig. 6. The location of Norton Priory's properties.

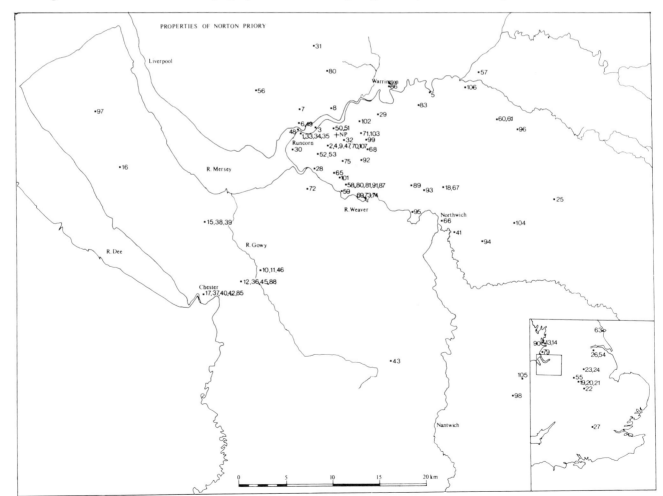

1,200 acres, if a bovate is assumed to be 15 acres – Tait 1939, 12).

The move to Norton involved a relatively simple adjustment of the original endowment. The new charter granted the canons the manor of Norton, and changed their habitation from Runcorn to Norton. In exchange for their new manor, the canons had to relinquish their three ploughlands in Staining (endowment number 14), one and a half ploughlands in Clifton (28 – which the charter mistakenly records as Aston) and the whole of Runcorn (1) with the exception of the church, half a ploughland and one fishery. The four new items listed in the Norton foundation charter are therefore:

32. The manor of Norton
33. The church of Runcorn
34. Half a ploughland in Runcorn
35. One fishery in Runcorn

The total exchange was seven ploughlands, according to a charter of confirmation issued by Henry II (Beamont 1873, 151). It must have been of great benefit to the canons, for by divesting themselves of their holding in the distant manor of Staining, and the two holdings in Runcorn and Clifton, they were able to acquire a single but extensive manor within which their new priory could be established. It is interesting to note that the figure of seven ploughlands mentioned in the Henry II charter is close to the Domesday assessment of Norton which in 1086 was stated to have 'land enough for six ploughs' (Tait 1920).

The date of the foundation of the priory at Norton is generally accepted as being 1134, which is the year given by the *Annales Cestrienses*, although the dates 1133 and 1135 have also sometimes been mentioned (Tait 1939, 2 – followed by Dickinson 1950; Knowles and Hadcock 1971, 168; and *VCH Chester* 3, 165).

Further gifts

William fitz William's foundation charter, whilst it confirmed existing grants and consolidated the greater part of the land holdings through exchange, did not bestow any extra gifts on the canons. However, as the twelfth century progressed a series of new and valuable benefactions took place. In most cases the precise date of a gift is not known, and it is through various charters of confirmation that the growth in the priory's possessions must be traced.

One particular grant is unusual and interesting. By 1144 or 1145 William fitz William was dead and had been succeeded as baron of Halton by the husband of his elder sister Agnes. Eustace fitz John had by his previous marriage added the baronies of Malton and Alnwick to his original inheritance of Knaresborough. The acquisition of the important barony of Halton extended his influence to the west of the Pennines. The constableship of Cheshire was conferred on him by Earl Randle Gernons, and it was while fighting in that office against the Welsh that he met

his death in 1157 (Beamont 1873, 11). It was therefore sometime during the period 1144–57 that the grant was made by Eustace fitz John to Hugh de Cathewic of pasturage for one hundred sheep 'upon condition that a final end is made of building the church at Norton in every part according to the first foundation of William fitz Nigel' (Tait 1939, 16). The identity of Hugh de Cathewic, and the implications of the wording of the grant, will be considered later. Of relevance to the subject of benefactors however, is the acknowledgement by Eustace fitz John of the role of patron, ensuring the completion of work originally planned by his predecessor, William fitz Nigel.

Monastic patronage was an activity with which Eustace fitz John was familiar. He founded four religious houses. The first was Augustinian – the Priory of St Mary at North Ferriby (East Yorks.), which he established in about 1140 (Knowles and Hadcock 1971, 168). His interest then changed to the Premonstratensian order, for in 1147 he founded Alnwick Abbey (Northumberland) (*ibid.*, 185). Three years later he chose the order of St Gilbert of Sempringham for two more foundations in Yorkshire, Malton Priory and Watton Priory (*ibid.*, 196 and 198). He had already, in 1133, provided emergency assistance to the starving monks at Fountains (Gilyard-Beer and Coppack, 1986, 149).

Apart from the pasturage grant to the master mason there are no specific references to gifts by Eustace fitz John to the priory. However, a charter issued by Henry II and witnessed by Richard de Beaumis, who was bishop of London from 1152 until 1163, lists a number of properties in addition to those mentioned in the foundation charter without specifying the donor (Beamont 1873, 151). Some may have been given by fitz John. The additional properties are:

36. Half the township of Guilden Sutton
37. The church of St Michael, Chester, with one house
38. Two bovates of land in Stanney
39. The tithe of the mill at Stanney
    The canons are said themselves to have bought:
40. Two houses in Chester
    In the case of three gifts, the donor is named. From the estate of Warren de Vernon, the canons were given:
41. Two bovates of land in Shurlach (Davenham parish)
    From the fee of the bishop of Chester they received:
42. One plot of land without the gate of the city of Chester
    From the fee of Robert de Stafford came:
43. One bovate of land in Calvedon

Endowments in the later twelfth century

The endowment of the priory continued to grow in the later part of the twelfth century. A number of new properties appear in a charter of confirmation which Earl Roger, the seventh baron of Halton, issued in about 1195 (dated by Barraclough 1957, 26; published by Beamont 1873, 162–3). The possessions and privileges with two exceptions are stated to have been given or confirmed by Earl Roger's ancestors; he succeeded to the barony in 1190. The additional items are:

44. The whole chaplainship of the constableship of Chester with all its appurtenances
45. One ploughland between Guilden Sutton and the bridge of Stamford, called Dunnescroft, with a meadow called Witaker
46. The tithe of a mill which John fitz Richard (the sixth baron) built on the dam of Barrow mill
47. The tithes of other mills which John built in his territory of Halton
48. The tenth part of the profits of Runcorn ferry
49. Half the demesne tithes of Widnes
50. The land which Gilbert Follis held, which is before the canon's gate
51. One parcel of land called Roger's Croft, between the canons' fishpool and Astmoor wood
52. Two deer from the baron's park at Halton each year at the Assumption of the Blessed Mary
53. Rights of the canons' swine to forage for mast with the baron's swine

It is clear that only the last two items are new grants by Earl Roger himself. In addition to the above, a number of gifts had been made by benefactors other than the baron's family. Roger fitz Alured gave for the soul of Leceline, his wife:

54. One house in Burton on Stather

The same Roger gave for the soul of Matilda, his wife:

55. One house in Derby

The charter lists other properties that had been granted by the knights of the barony, and confirmed by Earl Roger's ancestors:

56. One bovate of land in Tarbock
57. Two thirds of the demesne tithes of half of Warburton on Mersey
58. Two thirds of the demesne tithes of Aston held by Roger fitz Alured
59. One third of the tithe of the fisheries of Aston
60. The mill of Millington
61. One parcel land in Millington called Mulincroft

The charter repeats the usual formula discharging the canons from all secular sevices, but mentions for the first time:

62. The right of the canons to hold their own court

In only three cases are the gifts made by people other than the baron's family attributed by name – numbers 54, 55 and 58, all of which were given by Roger fitz Alured, who was related by marriage to the Duttons (see below).

It can probably be asssumed that number 59 was also given by fitz Alured. The grant of a bovate of land in Tarbock, number 56, was renewed by Robert de Tarbock in the late thirteenth century (*VCH Lancashire* 3, 177) and

was presumably a gift made by one of his ancestors. The donor of tithes in Warburton (number 57) was probably a member of the Dutton family, which held land there.

It is fortunate that a later charter of confirmation obtained from Edward III in 1329 names the donor of the Millington properties (numbers 60 and 61) as Wrono Punterling (Beamont 1873, 171). He had been given half the manor by John, constable of Chester, in the reign of Henry II; the grant, which was witnessed by Hugh Dutton and his son Adam, names him as Wrono of Stretton, a manor near Millington, which must have been his main possession (Ormerod 1882, 1, 447).

The total endowment listed in the charter of 1195 represents a considerable expansion compared to the properties and privileges listed in the 1115 and 1134 foundation charters. This is of particular significance when the evidence of the excavation is considered. It was in the late twelfth century and at the beginning of the thirteenth that Norton Priory underwent a massive expansion. The evidence is that the number of canons was doubled, with buildings erected capable of housing two dozen or so brethren. To finance the new building programme, and to provide for the increased running costs of the community, extra endowments would have been needed; the evidence of the charters is that such support was indeed forthcoming.

The increase in the endowment of the priory is clear when each of the categories of possession or privilege is compared:

1134	1195
Seven churches	Eight churches
Two houses	Five houses
Three mills, and a quarter of another	Four mills, and a quarter of another
Tithes of four mills	Tithes of (at least) eight mills
A proportion of tithes of six manors	A proportion of tithes of nine manors
Eight parcels of land	Seventeen parcels of land
Rights of common in three townships	Rights of common in four townships
One fishery, and half of two other fisheries	One fishery, half each of two other fisheries, and a proportion of tithes of another
	The chaplainship of the constableship
	One tenth of the profits of Runcorn ferry
	Two deer each year

The relationship of Norton Priory with the barons of Halton after 1200

By the end of the twelfth century the pattern of new endowment for Norton Priory was beginning to change. Since 1115 the initiative had lain with the founders, and their successors as barons of Halton, who continued to act as patrons. It was they who provided Norton with its substantial endowment, mainly by direct gift but also through the encouragement of their knightly retainers. By 1200 however the flow of gifts from the patrons had slowed to a trickle, and henceforth the barons of Halton played little part in the development of the priory.

One reason for this was the establishment, in 1178, of the Cistercian abbey of Stanlow by John fitz Richard, the sixth baron of Halton. Stanlow became the burial place of

Fig. 7. Skeleton of a man who had suffered from Paget's disease. The coffin lid with shields (fig. 8) sealed this coffin; the bones are *in situ*. Note the collapsed cranium, and the burial of the corpse with forearms crossed.

the barons, whose graves are said to have been removed to Whalley when the monks moved there in 1296 (*VCH Lancashire* 2, 131–3). The location at Stanlow, established with Cistercian fervour in a particularly inhospitable spot on the fringe of the Mersey estuary, proved too severe. Whalley was eventually granted to the monks by Henry de Lacy. As the place of burial, Stanlow had a clear advantage over Norton when further benefaction was being considered.

There is no evidence that any of the five barons who died after the foundation of Runcorn Priory in 1115 and before the foundation of Stanlow Abbey were buried at Runcorn (in the case of William fitz Nigel) or at Norton (in the case of William fitz William and his successors). William fitz Nigel was apparently buried at Chester (Beamont 1873, 9), and his son, who died in Normandy (*ibid.*, 11) was probably buried there. Eustace fitz John may have been buried at Norton, but it seems more likely that his body was taken to one of the religious houses he himself had founded. The burial place of his son, Richard is not known; it was Richard's son, John, who founded Stanlow, but he died in Palestine in 1190 while taking part in the Third Crusade (Barraclough 1957, 19).

Only two members of the baronial family are definitely known to have been buried at Norton. One was Richard, the brother of Roger, the seventh baron, buried at Norton in 1211 (*ibid.*, 164). Richard was a leper, and it is possible that he had spent his last days in the priory infirmary. Leprosy was a term which covered a great many diseases in the medieval period, and there is a possibility that one of the graves excavated within the nave of the church was that of Richard. In a sandstone coffin with an impressively carved lid was the skeleton of a man who had suffered from Paget's disease, a cancer which affects the structure of the bone of the skull (fig. 7). In this case the skull had become thickened and spongy, and the anterior lobes had collapsed. The coffin lid (fig. 8) was carved in relief with a cross within a roundel, the shaft terminating in a simple calvary. On either side of the shaft, also in relief, was a shield – a symbol of a knight. Alongside this grave was another sandstone grave slab that had covered the position of a wooden coffin with a sword (another knight symbol) carved in relief alongside the cross shaft. Nearby were two more grave slabs, one plain and the other of twelfth-century type with an incised cross, and an incised rectangle (representing the book of a cleric?). The group of coffins was situated on the south side of the nave, near the screen which separated it from the choir. In front of the screen were the fragmentary remains of an altar. Thus although the identification of the occupant of the coffin with shields with Richard must be tentative, the possibility does exist that it was he who was buried in the nave chapel.

The second person associated with the baronial family known to have been buried at Norton Priory was

Alice, niece of William, Earl Warenne, the sixth earl of Surrey, who granted the prior of Norton in order to maintain a pittance for her soul:

63. Thirty shillings a year from Sewerby (Yorks.)

Knowledge of the grant is due to an entry in the *Calendar of Close Rolls 1323–1327* (page 245) for 16 December 1324, when the rent was in arrears. The date of the original grant must be before 1240. Alice was probably a daughter of Ela, sister of William of Warenne (1202–40) (Clay 1949, 233–4). Ela married Robert de Lacy, who died in 1193. She was dowered in various lands in the Lacy fee (Clay 1949, 21). As a member of the family of the baron of Halton Alice presumably lived in the vicinity of Norton.

The involvement of the barons of Halton with other religious houses, particularly Stanlow, was one of the reasons why the flow of benefactions to Norton Priory from that source ceased in the late twelfth century.

Fig. 8. Coffin lids, one with shields and another with a sword (the latter damaged in the nineteenth century) found in the nave. The cross and sides of the large lid are expertly carved, the shields less so.

Successive holders of the title had in any case provided Norton with a generous endowment. There was another reason however for their interest to slacken. The descent of the barons was marked by union with other titles (ultimately with the House of Lancaster) through marriage or inheritance, which had the consequence of weakening the link with Halton.

When Norton Priory was granted the status of abbey by Pope Boniface IX in 1391 John of Gaunt, duke of Lancaster, was named as patron, and petitioner with the prior and convent of Norton to Boniface (*Cal. Papal Reg.* 4, 405). Two centuries after endowments from the barons had ceased, John of Gaunt was still prepared to acknowledge his hereditary role as patron, and was willing to lend his weight to Norton's petition to Rome.

The Dutton family and Norton Priory

The involvement of the Duttons with the priory began with gifts from Hugh, son of Odard, and his brother Gilbert as part of the original endowment (numbers 29 and 31). As the interest of the barons of Halton waned in the late twelfth century, the Dutton family assumed the role of principal benefactors of the priory. There were two main branches, one living at Dutton itself, the other at Sutton Weaver. Parts of the manor house at Sutton still exist. Hidden by the brick exterior of the large farmhouse of Sutton Hall Farm is a large timber-framed building. In the attics of the farmhouse are substantial remains of a fifteenth-century camber-beam roof, with windbraced rafters and purlins forming a pattern of quatrefoils. There can be little doubt that this manor house was one of the homes of the branch of the family that moved to Warburton and assumed that name. The branch originated in Adam de Dutton, the younger son of Hugh de Dutton, and grandson of Hugh fitz Odard. Adam possessed all of Warburton in the time of Richard I (Ormerod 1882, 1, 567). He cleared land near Stockham, which was granted to him by the canons of Norton, *c.* 1195–1205 (Barraclough 1957, 24–6). In return, he agreed to pay a rent at the feast of St Bertelin of:

64. Twelve pence each year

Adam also gave to the canons of Norton (Ormerod 1882, 1, 728):

65. Three shillings yearly from his mill at Sutton and after his death the mill itself
66. A salt house in Northwich (Barraclough 1957, 21)

It seems likely that he was the donor of the tithes of half of Warburton (number 57), and was no doubt influential in securing the support of his father-in-law, Roger fitz Alured (numbers 54, 55, 58 and perhaps 59). He died in about 1205 (*ibid.*, 21). Adam's successors retained the name Dutton until Peter Dutton made Warburton the principal manor in about 1300; henceforth they adopted the name of Warburton (Leycester 1666 in Ormerod 1882, 1, 642).

The main branch of the family lived at Dutton itself, though Hugh, son of Odard, must have had a dwelling at Keckwick, for it was there that he was visited on his deathbed by his lord William fitz Nigel and his son William. He surrendered his coat of mail and war-horse, and William fitz William was given a riding horse and a hawk; Hugh's son, Hugh, was confirmed in his inheritance (Ormerod 1882, 1, 690). It is the latter who appears to have been commonly called Hugh de Dutton, so perhaps it was during his lifetime that the manor house at Dutton was established.

It has been suggested that the baron of Halton, like Robert fitz Hugh of Malpas, had ten knights (Husain 1973, 105). Of the ten, the Dutton line seems to have been pre-eminent. Odard's original holding in Dutton (the largest of three parts) was held directly of the earl. His other holdings in the four townships of Halton, Aston, Weston and Whitley were held of the baron of Halton; Barraclough comments:

'among the Cheshire tenants of the constables of Chester none were more outstanding than the Duttons'(Barraclough 1957, 20).

The association of the two branches of the Dutton family with Norton Priory was strengthened during the thirteenth century by the provision of chaplains for two family chapels. Sir Thomas de Dutton built a chapel at Poolsey, a part of the township of Dutton situated on the north bank of the River Weaver. The name is derived from the position between the park pool and the river on a virtual island (Dodgson 1970, 113); in Leycester's time the chapel was still in existence but was described as being ruinous. Sir Thomas obtained permission for mass to be celebrated in the chapel, and in 1236 the prior covenanted with Hugh fitz Hugh de Dutton to find him a chaplain there for ever (Ormerod 1882, 1, 643). Twenty-six years later a similar agreement was made to permit the celebration of divine offices in the manor house at Sutton Weaver. Prior Roger and his convent granted the licence to Sir Geoffrey de Dutton, with the proviso that in the great festivals of the church his family were to attend the parish church at Runcorn and there make their offerings. The chaplain at his first entrance was to swear to be faithful to the church, and in no way defraud her. Sir Geoffrey and his wife, in the chapter house at Norton before the whole convent and many others, swore to observe the agreement (Beamont 1873, 166). It is interesting to note that the chapter house was used for this purpose, and that even a prominent benefactor was expected to present himself at the priory to swear to observe the terms that had been agreed.

Sometime in the reign of Henry III, Geoffrey de Dutton had made a grant to Norton Priory of:

67. One third of the lands of Budworth

The grant was made on the condition that the canons should pray for his soul for ever more (Ormerod

1882, 1, 605). This was a valuable gift in the centre of the parish where they already possessed the church.

In 1290 licence for another Dutton gift was granted by Edward I. Peter de Dutton was permitted to grant the prior and convent (*Cal. Patent Rolls* 54, No. 41, p. 336):

68. A dwelling and fourteen acres in Newton near Preston on the Hill

Relations with benefactors were not always smooth. In 1315 it was necessary for Sir Hugh de Dutton to complain to the bishop of Lichfield and Coventry's officers that the prior and convent had not provided a chaplain and a lamp at Poolsey chapel acccording to the agreement of 1236. The prior was ordered to correct the situation (Beamont 1873, 170). This dispute does not appear to have caused lasting harm, for in 1329 recent gifts from Hugh de Dutton's son, another Hugh, were licensed under the Act of Mortmain. They comprised:

69. Two shillings and eight pence from the rent of Poolsey
70. Four shillings from the land of John the Digger of Halton
71. Timber from the wood of Keckwick to repair the mill of Keckwick
72. Land in Frodsham with its appurtenances
73. Land in Poolsey with the chapel
74. All the cleared land in Poolsey and pasture there for sixty beasts

The gifts are stated to have been made before the publication of the Statute of Mortmain, which placed restrictions on gifts to the Church (Beamont 1873, 171). The total amount of land that the canons acquired in Poolsey was substantial – in a later document it is described as the 'manor of Poolsey in Dutton' (Beamont 1873, 178). It is likely that the grant of the chapel at Poolsey to the canons was a result of Thomas de Dutton's addition of a chapel to the manor house at Dutton in 1272 (Anon. 1901, ix). The new chapel would have been much more convenient, and it is likely that the privileges previously granted to the Poolsey chapel were transferred to it.

Burial of the Duttons at Norton

The gifts that were confirmed in 1329 are the last big donations to the priory by the Dutton family for which records exist. Later gifts are minor in comparison, taking the form of bequests linked with burial of the donor at the priory, or specific requests for prayers for the dead.

There are three wills in which Norton Priory is specified as the intended burial place of a member of the Dutton family. The earliest is dated 1392, in which Lawrence de Dutton bequeathed his body to be buried at Norton, giving his black horse to the convent of Norton as a heriot (a death gift), also sixteen torches and five tapers about his body on burial day, with sixteen poor men in gowns to carry the lights, also ten marks to the poor, and thirty pounds to sufficient chaplains to celebrate for his

soul the next year, two in the church of Budworth and four in the chapel at Dutton (Ormerod 1882, 1, 648).

Lawrence de Dutton makes no large donation to the canons – his only gift is his black horse. Instead of requiring the canons to pray for his soul, he makes arrangements for six chaplains to carry out the task at Budworth and Dutton. Of particular interest is the information the will contains about the form of the funeral, clearly a solemnly impressive ceremony.

The will of a member of the second branch of the Dutton family was made on 1 September 1448. Sir Geoffrey Warburton wished to be buried within the monastery at Norton, between the high chancel and the chapel of the blessed Mary. He left to the priest celebrating before his tomb for the year one hundred shillings; to the abbot of Norton he left his best horse; to Thomas de Sutton (chaplain at the Sutton Weaver manor house?) one hundred shillings out of the farm of his church at Wrexham to celebrate for his soul for a year; and he left one hundred shillings to John Humbleton, chaplain, for the same purpose (Ormerod 1882, 1, 572).

There are a number of interesting aspects of this will. One is the reference to the 'chapel of the blessed Mary', the location of which will be discussed later. Provision for prayers to be said for his soul consists of money payments (at the same rate as in Lawrence de Dutton's will) to three named clerics; there is no general gift to the abbey. The abbot is to receive a heriot in the form of Sir Geoffrey's best horse, a similar gift to that received on the death of Lawrence de Dutton.

One person, not buried at Norton, nonetheless bequeathed money. Lady Strangways, the wife of Sir Richard Strangways, died in a friary in York in 1500. She had previously been married to Roger Dutton, and bequeathed ten marks to Norton for prayers for her soul and that of her first husband (*Testamenta Eboracensia* 4, Surtees Soc. 53, 1868, 188).

The third will of a person buried at Norton to have survived is that of Lady Strangways's son, Sir Lawrence de Dutton, made on 4 October 1527. In the will he stated:

I bequeath my soul to Almighty God, beseeching humbly our Blessed Lady, and all the holy company of heaven, to be mediators for me to the Holy Trinity, to receive the same to the eternal bliss of heaven. And I will that my body shall be buried and interred amongst my ancestors in the chapel of our Blessed Lady within the monastery of Norton. And I will that every priest that shall be at my burying shall have, to pray for my soul, twelve pence, and every clerk, four pence, and every poor man and woman one penny.

In addition he left money for the 'reparation and ornamentation' of Budworth church, and a gift to the mother church of Coventry and Lichfield (transcript Chester Record Office EDA 2/1.15b).

Again in this will there is reference to a Lady Chapel, which is regarded as the traditional burial place of the family. The rate of payment to priests and others praying for the soul of the deceased (admittedly not specified as

Fig. 9. Burials in the north east chapel. Wooden coffins had been used for these burials of members, almost certainly, of the Dutton family. The skeleton of a child is a reminder of high infant mortality levels in the medieval period.

being for one year) is much smaller than in Sir Geoffrey Warburton's will made in the previous century. No heriot is promised and there is no general bequest to the canons.

It is unfortunate that no more than three wills of those buried at Norton exist. However, the three do demonstrate that descendants (calling themselves Dutton and Warburton) of Hugh, son of Odard, a benefactor at the foundation of the priory at Runcorn, expected centuries later to be buried within the monastery. Indeed it is likely

that the great majority of the 140 burials that have been excavated at Norton belonged not to the canons, but to their lay benefactors.

The most impressive group of burials was found in the chapel that was built in the angle between the east side of the north transept and the north side of the chancel (fig. 9). The great visual impact of the burials when excavated was created by the presence of many sandstone coffins in

Fig. 10. Coffins in the western (earlier) part of the north east chapel. Most are made from single blocks of sandstone, shaped to accommodate a corpse, others consist of slabs of sandstone.

the western part of the chapel (fig. 10). Ornately carved lids still covered a number of the coffins (figs. 76, 77). Confirmation that this was the burial chapel of the Duttons was provided by the discovery of an unusual and important group of floor tiles.

None of the tiles were found *in situ*. Some, in garden soil, had been disturbed by eighteenth- and nineteenth-century digging. Others were in the (rather slight) demolition deposits. Others were in the fill of graves in the chapel. The 'special' tiles belonged to a line-impressed mosaic floor made at the beginning of the fourteenth century. Over most of the eastern part of the church, and

the chapter house, the floor consisted of bands of geometric pattern. The special tiles occurred in only three locations. The majority came from the chapel. One special tile was found associated with the chapter house. The remainder were wasters (defective tiles) found during the excavation of a tile kiln, and had such an affinity with those in the chapel area that it is reasonable to assume

that they had been intended for that location. There is therefore a firm association between the special tiles and the north transept chapels. The tiles can be divided into five groups:

1. Elements of large mosaic lions
2. Elements of one or more panels of picture mosaic
3. Rectangular tiles bearing parts of one or more inscriptions
4. Tiles with a surface decoration intended to represent chain mail
5. Tiles that formed part of heraldic shields

Fig. 11. Tiles associated with burials in the north east chapels. In the centre is the Dutton coat of arms, at the top is part of a marginal inscription, and surrounding are four 'chain mail' tiles.

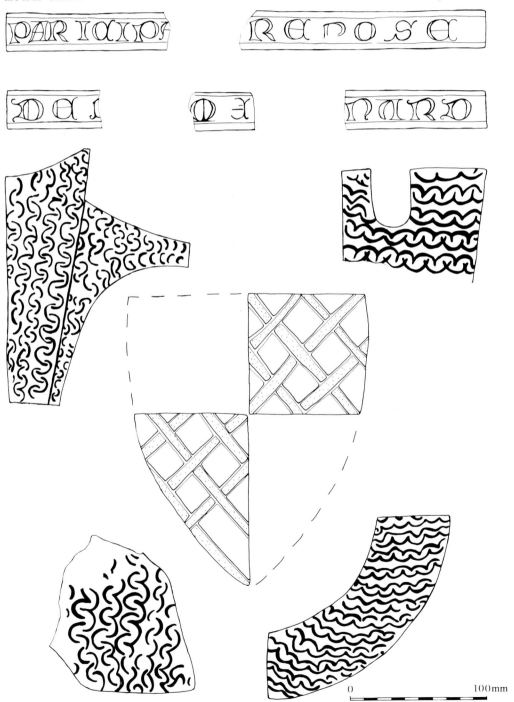

The first two groups of tiles, and the affinities of the floor as a whole, are described later. It is groups 3, 4 and 5 that are of particular relevance to the subject of the burial of the Duttons, for all would seem to be part of tiled grave covers (fig. 11). Rectangular tiles with finely drawn Lombardic lettering must have formed a marginal inscription around a grave cover. Three waster fragments from the kiln read PAR ICI P(ASSEZ) . . . REPOSE – part of a standard formula requesting prayers for the soul of the individual lying in the grave from those passing by. The chain mail tiles must have been assembled to form one or more lifesize figures of knights in the manner of a memorial brass; doubtless the marginal inscription was intended to form the surround of the figure. A waster tile bearing a design intended to represent a crocketted canopy is also likely to have been part of a grave cover – it is another feature frequently found on brass memorials. The tiles that were part of heraldic shields provide conclusive evidence that this was the burial place of the Duttons. Pieces of at least three small shields, 0.2 m high, came from the chapel, and from the kiln parts of a large shield about 0.5 m high. All bore the fret that was the characteristic feature of the Dutton coat of arms: *quarterly argent and gules, in the second and third quarters a fret or.* The tiles indicate that at the beginning of the fourteenth century the north transept chapels were provided with a fine tile floor, incorporating picture mosaic and one or more tile tomb covers representing a knight with a marginal inscription in French, and heraldic references to the priory's principal benefactor, the Duttons. It is probable that it was the Duttons who provided the finance for the installation of the complete floor which was such a striking embellishment for the church and the chapter house.

Visual reminders of the Duttons' patronage were not restricted to the tile floor. According to a survey of Cheshire heraldry made in 1572, the Dutton arms were to be seen in the windows at Norton Abbey along with those of other local families (Anon. 1901). Similarly, Great Budworth church, owned as it was by Norton, was the subject of Dutton patronage. One of the Randle Holme family visited the church in 1568 and noted the heraldry in the window glass (British Library Harleian MS, 2151, f.71). Lawrence de Dutton, whose will made in 1527 was quoted above, gave a window to the church which contained the arms of Dutton, and the figure of a knight wearing the arms on the coat and shield. The tower of Great Budworth church bears the Dutton arms, with those of Warburton and Norton Priory, repeated several times above the west door.

Other aspects of Norton Priory's relationship with the Duttons

The relationship between the priory and the Duttons was not restricted to the role of provider of burial places,

prayers and a chaplain for the manorial chapel on the one hand, and benefactors on the other. Both were large landowners whose lands in many cases shared a common boundary. By the Dissolution the Warburton and Dutton landholdings were considerable: Leycester described the latter's demesne as being 'the largest and best within our country' (Ormerod 1882, 1, 642). Adam de Dutton's clearance near Stockham is an example of two neighbouring landowners needing to resolve a problem of land of uncertain ownership (Barraclough 1957, 24–6). Later agreements involved such matters as the lease of the corn tithes of Appleton to Sir Geoffrey de Warburton for a year in 1371 (Beamont 1873, 175), repeated for six years in 1381 (*ibid.,* 178), and the lease of Poolsey to Sir Peter Dutton for ten years in 1430 (*ibid.,* 178). There were probably many more examples of the Warburtons and the Duttons renting Norton lands, the records of which have not survived.

It is in this context that the part Sir Piers Dutton played in the Dissolution of Norton Abbey must be seen. He was a member of the Hatton branch of the family, and had engaged in seven years of litigation to claim the inheritance of the Dutton lands following the death without issue of Lawrence Dutton, whose will has been described above. The daughters and co-heirs of Lawrence's uncle, Sir Thomas Dutton who had been killed at the battle of Blore Heath in 1459, had also claimed the inheritance. The dispute was settled in favour of Sir Piers Dutton in 1534 by Henry VIII (Leycester 1666, in Ormerod 1882, 1 649). The following year Sir Piers was made a Royal Commissioner for the County of Chester, and also specifically for Frodsham Deanery (*Valor Ecclesiasticus* 5, 209–10). The manner in which he carried out his task with regard to the valuation of Norton Abbey, and the events at the time of the dissolution of Norton (particularly an attempt at perjured evidence against the abbot) raise many questions about Dutton's attitude to the abbey. These will be dealt with in detail later, but it can be suggested that Dutton intended to acquire the Norton lands. They were alongside his own, some had been rented by Duttons, and a substantial proportion of them had been given by Duttons in the first place. He was clearly not a man of sentiment, and in any case his dispute with the descendants of Lawrence probably lessened any compunction he may have felt about encouraging the closure of the abbey that was their traditional burial place. It is nonetheless ironical that Hugh, son of Odard, ancestor of the Duttons, was one of the founders of the monastery of Norton, and Sir Piers Dutton was prime mover in its closure. As one of the commissioners, Sir Piers recorded, among the alms of the priory, a stipend of 100 shillings for prayers for the souls of the founder – and Hugh Dutton.

The pedigree of the Duttons of Dutton

Odard
(first mentioned in Domesday, 1086)
Hugh
(whose lands were confirmed directly by the earl of
Chester)
founder benefactor, with his brother Gilbert, of Runcorn
Priory in 1115
Hugh de Dutton
(who received confirmation of his lands from William fitz
Nigel at his father's deathbed)
Hugh Dutton
(his brothers were Adam, who founded the Warburton
line, and Geoffrey who was ancestor
of the Duttons of Cheadle). He married the daughter of
Hamon Mascy, baron of Dunham Massey
Hugh Dutton
(built Poolsey chapel in 1236; died without issue. His
younger brother succeeded him;
he also had brothers John and Adam)
Thomas Dutton
(was living in 1249, built the chapel at the Dutton
manor house;
married Phillipa daughter of Vivian de Sandon)
Hugh Dutton
(had brothers Thomas and Robert; married Joan,
daughter of Sir Urian de Sancto Petro;
he died in 1294)
Hugh de Dutton
(born 1276, married Joan, daughter of Sir Robert
Holland, the steward of Halton; died 1326)
Thomas Dutton
(born 1314; made governor, seneschal and receiver of
Halton; founded a chantry in Warrington friary
in 1379; a Sheriff of Cheshire and a knight; died 1381)
Lawrence Dutton
(married Alice and then Margaret but had no surviving
issue; died and was buried at Norton 1392.
He was a knight and Sheriff of Cheshire. The inheritance
passed to the son of his brother Edmund)
Peter Dutton
(married Elizabeth, daughter of Sir William Boteler of
Bewsey, the lord of Warrington;
knight and deputy seneschal of Cheshire; died in 1433.
His first son died during his lifetime,
so his second son succeeded him).
John Dutton
(married Margaret, daughter of Sir John Savage of
Clifton, died 1445)
Thomas Dutton
(married Anne, the eldest daughter of James, Lord
Audley; he and his son, Peter, were slain at
the battle of Blore Heath in 1459; his second son
succeeded)

John Dutton
(married Margaret, daughter of Richard Molyneux of
Sefton; made steward of the abbot of Norton
for life in 1459 for the fee of £3 per annum. Died
without issue, so he was succeeded by his uncle,
the younger brother of Thomas Dutton)
Roger Dutton
(married Joan, daughter of Sir Richard Aston; died in
1499 and she then married Sir Richard Strangways)
Lawrence Dutton
(married Joan, daughter of Robert Duckenfield; died
1527 without issue; buried at Norton.
Law suits between Piers Dutton of Hatton, and
daughters and co-heirs of Sir Thomas Dutton
lasted seven years, eventually decided in favour of Sir
Piers)
Piers Dutton
(possessed the Dutton estate from 1534; involved as a
royal commissioner in the closure of Norton Abbey)

The Aston family and Norton Priory

The principal gift from the Aston family was made in the
time of King John, when Richard fitz Gilbert de Aston gave
to Norton Priory:
   75. 'all his land in Hendeley, with all its appurtenances'
       (Ormerod 1882, 1, 680)
    The identification of Hendeley with Eanley, and its
location and extent, will be discussed later. It suffices to say
here that Eanley was situated in the south east corner of
the manor of Norton, within which it became an integral
part.
    The gift of Eanley was not made purely out of piety
and concern for Aston souls. A dispute in the fourteenth
century provides an interesting description of a corrody (a
perpetual commitment) that the canons of Norton had
granted the Astons – probably in return for the gift of
Eanley. In 1354 it was stated that Sir Richard Aston,
knight, Hugh and Richard his sons, and Sir Robert Aston,
knight, father of Sir Richard Aston, possessed a corrody at
Norton. Under its terms, 'each of them had the finding of a
yeoman and a page, with three horses, a brace of
greyhounds and a goshawk, according to their estate,
with their chambers, and such easements as belonged to
their degree; all of which the priors of the said monastery
(considering the great possessions that had been given to
them from the lordship of Aston) had always consented to,
granted and yielded as their right of old time granted'
(Ormerod 1882, 1, 722). The terms are onerous for the
canons; as hunting personnel and animals were lodged at
the priory it cannot have been conducive to a spiritual
atmosphere. The 'great possessions' seem to have been
dearly acquired.
    Another source of friction was the chapel of Aston.
In 1425 Richard, son of Sir Robert Aston, was forced to
complain that the chapel of Aston was out of repair and

services were intermittent. The archdeacon of Chester ordered the abbot and convent to redress the evil following the mediation of Thomas Dutton and his wife (Leycester 1666, in Ormerod 1882, 1, 720).

There is no documentary or archaeological evidence that members of the Aston family were buried at Norton. The family became established at Aston by the reign of Henry II when Gilbert de Aston, father of the donor of Eanley, acquired the township. The family held it by a continuous line of descent throughout the medieval period (*ibid.*, 720). The arms of Aston were amongst those recorded at Norton in 1572 (Bostock's Collections, Harleian MS. 139). The chancel of Runcorn church contained, in the seventeenth century, two stones, one bearing the inscription 'Hic jacet Rics Aston, miles, qui obit Ano dni (1493)' and one for Matilda Aston (British Library Harleian MSS. 2129 and 2151). Runcorn church rather than Norton Priory may therefore have been the traditional burial place for the family.

Other miscellaneous gifts and acquisitions

So far in this account of the properties of Norton all the gifts of the barons of Halton have been listed, as well as those given by others and confirmed in the barons' charters, and also various additional gifts by the families of Dutton, Warburton and Aston. There remains a collection of other miscellaneous properties, the donor and date of gift of which are sometimes known, but which in many cases lack these details. They are dealt with briefly here.

The first three benefactions to be described all concern rights and privileges given to the canons. In 1232 or before, a charter (British Library Harleian MS. 280 f. 78) was obtained from the earl of Chester which:

76. Freed the priory from all taxes, aids and works in castles

Whether this privilege was simply given, or granted to the canons in exchange for payment is not known. Two charters (Ormerod 1882) were obtained from Henry III, one of which granted the priory:

77. Exemption from various taxes, duties and secular services

The other granted the canons:

78. Exemption from all salt passage and customs

This must have been a useful privilege in view of Norton's ownership of one of the Northwich salthouses (number 66).

In about 1200, Ralph de Diva, prior of the Hospitallers, gave to Norton Priory:

79. Stotfoldshaw near Ormskirk (Kuerden MSS. 11, 269b, n. 80 quoted in *VCH Lancashire* 3, 281)

At a similar date Richard de Bold, who paid scutage (feudal dues) in 1201, granted to the priory of Norton (*VCH Lancashire* 3, 403):

80. A ridding (an area of farmland cleared from the waste) in Bold

In the late thirteenth century an agreement was made with Vale Royal Abbey for Norton Priory to assume responsibility for the chapel of Middle Aston, where the monks of Vale Royal were committed to ensuring that divine service was celebrated three days a week. In return for the payment to Vale Royal of forty shillings yearly, and for causing mass to be celebrated on Sundays, Wednesdays and Fridays for ever, Norton acquired:

81. Two bovates of land in Middle Aston, with all tithes of the township, fisheries, commons etc., except for small tithes, oblations and mortuaries (donations) (Beamont 1873, 167)

Norton had already been given:

82. Land in Middle Aston

The donor was Mathilda, the widow of Collini de Loches. It was confirmed by John Lacy, the eighth baron in about 1236; he granted the canons acquittance from all services due from that land (Ormerod 1882, 1, 720).

In about 1300 Norton must have been given:

83. The church of Grappenhall

The circumstances of the grant of the church, which is in Cheshire to the south east of Warrington, are unclear. Norton appears in the records as patron (though not rector) in 1302, 1311, 1346, 1377, 1423 and 1450. In 1460 however the connection was severed (Ormerod 1882, 1, 600) although Norton still received a pension from Grappenhall at the Dissolution (*Valor* 5, 209).

Throughout the twelfth and thirteenth centuries all the gifts to the priory were in the form of properties, tithes, rents or privileges. One record of a gift of money dates from the beginning of the fourteenth century. In 1306, William Danyers of Daresbury left the priory and convent of Norton, as part of his will, the sum of:

84. Twenty shillings (Ormerod 1882, 1, 733)

Other gifts of money associated mainly with burial have already been mentioned in connection with Dutton and Warburton wills. It is not known where the Danyers family (who owned Daresbury at least from the beginning of the fourteenth century) were buried. However, grave slabs bearing floriated crosses and swords were noted in the seventeenth century at the parochial chapel of Daresbury (British Library Harleian MS. 2151, 108).

In 1352 a jury found that the priory was entitled to:

85. Rent of twelve pence from land and tenements in Northgate Street, Chester, which had been granted by the earl of Chester (Jones 1957, 95, quoting PRO Chester C/1 23 Ed. 111)

In 1390 the Boteler Annals mentioned another urban property of Norton's that must have been acquired some time previously (Beamont 1873, 176):

86. One burgage in Warrington

This may be the same property as 'Marbury's land' which Norton owned in Warrington (*VCH Lancashire* 3, 322).

Other sources of information about Norton's properties

There are general sources of information about monastic properties that provide a guide to those of Norton's possessions that have escaped notice in records of Norton itself. The earliest is the so-called Pope Nicholas IV Taxation of 1291, by which Edward I was enabled to collect tenths of ecclesiastical income to finance a crusade to the Holy Land. An edition of the 1291 Taxation was published by the Record Commission in 1802, unfortunately in a form which is very difficult to use. The index in particular is notoriously unreliable, and this is no less true in the case of Norton than for other religious houses. Thus Robinson, in listing Augustinian spiritualities noted in 1291, was unable to find any churches owned by Norton, and only pensions from Donnington, Kneesall, and Radcliff, and a portion from Poulton le Fylde (Robinson 1980, 415). Important possessions like Runcorn, Great Budworth and Pirton do not appear in the index references to Norton, nor are they listed in the text under Norton Priory itself. By diligent search however it is possible to find them assessed within their deaconries. As a means of discovering otherwise unknown properties of Norton this is clearly unsatisfactory.

The entry for Norton Priory itself however does have its value as it lists a number of temporal properties and their annual worth (*Pope Nicholas Taxation* 259). Some have been encountered previously, others are new items – they are numbered accordingly:

Middle Aston – £1 0s 0d (82)
and in the same place two carucates (areas of land) with an annual value each of 10 shillings (81)
and a fishery there worth 6s 8d (81), and

87. a mill with the value of 8 shillings
and meadowland worth 1 shilling (81/82)
Frodsham – two carucates with an annual value of 10 shillings each (72)
Guilden Sutton – two carucates with an annual value each of 15 shillings (36)
annual rent of £2 10s 0d (36)

88. a mill with the value of £1 0s 0d
Walton – a mill with the value of 11 shillings (29)

89. Coggeshall – a mill with the value of 13s 4d
The sum of the above is given as ten pounds, with the tenth assessed at one pound.

The surprising aspect of this entry in the Taxation is that it is detailed about a few of Norton's properties, but it omits a much greater number altogether. With a valuation of its temporalities of only ten pounds, and consequently an assessment of just one pound, Norton succeeded in escaping the burden of taxation lightly.

The ecclesiastical properties of Norton that can be traced in the Pope Nicholas Taxation do not add anything to what is already known from other sources; their values in 1291 are given in the appendix listing all the properties.

There is one exception however. In the list of spiritualities it is recorded that Norton received:

90. A portion of two pounds from Poulton (le Fylde) (*Pope Nicholas Taxation* 307b, repeated 309)
It is possible that this item is identical with the tithes of Staining (number 13) which is within Poulton parish.

The *Valor Ecclesiasticus* and the Suppression or Ministers' Accounts

Apart from the Pope Nicholas Taxation of 1291, the only other general surveys of monastic income available are those drawn up at the Dissolution. In the case of Norton, there are discrepancies between the two sixteenth-century documents. The list of properties in the *Valor* (vol. 5, pp. 209–10 of the published version cover Norton) are given in full here, with their values. The commissioners for Frodsham deanery, who therefore assessed Norton, were directed by Sir Piers Dutton. In the list of temporalities that are given here, the number of each of those that has been noticed so far in the text is given in brackets. Properties not previously encountered are assigned numbers.

	£	s	d
Cheshire:			
Norton (32)	45	1	11
Walton (29)	1	0	0
Stockham (32)	5	0	0
Runcorn (34, 35)	3	0	0
Halton (2, 9)	1	5	4
91. Aston	8	11	4
92. Preston	0	8	0
Newton (68)	1	19	0
Moore (102)	0	12	7
Budworth (67)	8	9	6
93. Comberbach	4	0	0
Northwich (66)	1	10	0
94. Lache	3	0	0
Shurlache (41)	0	13	4
Nether Peover (104)	0	6	0
Cogshall (89)	0	2	0
95. Barnton	0	2	6
Guilden Sutton (36, 38)	16	6	6
Frodsham (72)	0	18	4
96. Rostherne	0	16	0
Great Barrow (10)	0	10	0
97. Landican	0	10	0
Millington (60, 61)	0	3	4
98. Haslynton	1	10	0
99. Daresbury	0	9	0
	106	4	8
City of Chester:			
Rent per annum (17, 85)	4	13	4
Lancashire:			
Rent in Warrington (86)	0	4	4
Rent in Tarbock (56)	0	10	4
	0	14	8

Yorkshire:

	£	s	d
Rent in Sewerby (63)	1	10	0
Total (temporalities)	£113	2	8

The spiritualities listed in the *Valor* were as follows:

	£	s	d
Cheshire:			
Budworth rectory (tithes, oblations, etc.) (18)	58	0	0
Runcorn rectory (gross) (1, 33)	38	11	0
Guilden Sutton (great tithes) (15)	2	0	0
Grappenhall (pension) (83)	0	2	0
Warburton (great tithes) (57)	0	16	0
	99	9	0
Oxfordshire:			
Pirton rectory (gross) (27)	22	0	0
Lancashire:			
100. Halfield (great tithes)	1	0	0
Sutton (great tithes) (31)	1	0	0
Lincolnshire:			
Burton rectory (gross) (18)	6	0	0
Leicestershire:			
Donnington rectory (gross) (19)	16	0	0
	46	0	0
Total (spiritualities)	£145	9	0
Grand Total	£258	11	8

Expenses totalled £78 4s 1d, leaving a net income of £180 7s 7d, bringing Norton within the list of those to be dissolved, with an income of less than £200.

It would have been very surprising if records of the gift of all of Norton's properties had survived. In fact, ten of the properties listed by the *Valor* commissioners are new items, at least under the name used to record them.

The *Valor Ecclesiasticus* is clearly a very useful list of Norton's income-producing assets, but it is surpassed in quality by the Augmentation Office Ministers' Accounts drawn up immediately following the dissolution of Norton (PRO SC6/Henry VIII/410 26259). A summary of this was published by Beamont (1873, 194–5) and a fuller account was given by Selby (1882, 102–5). The writer has examined the complete record himself – the documents survive in an excellent state.

The main heads of the items in the account refer to the following places, with their values (again, the numbers of all those that have been recorded so far are given in brackets, and new items are assigned numbers).

	£	s	d
Site of the abbey and demesne (32)	42	16	0
Pasture to farm once in the abbey demesne (32)	3	12	0
Norton, rent and farm (32)	22	3	$4\frac{1}{4}$
Aston, rent and farm (91)	12	5	4
101. Aston by Sutton, rent	0	2	0*
Halton, rent and farm (2, 9)	2	8	0
102. Moore, rent and farm	1	13	6
Preston, one tenement (92)	0	7	0
Guilden Sutton, rent etc. (36, 88)	20	15	8
City of Chester, rent (17, 85)	0	15	8
Walton, water mill (29)	1	0	0
Newton, land and tenement etc. (68)	1	19	0
Daresbury, farm, land etc. (99)	0	9	0
103. Keckwick, rent from antiquity for providing a lamp	0	4	0*
Stockham, rent from 7 tenements (32)	9	19	1
Runcorn abbot (Lower Runcorn) tenement etc. (34, 35)	3	1	4
Northwich, saltworks etc. (66)	3	5	8
Lache Dennis, land (94)	2	0	0
104. Nether Peover	0	6	0
Budworth (67), Comberbach (93), Shurlach (41), and Barnton (95), diverse premises	17	2	8
Landican, rent (97)	0	10	0
Frodsham, rent (72)	0	18	4
Rosthorne, one messuage (96)	0	16	0
Millington, one mill (60)	1	0	0
105. Wynstanley, one messuage	1	10	0*
Warrington, rent (86)	0	4	4
106. Bold (80) Penkrich and Rowsiche	0	1	0*
Tarbock, rent (56)	0	6	8
Stotfield Shaw, rent (79)	0	4	0*
107. Oldegreve by Lymm, rent	0	3	4*
Sewerby, alms (63)	1	10	0
Runcorn rectory (1, 33)	50	15	0
Budworth rectory (18)	82	2	8
Guilden Sutton, tithes (15)	2	0	0
Halfield (100) and Sutton beyond the Mersey (31), tithes	2	0	0
108. Haltonfield and Astmoorfield, tithes	0	5	0*
Pirton, rectory (27)	26	0	0
Donnington, rectory (19)	20	0	0
Burton Stather, rectory (18)	6	0	0
Pensions (83?)	1	2	0
Sale of wood		nil	
Perquisites		nil	
	£343	13	$7\frac{1}{4}$

Those items marked with an asterisk are the ones which are mentioned in the Ministers' Accounts but not in the *Valor*. Their total value is only £2 9s 4d, and therefore do not account for the great disparity between the two assessments of income (£343 13s 7¼d against £258 11s 8d). The difference is mainly made up of markedly different assessments for the manor of Norton (£68 11s 4¼d against £45 1s 11d); Runcorn rectory (£50 15s 0d against £38 11s 0d) and Budworth rectory (£82 2s 8d against £58 0s 0d).

It is inconceivable that the annual value of these possessions could have altered so radically in the short time between the two surveys. It follows that the difference can be accounted for only if it is assumed either that the valuation took place on the basis of different standards of assessment, or that the figures were deliberately modified during some stage of the process of collection.

The first alternative may be the correct explanation. For England as a whole the assessed values in the *Valor* and those in the Ministers' Accounts show a 27.8% rise (Robinson 1980, 137). The difference in the case of Norton is 33%. The reason may be that the Crown stood to benefit from higher assessments when it came to selling the possessions of the dissolved houses, though this might be expected to show itself in the assessment of temporalities rather than spiritualities, which account for a substantial part of the Norton increase.

Alternatively, it is possible that the valuation for Norton was deliberately lowered by the *Valor* commissioners to bring it within the net of those with an annual income of less than £200, and therefore ripe for closure (Knowles and Hadcock 1971, 168). The commissioners found expenses of £78 4s 1d, leaving just £180 7s 7d net (*Valor* 210). It is tempting to see Sir Piers Dutton, one of the two royal commissioners for the county of Chester, as the person most likely to falsify the figures. He was involved in the assessment of Norton itself as the leading commissioner for the deanery of Frodsham. A substantial part of Norton's endowment had been given by the family to which, after protracted litigation, he became heir. His own extensive landholdings bordered those of the abbey at many points. He had already arrested Thomas Birkenhead, the abbot of Norton, on a charge of forgery, had been forced to release him, and was subsequently to re-arrest him and would present perjured evidence, unsuccessfully, against the abbot. His career was marked by numerous similar incidents, including involvement in murder. He could have profited considerably by the closure of Norton had he been granted the abbey's lands. The manipulation of the figures in the assessment of Norton, either to bring it within the £200 income range, or simply to make acquisition from the Crown cheaper, would be one of Dutton's lesser misdemeanours. It must be emphasised however that evidence of malpractice in the assessment of Norton by Sir Piers Dutton is entirely circumstantial, and the more prosaic explanation put forward above may be the correct one.

One of the last gifts that Norton Abbey is known to have received was, ironically, from Henry VIII. He signed, to make into a warrant, a request by Abbot William Merton (abbot from 1510 to 1517) for permission to take thirty oaks from Delamere Forest, for repairs to Norton (conversion to boards and shingles) following the 'misfortune of fire' (Cheshire Record Office, DAR/G/50/1).

A comparison between the endowment of Norton Priory and that of other Augustinian houses

David Robinson, in his study of the geography of Augustinian settlement, has drawn together a considerable body of information about Augustinian houses and their possessions and finances (Robinson 1980). The study provides a useful measure against which the particular circumstances of Norton Priory can be compared.

It has already been mentioned in this account that Runcorn (later Norton) Priory was, like most of the other Augustinian houses before 1135, founded by a person of considerable rank and with a generous endowment. As the great majority of Norton's endowment came from the baron of Halton and his retainers, the distribution of properties is largely a reflection of the extent of the barony. Norton's spiritual possessions, especially its churches, were consequently widely spread. Pirton was 145 miles (250 km) from Norton; Burton Stather was 85 miles (140 km); Radcliffe on Soar was 75 miles (120 km); Kneesall was 70 miles (110 km); Castle Donnington was 65 miles (100 km). The Cheshire churches were St Michael's Chester, 14 miles (23 km); Grappenhall, 6 miles (9 km); Great Budworth, 8 miles (13 km) and Runcorn, 2 miles (4 km). Thus five out of the nine churches that Norton owned at some stage of its history were in no sense local, and of the five appropriated churches still owned at the Dissolution, three (60%) were at a considerable distance. This contrasts with the national situation in which less than 16% of appropriated churches were more than 30 miles from their mother house (Robinson 1980, 222).

It is more difficult to assess the extent to which Norton's ownership of manors and granges conformed to the norm. According to Robinson 115 houses listed in the *Valor*, the Ministers' Accounts or elsewhere possessed 747 manors at the Dissolution. Thirty-six houses however had none (Robinson 1980, 313). Norton is credited with no manors or granges but Aston, Great Budworth, Guilden Sutton, Norton and Stockham are listed in Appendix 28 (*ibid.*, 496) as 'Lands, Tenements or Rents assessed at over £5'; twenty-two other properties valued under £5 are also mentioned. The difficulty must arise as a result of definition of what is a grange or manor, and the vagueness of medieval use of the terms – indeed Robinson states that by 1535 the distinction between the two was far from clear. Many properties listed in the *Valor* as manors appear in the Ministers' Accounts as granges and vice versa. In the case of Norton the *Valor* uses neither term, but as we have seen Norton and Stockham comprised a manor in every characteristic, while Middle Aston is described in some accounts as a grange. The substantial holdings in Guilden Sutton and Great Budworth must be considered in the same category. The term 'grange' would appear to refer to large farms which might originally have been run directly by the priory, but which by the Dissolution were rented out, and is not used in the early Cistercian sense of monastic property run by lay brothers (Platt 1969). The glebe land belonging to two of the more distant churches, Pirton and Castle Donnington, provided a nucleus around which holdings of at least partly manorial status had developed. This was a widespread characteristic of the possessions of Augustinian houses (Robinson 1980, 311). Thus Norton had in fact six units of land that can be regarded as being either of manor or grange status. This is of the same order as the average (6.5 per house) for the 115 monasteries for which Robinson has calculated total holdings (*ibid.*, 313). The manor of Norton remained the canons' most extensive and valuable temporal property throughout the history of the house.

According to the *Valor*, the yield of Norton's possessions was in total less than the national average. In the *Valor* Norton's net income was £180, which compares with an average net income for 154 Augustinian houses of £203, and for Cistercian houses of £233 (*ibid.*, 128). In both cases only about twenty per cent had values greater than £300. The remarkable discrepancy between the *Valor*'s assessment of Norton's income and that in the Ministers' Accounts creates a rather different impression. Norton's income in the latter survey totalled £319 compared to an average for 117 houses of £262 (*ibid.*, 392). Norton was therefore one of only twenty-eight per cent of Augustinian houses with a value greater than £300 in this survey.

When the income from spiritual possessions is compared to that from temporalities for all houses for which the figures are available, the value of the former to the Augustinian order is clear. Thirty-six per cent of Augustinian income was derived from spiritualities in 1535, compared to twenty per cent for all the orders at that date (*ibid.*, 273). In the specific case of Norton, the situation is still more extreme. Again using the *Valor* figures, fifty-six per cent of net income was derived from spiritualities (precisely the same proportion is revealed by the Ministers' Accounts). The average figure for 124 Augustinian houses was £68 net (*ibid.*, 208) but despite Norton's overall *Valor* assessment being lower than average, its spiritual income was £98 net.

At the Dissolution Norton possessed five appropriated churches. The average number for Augustinian houses was 7.1. The fact that a much higher than average income was derived from a lower number of churches is a reflection of the wealth of four of the churches. The average national value of appropriated churches has been calculated at £11 14s 0d (*ibid.*, 256). Burton on Stather was below this level according to the *Valor* (£6), but Donnington was valued at £16, Pirton at £22, Runcorn £38 11s 0d, and Budworth £58. The Ministers' Accounts valued them even more highly. Budworth was still £6 but Donnington was £20, Pirton £26, Runcorn £50 15s 0d and Budworth £82 2s 8d. The possession of the two enormous multi-township Cheshire parishes in particular more than compensated for Norton's lower than average total number of appropriated churches.

The means of exploitation of land owned by Augustinian houses has been examined in a number of cases where detail survives for a sufficient span of time (Robinson 1980, 296). There appears to have been a fairly widespread change in the method of estate exploitation during the later Middle Ages away from demesne farming (i.e. directly, as a manorial estate) towards renting and leasing. The decline of demesne farming through the grange system in particular has been studied (Platt 1969, 94–117). By about 1300 the leasing of granges to lay tenants was familiar, and a century later it was widespread. The change to leasing did not mean the end of monastic demesne farming however. Most monastic houses retained at least a home farm in hand to supply the needs of the establishment. In the case of Norton little is known of the priory's land management policy for all but its last years. The detail in the Ministers' Accounts however provides a clear picture of the situation at the time of the Dissolution. It has been calculated for a sample of thirty-one Augustinian houses listed in the *Valor* that only 17.7 per cent of gross temporal income was from lands still held in demesne in 1535 (Robinson 1980, 298). In the case of Norton, practically all the temporal possessions apart from the manor of Norton itself were being rented or leased. In the entry in the Ministers' Accounts for Guilden Sutton, for example, the land was being rented or leased by twelve different persons. None was kept in hand by Norton. However, there is no sign of a rush to lease out Norton's lands on the eve of the Dissolution. The three Guilden Sutton leases had all been signed in the third year of Henry VIII (1511), two with terms of 51 years, one with a term of 24 years. The year 1511 is one that occurs in a number of the other leases listed in the Ministers' Accounts for Norton – presumably the decision was taken in that year to put out to lease a substantial number of properties, though it may also be a year in which a batch of earlier leases came up for renewal. The only lease known to the writer to have been signed shortly before the Dissolution, on 1 February 1534, conveyed a property in Norton already in the possession of one Agnes Fletcher to Robert and Margaret Jannyns (PRO E303/1/

62). This however was certainly not disposal of demesne.

Norton's demesne land lay entirely within the manor of Norton. Its extent and boundaries will be discussed later. Its annual value was £42 16s out of a total value of temporal properties of £145 14s 3¼d (excluding mills, saltworks and urban property). Thus 29.5 per cent of the income of Norton's land came from its demesne, compared to the national average of 17.7 per cent. Generally it was those houses with very large home farms that derived a higher than average proportional income from their demesne (Robinson 1980, 299); this was certainly the case with Norton.

The Ministers' Accounts reveal that just as most temporal properties were leased or rented, so too were sources of spiritual income. In Great Budworth parish, the great tithes of townships such as Barnton, Anderton, Marbury, Budworth itself, Aston near Budworth, Warburton, Tabley, Pickmere, Crawley, Stretton, Lower Whitley, Appleton, Marston, Little Leigh and Bartington were all farmed out for fixed yearly fees. The lessees were all local landowners.

The leasing and renting of temporal property and spiritual assets would have had considerable advantages for Norton. By converting the variable production of the land into fixed money rents, the hazards of poor harvests were avoided, and the level of income was predictable. It was also administratively much simpler to employ a bailiff to be responsible for collecting rents from each locality than to be involved in the management of each agricultural unit, or in the collection of tithes.

Eight bailiffs are named in the *Valor* amongst the expenses of the abbey. John Jannyn, who received £3 6s 8d, appears to have been the bailiff of the abbey demesne. Three bailiffs are listed whose responsibility is not specified – John Birked, £3 6s 8d; William Malbon, £2 0s 0d; John Smethurst, £2 0s 0d. Four more are listed with their office; Thomas Davy of Pirton, £2 0s 0d; John, parson of Donnington, £1 0s 0d; William Williamson of Burton, 10s 0d; William Wright of Aston (presumably Middle Aston), 6s 8d – he also received £1 6s 8d for unspecified duties.

In the late thirteenth century Norton is likely to have had a shrine. The restoration of speech and sight by the 'holy cross of Norton' was recorded in the annals of Whalley Abbey for the year 1287 (Taylor 1912). The chapel added to the east end of the church in about 1300 may have been built to house a shrine for the miracle-working relic. No income from a shrine is recorded at the Dissolution, however. This need occasion no surprise, for by then the age of lucrative shrines had ceased. Even the shrine of St John at the Augustinian priory at Bridlington did not warrant a reference in the *Valor*. Walsingham, also Augustinian, was the spectacular exception, with an income of £260 from its shrines (Robinson 1980, 257).

Summary

William fitz Nigel's foundation of an Augustinian priory at Runcorn was a pioneering act, establishing only the second religious house in the earldom of Chester, and introducing to the north west an order that was still relatively new to England. The original endowment of the priory at Runcorn was a generous one, and provided the canons with many of the properties that over the following four centuries were to prove most valuable, in particular the churches of Runcorn, Great Budworth, Castle Donnington, Pirton, and to a lesser extent Burton Stather. Their true value however was fully realised only when they had been fully appropriated, and in particular when canons of Norton were permitted to act as vicars. The two other churches in the original endowment, Kneesall and Ratcliffe on Soar, had to be disposed of when the priory got into financial difficulties. Norton's other two churches, St Michael's, Chester, and Grappenhall, were both acquired after the move to Norton; like the Nottinghamshire churches they were not fully appropriated and were disposed of in due course.

The important land holdings owe their origin more to the refoundation of the priory at Norton than to the original endowment, although the land in Castle Donnington continued to be a useful manor. The granting of the whole of the large manor of Norton was an important development – to have this major land holding where the priory was situated was a great asset, particularly when so many religious houses took decades or centuries to aggregate their holdings into manageable manors. The next chapter will examine in detail the landscape and settlements of the manor of Norton.

By the second half of the twelfth century Norton had been given half of Guilden Sutton by one of the barons of Halton – a gift that was added to by the end of the century. Again, this formed a financially valuable, compact unit.

From the late twelfth century the two branches of the Duttons became the major supporters of Norton. The 'manor' of Poolsey was one land gift from the family, but by the Dissolution it had reverted to their ownership. A gift which remained as one of the canons' possessions however was one third of Budworth.

Middle Aston (Middleton Grange) was another substantial but compact land holding, acquired by gift from Mathilda, wife of Collini de Loches, in the early thirteenth century, and added to at the end of the century through agreement by the canons to serve the chapel there.

The various land holdings required bailiffs, whose remuneration is recorded in the *Valor*. The largest single expense connected with land ownership was £7 0s 0d for 'diverse operations for defence against the sea' – doubtless construction and maintenance of the embankment along the south bank of the Mersey to protect the reclaimed northern part of the manor of Norton.

Urban property formed only a small part of Norton's income. Chester accounted for most; Warrington was the only other town where Norton held property at the Dissolution. Land was also held in Frodsham and Halton townships whose settlements both had a degree of borough status, but the property there can hardly be described as urban.

Norton's substantial endowment of properties and spiritual possessions provided the means to increase the number of canons, and to expand and embellish the buildings. The basis of wealth also enabled the priory to recover from the financial mismanagement of the fourteenth century to achieve Abbey status. In the end however, whether through miscalculation or as a result of deliberate underestimation of its income, Norton was unable to escape the first round of suppression in 1536.

2

The landscape and settlements of the manor

Changes during the last two centuries

The landscape of the manor of Norton, like the landscape of most areas of England, has been subject to a process of gradual transformation. The changes that occurred during the medieval period were followed by other alterations which in the last two hundred years have been of a more drastic nature. Whereas the earlier effects on the landscape were alterations to the surface appearance, many of the changes which have occurred since the mid-eighteenth century have been of a kind that involved earth-moving on a large scale. Thus, to attempt to investigate the medieval landscape of Norton, it is first necessary to describe some of the more recent changes that have left their mark upon it (the situation in 1843 is shown on fig. 12).

In 1770 the duke of Bridgewater decided to construct a canal from Manchester to Runcorn. The canal would permit traffic to pass between Liverpool and Manchester avoiding the tidal and navigational problems of the Mersey and Irwell Navigation. This event was revolutionary in national terms, as the success of the canal was the catalyst that led to the canal boom that swept England. It was no less revolutionary in its effect on the manor of Norton. Until this time the changes which occurred within the manor were ones that were initiated by the owners of Norton Priory (the canons and subsequently the Brooke family) and their tenants. The duke of Bridgewater's attempt to cut a canal across the estate was a new situation, which was resisted with vigour by the fourth baronet. Sir Richard Brooke engaged the duke in a war of litigation taken all the way to the Palace of Westminster. When parliamentary tactics by a coalition of landowners, MPs and peers failed to preserve the inviolability of a gentleman's pleasure grounds, obstruction by litigation (usually by disputing compensation terms)

was initiated. Brooke managed to hold out for six years before conceding defeat, though with the duke's debts nearing £250,000 by 1776 when the canal opened (Malet 1977, 179) victory was almost within his grasp.

The cutting of the contour canal was an enormous undertaking. As well as digging the broad trench for the canal, embankments had to be built, towpaths, bridges and wharfs constructed, and streams culverted under the canal – Brooke denied Bridgewater any water from his land.

The effect was to usher in a period of rapid change in the landscape. Within a generation, the pattern of small fields in scattered tenancies was replaced by one of large fields with straight, surveyed boundaries held in compact tenurial blocks. The contrast is vividly illustrated by comparing the J.E. 1757 estate map (fig. 14, p. 27) with the situation shown on the estate maps in Dunn's book (1806–11) and the 1843 Tithe Map (fig. 12). Similar changes in field patterns occurred during the eighteenth and nineteenth centuries on a wide scale throughout England, but it is probably no coincidence that in the case of the Norton estate, rationalisation followed hard on the heels of the construction of the canal. The reasons are probably twofold. The canal cut a swathe through the small fields, and the complexity of agreements on compensation for Brooke's tenants with their scattered holdings could have provided the impetus for reorganisation. The second factor may have been the compensation paid by the duke – this could have provided the means by which the introduction of a new system of estate management was financed. In addition, the physical impact of the canal was such as to require a new approach to the areas it affected.

The next major impact on the landscape was the construction of the Grand Junction Railway in 1837. A second railway, the Warrington and Chester Railway, was opened in 1850; part of its route was tunnelled through the estate. The two railways were set on embankments and in cuttings in the south east part of the manor.

The north of the manor was affected by a second canal. The Latchford Canal (also known as the Old Quay Canal) was built as a rival to the Bridgewater Canal, and superseded the Mersey and Irwell Navigation. Whereas the latter was essentially a modified form of river passage, with all the problems of a tidal river, the new undertaking was a genuine canal, following a course alongside the Mersey. It had the effect of detaching the northern, low-lying part of the manor, which henceforth became a virtual island accessible only by the occasional canal bridges.

In the late nineteenth century, the northern area became still more isolated. The Latchford Canal was replaced by the largest inland waterway in Britain, the Manchester Ship Canal, which opened in 1894. Only one bridge (and that a swing bridge) linked the two parts of the manor.

Fig. 12. The manor of Norton in 1843, based on the
Tithe Map.

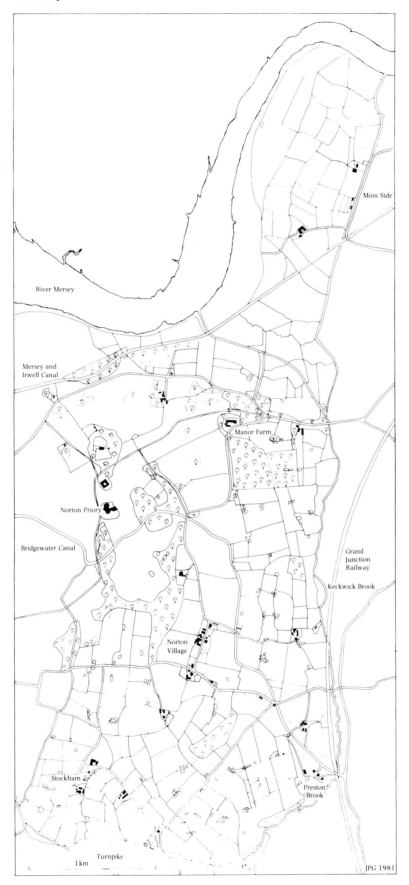

River Mersey

Mersey and
Irwell Canal

Manor Farm

Norton Priory

Bridgewater Canal

Grand
Junction
Railway

Keckwick Brook

Norton
Village

Stockham

Preston
Brook

Moss Side

Turnpike

1 km

JPG 1981

The Vyrnwy aqueduct carrying water from Wales to Liverpool was dug in 1890. At the highest point in the manor a large water tower was built to permit equalisation of pressure in the piped system. More recently, underground pipelines have been installed to serve the chemical industry, carrying for example brine and ethylene. They have had their effect on the landscape, through the creation of easements within which any building and below-ground activity is prevented.

The most recent series of changes resulted from the designation of Runcorn as a New Town in 1964. With modern earth-moving machinery, Expressway and Busway routes and areas of new housing can be imposed on the landscape, rather than be shaped by it. Much of the manor of Norton has been built upon by the Development Corporation. Fortunately however a large area has been kept free of development as the 'Town Park', woodland and fields about 100 hectares (240 acres) in extent. The site of Norton Priory lies within the Town Park.

The changes that have affected the manor over the last two hundred years have had the effect of concealing the earlier landscape. Despite this, it is possible to investigate that landscape, and to attempt to describe it.

Sources of information

Five sources of information are available for the manor of Norton.

1. The existing landscape

In spite of the developments of the last two centuries, there are surviving features that have their origins in the medieval period. The whole of the area under discussion has been examined on the ground by the writer since 1971.

2. Aerial photographs

Two sets of aerial photographic cover are particularly useful. The RAF series taken in 1947 and cover taken for the Development Corporation during its major planning phase in 1965 both record the landscape as it existed before building of the New Town began.

3. Maps

Compared to many other counties there are relatively few eighteenth-century estate maps extant for Cheshire. Due to the fragmentation of many large estates even the best plans of the period only show portions of townships (Harley and Laxton 1974, 20, n. 122). It is therefore very fortunate that an excellent map of Norton and Stockham townships has survived (fig. 13). The inscription at the top states 'A map of the Manor and Lordship of Norton in the parish of Runcorn and County Palatine of Chester together with a Plan of Norton Hall the Seat of Sir Richard Brooke, Baronet, surveyed 1757 by J.E.' J.E. is likely to be John Eyes, a surveyor working in Liverpool during this period, who carried out a number of estate surveys on manors near Liverpool, and in 1755 surveyed the route of the Trent and Mersey canal (Stewart-Brown 1911, 143–74).

The accuracy of the map (which has been checked from surviving topographical features) and the quality of draughtsmanship are of a high order. It was drawn at a scale of twelve perches to the inch (about 1 to 3,300). Each field and dwelling is marked with a letter and a number. Although no estate book of this date has survived, it is clear that each letter represents an individual tenancy, and the numbers distinguish between each item in the tenancy. The southern part of the map has field names added to it. Fig. 14 is based on the map.

Another cartographic document that formed part of the Brookes' estate record is a book of maps at various scales drawn by J. Dunn in 1806 and 1811 (Cheshire Record Office, DBNC (part) 1443 – Potts Collection; referred to henceforth as 'Dunn 1811'). Like the J.E. 1757 map, each tenancy has a letter, and each field a distinguishing number. The book contains tables of acreages (both Cheshire and Statutory), with each field named. A distinction is also made between titheable and demesne land; the boundary between the two is shown.

The 1843 Tithe Map and apportionment (Cheshire Record Office, EDT 307/1 and 2) is a valuable record of the landscape and of field names, in the mid-nineteenth century (fig. 12). The first edition Ordnance Survey map (1842) is another source of information. Other maps of more limited use are the county maps of John Speed (1610), P. P. Burdett (1777) and Bryant (1831).

4. Documentary evidence

The lack of Norton Priory's own documentation and the sparse nature of the records of the post-Dissolution manor are handicaps to the investigation of the landscape. The few references that can provide clues to the topography of Norton are cited where relevant in the following account.

5. Environmental evidence from excavation

Two sites have been excavated within the area under discussion, Norton village and Norton Priory. The former was found to have been thoroughly ploughed, and therefore lacked nearly all medieval ground surfaces (Greene and Hough 1977). From Norton Priory there is a body of useful botanical information which illuminates to a limited extent the vegetational history of that site.

The extent and boundaries of the manor (fig. 15)

The area encompassed by the manor was with one exception part of the endowment of the priory at its foundation at Norton in 1134. The exception, Eanley, became an integral part of the manor some years later. After the Dissolution the manor was sold in its entirety to the Brookes, and it remained intact in their ownership until the 1920s (with the exception of those tracts sold to the various canal and railway undertakings in the eighteenth and nineteenth centuries). Consequently the development of the area from the twelfth century was in the hands of two successive owners of Norton Priory.

The boundaries of the manor are shown on the J.E. 1757 estate map (fig. 14) and later maps. They consist of

Fig. 13. A detail of the J.E. 1757 estate map. The
Georgian country house (see fig. 99) is in the centre,
surrounded by a network of moats on three sides and
the millpond (labelled A.24). The gatehouse and other
earlier buildings still stand close to the house on the
west and north. The courtyard building (A.11) north of
the Halton–Moore–Warrington road is the newly built
stables.

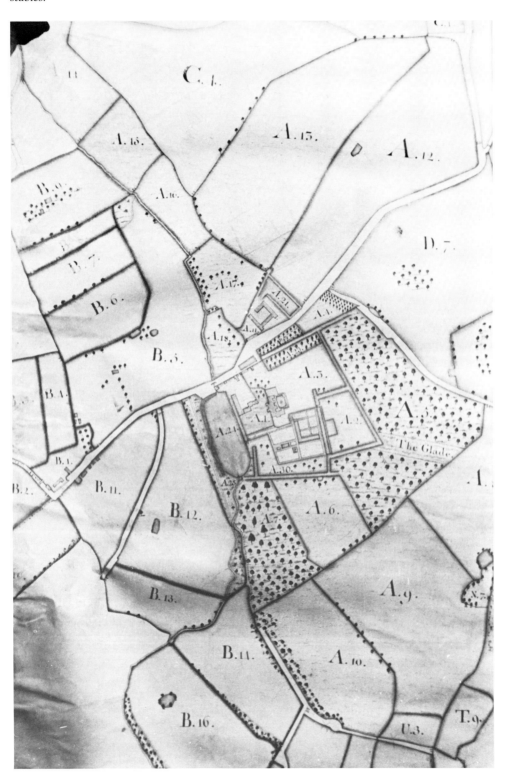

Fig. 14. The manor of Norton in 1757, based on the J.E.
1757 estate map.

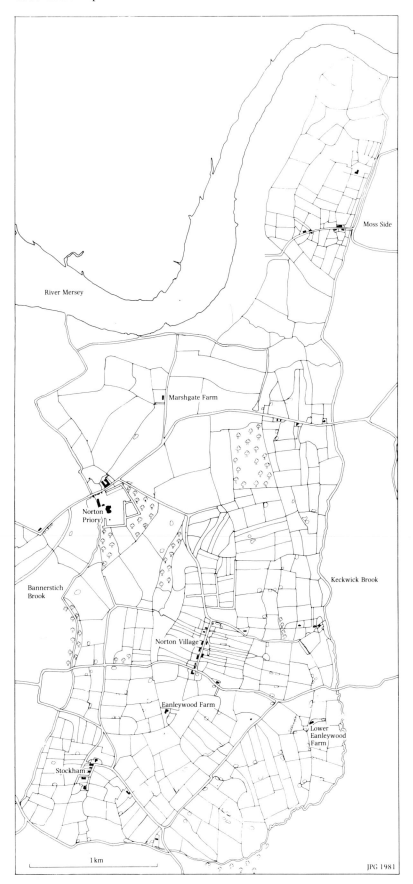

Moss Side

River Mersey

Marshgate Farm

Norton
Priory

Bannerstich
Brook

Keckwick Brook

Norton Village

Eanleywood Farm

Lower
Eanleywood
Farm

Stockham

1 km

JPG 1981

natural features for nearly all their length. The northern limit is the south bank of the river Mersey. On the east is Keckwick Brook, which rises on the southern side of the manor, flows eastwards and then for much of its course ran almost due north to the Mersey before canalisation in about 1800 altered its course. On the west is another stream which rises a short distance from the source of Keckwick Brook, but which flows west and then northwards to the Mersey. The boundary followed the stream for most of its course, apart from one length near the priory where it diverged to the west. This stream is not named on any map, but the name 'Bannerstich' was given to a number of fields in its vicinity on the J.E. 1757 map and Bannersludge in Dunn 1811. However, it is still

Fig. 15. The central part of the manor of Norton looking south east from the air, 1974. The site of the priory can be seen in the woodland in the foreground. Beyond, another area of woodland occupies the ridge of Windmill Hill; Norton village is on the far side. The impact of a cutting for a future road, and levelling for playing fields, can be seen in the vicinity of the priory.

known by local people as the Bannerstich and this name will be used in this account. The name has a long history. The Dutton charter of 1199–1203 referred to the 'Banalsiche' as a boundary (Barraclough 1957).

The shape of the manor was thus approximately rectangular, with a long axis running north–south, about 6 kilometres (*c.* 4 miles) long and 2 kilometres (*c.* 1.3 miles) wide. Within it were the two townships of Norton and Stockham, which were probably combined to form one manor in the late eleventh century on the evidence of Domesday Book. The Domesday entry for Norton stated that: 'The same William [fitz Nigel] holds Nortune and Ansfred [holds it] of him. Uhtred and Tokig held it as two manors and were free men. There are two hides that pay geld. There is land for six ploughs. In the demesne there is one [ploughland] and two serfs, and there are three villeins and one plough. There is one fisherman and three acres of meadow, and four acres of wood and two hays. It was worth sixteen shillings in the time of King Edward; now nine shillings and four pence. He found it waste' (Tait 1916, 171).

Stockham was not mentioned in Domesday, so it is likely that it was one of the two pre-Conquest manors referred to in 1086. It was also omitted from the 1134 foundation charter of the priory where it is probable that the manor of Norton was assumed to include it.

The third area within the boundaries of the medieval manor was Eanley. Domesday recorded that: 'The same William holds Enlelei. Wighe held it. There is half a hide that pays geld. There is land for half a plough. It was and is waste' (Tait 1916, 171; Enlelei is probably a copyist's error for Enlei). In the time of King John, Richard fitz Gilbert de Aston gave to Norton Priory 'all his land in Hendeley, with all its appurtenances' (Ormerod 1882, 1, 680). There are today two farms known as Eanleywood Farm (SJ 533 814) and Lower Eanleywood Farm (SJ 564 813). Dodgson decided that Enlelei, Hendeley, and Eanley are all forms of the same name, which has also been recorded as Hendley (c. 1230), Hemley (1538), Henley Wood alias Endley Wood (1691), Eanley Wood (1709) and Hindley Wood (1842) (Dodgson 1970, 173). There can therefore be little doubt about the identification of Eanley with Hendeley, and that from the early thirteenth century it was regarded as an integral part of the manor of Norton. Indeed, Leycester in the early seventeenth century stated that 'there is a certain place or hamlet called Endley, now belonging to the township of Norton, and enjoyed as part and parcel of the same' (Ormerod 1882, 1, 680).

Thus, from the early thirteenth century the manor comprised the townships of Stockham and Norton and incorporated Eanley. The pre-Conquest boundaries continued in the form of the township boundaries of Norton and Stockham and were destined to survive for a further nine centuries after the Conquest.

The pattern of pre-Conquest land holdings in the area

The origin of the pattern of land holdings is hazy, but clues are provided by the place names of the Runcorn area. The group with names derived from the cardinal points (Norton, Aston, Sutton and Weston) have given rise to a number of explanations. It may be thought that they refer to the location of settlements in relation to the central settlement of the area, Halton. Examination of the township map (fig. 16) shows that this cannot be so: Aston and Norton are not east and north of Halton. It has been suggested that the position of settlements relates to rivers (Dodgson 1970, 161). This is equally unlikely. The best explanation is to suggest that there was a large estate sometime in the pre-Conquest period occupying the promontory between the Mersey and the Weaver. Its eastern limit might have been marked by Keckwick Brook and the eastern side of Aston township, which run in an approximately north–south line across the promontory from the Mersey to the Weaver. The various farms or

settlements situated within the estate would have been distinguished by their positions – Norton being the most northerly, Weston the farm on the west, Sutton in the southern part of the estate, and Aston alongside the eastern limit of the estate.

A similar conclusion was reached by W. J. Ford in his examination of the settlement patterns of the central region of the Warwickshire Avon (Sawyer 1976, 186). A group of manors centred on Brailes included in their area Norton, known from field name evidence, and Sutton – a village which still exists. Ford concluded that 'it is reasonable to suppose that these two settlements were so called because of their original positions in which was probably a single estate', though he suggested the naming related to Brailes in the centre of the estate. Ford also examined the dating evidence for settlements with names incorporating the cardinal points. They occur frequently in documents of ninth-, tenth- and eleventh-century date, and the earliest reference is in a charter for Aston near Stoke Priors in Worcester, A.D. 767.

The other settlements on the promontory represented by townships are of a similar name type. Both Halton and Clifton, like the four discussed above, are a combination of topographical/geographical and habitative elements; Runcorn however is purely topographical. None contains a personal name. With the habitative element *tun* common to six of seven, and with the presence of the four geographical names in the group, a unity is apparent which supports the suggestion that all were once part of a large estate.

It is also possible to speculate that the parish of Runcorn, with its twenty townships in 1843, was based on a large unit encompassing the Mersey–Weaver promontory and a strip of land to the east along the south banks of the Mersey. The origins of the large multi-township parishes of Cheshire are not known, but they may have been similar to those in other parts of England. It has been suggested (e.g. Sawyer 1978, 244–8) that the original parish churches were those situated at royal centres, and that as lay estates gradually obtained privileged status by charter, churches serving the proprietors of the estates became parochial with parish boundaries coinciding with estate boundaries. In the case of Cheshire, the original parishes that developed following the missionary activities of Bishop Chad in Mercia, which began in 669, may have been based on those centres where royal privileges are likely to have existed from an early time, particularly the salt wiches. The large estate parishes may have become established in succeeding centuries with some township manors eventually becoming small parishes, but, for some reason, many large multi-township parishes continuing. Runcorn was one of these, and in its extent we may see the size of a Saxon estate within which were smaller units that eventually became the townships recorded in Domesday.

Runcorn however could be something of a special case, for the establishment of a burgh by Aethelflaed may have been accompanied by the founding of a new church, dedicated to St Bertelin – a saint associated with the Mercian heartland of Staffordshire. If this supposition is correct, it may be that prior to Aethelflaed's creation of the burgh the parish church was situated somewhere else in the parish.

A strong candidate would be Daresbury, which shares the *bury* (OE *burh*, a stronghold) element with a

number of the principal settlements of large Cheshire parishes – for example Astbury (12 townships), Bunbury (12 townships), Prestbury (32 townships), Wrenbury (7 townships) and Wybunbury (18 townships). *Burh* certainly appears dominant when contrasted with the other place names of the parish, which are characterised by the *tun* habitative element (and one *wic* in Keckwick). Another piece of evidence that Daresbury may have been the original administrative centre of a large estate coterminous with the known bounds of the parish of Runcorn is the form of the township, which on the map has the appearance of a core from which the surrounding

Fig. 16. Norton and its neighbouring townships.

WALTON

ACTON GRANGE

MOORE

KECKWICK

DARESBURY

NORTON

HATTON

RUNCORN

HALTON

NEWTON

WESTON

STOCKHAM

PRESTON

CLIFTON

SUTTON

ASTON

DUTTON

ASTON GRANGE

MIDDLETON GRANGE

········ Norton's parkland in 1831

JPG 1981 AFTER BRYANT 1831

townships have been struck, one of which is Newton ('The new farm' *niwe tun*: Dodgson 1970, 154). Another nearby township, to the south, is Preston ('Priest's farm', *preost tun*: Dodgson 1970, 156). Was this the farm of the priest serving the household of the proprietors of the manor, one of whom bore the name *Deor* which is perpetuated in Daresbury?

Throughout the later medieval period Daresbury was a chapelry of Runcorn. That the situation may have been reversed before Aethelflaed's activities is supported by the presence of Thelwall within the parish of Runcorn. Thelwall is a detached township; significantly it was the site chosen for another burgh established for the defence of the Mersey hinterland by Aethelflaed in the same year that she founded the burgh at Runcorn.

The topography of the manor in the later medieval period

The area can be broken down into four main zones. At the northern end is the low-lying marshland alongside the Mersey. The central sandstone ridge, known as Windmill Hill, divides the middle part of the manor; to the west was Norton Priory and to the east was Norton village. These can be considered as two zones; the township of Stockham with the area known as Eanley in the southern part of the manor constitutes a fourth. There are no rigid boundaries between these zones, but as there are differences between them it is convenient to consider them separately.

The northern marsh

On the northern side of the manor the River Mersey flows in a north westerly direction before swinging south west. On the south bank of the river is a large area known as Norton Marsh. Today it is a virtual island, isolated by the Manchester Ship Canal. It is agriculturally very rich with above-average yields of root crops and cereals, and excellent grass. The potential of the area must have been recognised in the medieval period, when the marshes were enclosed, drained and used for agriculture. The earliest information on the priory's low-lying land is a reference to flooding in 1332. In that year Pope John XXII permitted the appropriation of Castle Donnington church, Leicestershire, by Norton Priory, following 'high tides and flooding of that area of sea called the Mersey which had diminished the fruits of the land of the said monastery' (*Cal. Papal Reg.* 2, 379). More flooding is recorded in 1429, when indulgences were granted to those giving alms to Norton (*Cal. Papal Reg.* 8, 169). It is reasonable to assume that the area which had been estuarine marsh was largely reclaimed by the date of the 1332 floods, and an embankment constructed to protect it. The maintenance of this embankment figures among the expenses of the abbey in the sixteenth century – no less than £7 0s 0d is recorded by the *Valor* as the annual cost of 'diverse operations for defence against the sea'.

The embankment is shown on the J.E. 1757 estate map (fig. 14) and all subsequent maps. Apart from stretches where it has been removed by the Ship Canal, it can still be followed on the ground. Visible on air photographs are vegetation marks caused by the meandering water channels of the marsh, which must have been filled in following reclamation.

There is field name evidence that the marsh was being used for agriculture in the late medieval period. The grant of Norton Priory to Sir Richard Brooke in 1545 (Beamont 1873, 201) mentioned by name the Kale Yards and the Wholroe. Both these names can be found on the 1843 Tithe map and apportionment, and are situated in the low-lying, drained area. Several fields bearing the name Calyards (which means calf enclosure, or possibly vegetable garden – Dodgson 1970, 175) are centred at SJ 565 860. Wholroe appears in the form of Hoo Row; two fields called this are centred at SJ 565 844. The Warth, mentioned in the 1536 Commissioners' accounts, can be identified with Wharf (Dunn 1811) which occupied the north western tip of the manor. The names are marked on fig. 24 (p. 43).

The drainage of marshland along the shores of the Mersey was not restricted to the manor of Norton. An enormous area in the royal manor of Frodsham was also enclosed, and further west at Ince, St Werburgh's Abbey owned substantial areas of drained marsh. The Frodsham marshlands were part of the demesne of the manor and like those of Norton were in danger of inundation – severe flooding occurred on at least five occasions in the fourteenth century (Booth and Dodd 1979, 45). Defence against the sea consisted of earthen banks and drainage ditches with sluices to control tidal inflow. The fourteenth-century Frodsham demesne marshlands contained a predominance of arable land, although following the Black Death the proportion used as pasture increased. The arable and meadow consisted of enclosed areas separated from each other by gutters and drainage ditches and were termed furlongs (*ibid.*, 40). It seems probable that the divisions shown on the J.E. 1757 map originated in the medieval period; drainage ditches by their nature tend to be enduring landscape features in a continuously cultivated area.

After the Dissolution some of the farms shown on the J.E. 1757 map must have been established, such as Marshgate Farm (SJ 553 839) and Manor Farm (SJ 558 837). Moss Side Farm however would seem to occupy the site of a much older settlement – in 1757 it was shown as a hamlet, and six dwellings were recorded there in a lease of 1780 (Cheshire Record Office, DBN A/7/1). The most significant indicator of its antiquity however is the block of 56 acres shown as titheable land surrounding Moss Side Farm in the early nineteenth century, when everything else in the area was regarded as demesne (Dunn 1811). This must mean that Moss Side was in existence prior to the Dissolution, when the distinction between titheable and non-titheable demesne originated.

The low-lying land extended into the valley within which Keckwick Brook flows. It included an area known as Sandymoor Wood. Today it is covered by scrub, though in 1843 the Tithe Apportionment referred to it as a 'plantation' – presumably some deliberate tree planting had recently taken place there. In 1815 an account was presented to Sir Richard Brooke for felling and carrying away 1,775 trees at Sandymoor (Cheshire Record Office, DBN/C/7B/16). In 1536 the Augmentation Office Commissioners' accounts included Sondewell Moor, classified as pasture. The suggested derivation is 'marsh at the sandy spring' *sandig*, *waella* and *mor* (Dodgson 1970, 174).

The road from Halton and Norton Priory to Moore and Warrington crossed Keckwick Brook at Keckwickford, where it skirted the original marsh edge. The J.E. 1757 map (fig. 14) shows a collection of four buildings at Keckwickford on the Norton side of the brook. Several field

Fig. 17. Seventeenth-century sketch plan of the Tudor mansion by Randle Holme. It should be compared with fig. 18.

names are marked on the J.E. 1757 map at this point, including Ridgalong Croft. By 1811 the name had changed to Riggotts; a group of fields occupying a large area to the north of the road had this name (Dunn 1811). The 'rig' element may refer to ridge and furrow; possibly Keckwickford was a hamlet with an area of open field where the Riggot names occurred in 1811; significantly the boundary between demesne and titheable land projected out to incorporate all the fields with this name in the titheable zone (Dunn 1811; marked on fig. 24, p. 43).

To the west of Keckwickford, but also on the margin of the marsh, is a wood still known as Oxmoor Wood (centred SJ 558 841). In that area four fields were named as parts of Oxmoor in the nineteenth century (1843 Tithe Map; Dunn 1811). It is probable therefore that the Oxmoor listed in the 1536 Augmentation Office Commissioners' accounts occupied that area. It must have derived its name from the practice of grazing oxen there – the rich grassland of the reclaimed marsh would have provided excellent pasture. The use of the marsh for grazing animals in the late medieval period is attested by a reference in the account of the special episcopal commission that investigated irregularities at Norton Priory in 1522 (Heath 1973, 90). One Thomas Ruttour

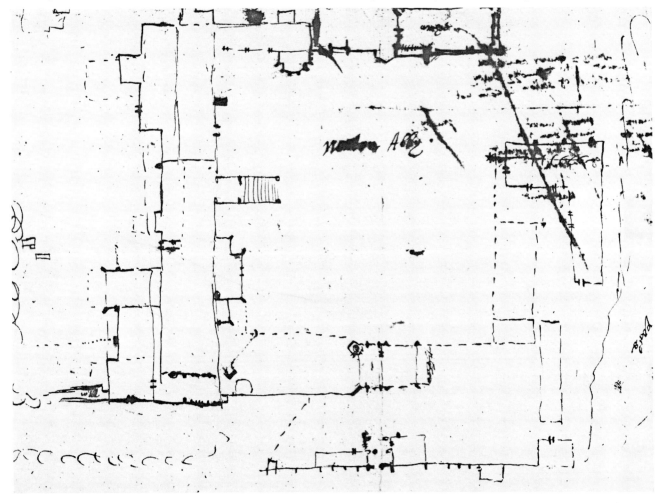

was stated to have supervision of the oxen, other cattle and horses at the 'Mershe'. The Oxmoor, like all the marsh except the block around Moss Side, was regarded as demesne in the early nineteenth century (Dunn 1811).

Norton Priory and its surroundings (fig. 15)

As well as the marshland, a substantial proportion of the rest of the township of Norton was regarded as demesne in the nineteenth century. The 1843 Tithe Apportionment recorded its extent: 'The demesne lands of Norton Priory, formerly the possessions of Norton Priory amounting to 1,193 acres . . . now the property of Sir Richard Brooke, Baronet, are and have been immemorially exempt from the payment of all Tithes.' The remaining titheable part of the township totalled 913 acres. There is therefore the explicit statement by the Tithe Commissioners to the effect that 57% of the township was free of tithes because it had formed the demesne of the medieval priory. This area cannot however be identified in its entirety from the Tithe Map and Apportionment, for only 600 acres are listed with no assessment for tithes, and even this figure includes 180 acres of woodland, which was normally free of tithes. It is therefore of considerable value that Dunn's various 1806 and 1811 maps show the boundary between demesne and titheable land, and the medieval Norton Priory's demesne can therefore be identified (fig. 24). The

Fig. 18. The Tudor mansion, engraving by S. and N. Buck, 1727. This is the view from the west – so the fall of the shadows is highly misleading! The medieval gatehouse is on the left, and beyond can be seen the tower house attached to the west range, the door to the passage of which is at the left hand end.

1536 Augmentation Office Commissioners' accounts valued the site of the abbey and its demesne at £42 16s 0d, with arable and pasture let out to farm worth a further £3 12s 0d, compared to a value of £22 3s $4\frac{1}{4}$d put on land outside the demesne. This ratio of valuations provides a rough guide to the division of land in the township, and supports the evidence of the 1843 tithe-free acreage that the medieval demesne occupied more than half the township.

Of the land surrounding Norton Priory, i.e. that lying between the marsh on the north, the western edge of the township, and Windmill Hill on the east, some reconstruction of the medieval topography is possible. Here too the J.E. 1757 estate map is an invaluable source of information, for many features shown on it can be correlated with earlier evidence (fig. 13). At the heart of the area was the complex of monastic buildings, which will be described later. However, the buildings of the outer courtyard and beyond have yet to be investigated, and knowledge of these is derived from a number of sources – the J.E. 1757 map, the Randle Holme sketch of mid-seventeenth-century date (British Library Harleian MS 2073 f. 107) (fig. 17), the Buck engraving (fig. 18), and an *inquisition post mortem* of Sir Richard Brooke who died 10 April 1632 (Chester Record Office CR63/1/226/n (102), transcription). Although the last two documents date from about a century after the Dissolution, there is reason to think that the situation they record is little different to that obtaining earlier. The Brookes' financial situation ensured that they adapted existing buildings rather than erecting new ones after their acquisition of Norton in 1545.

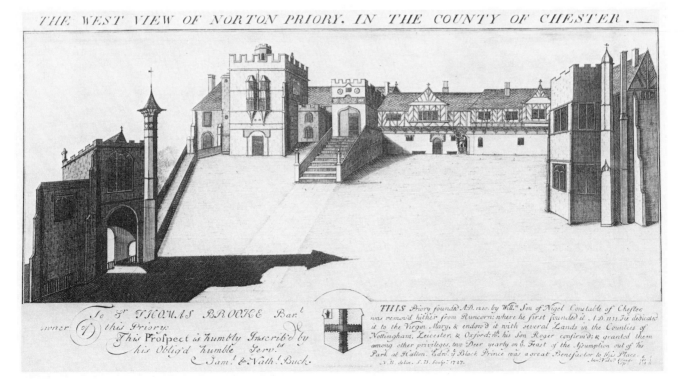

THE WEST VIEW OF NORTON PRIORY, IN THE COUNTY OF CHESTER.

The IPM, after listing the rooms of the main wings of the house (hall, chambers, butteries, porch, kitchen, and larders etc.) deals with those buildings that surrounded the courtyard; the brewhouse, the boulting house, with their passage, the dairy house, the dairy vault, and little storehouse, the kiln, the malt lofts, the hack house, the stable and slaughter house at the end thereof, and the vast room at the end thereof, the nearer barn, the cow-house, the outbuildings for swine and pullen, the garden house, the new buildings at the east end of the cow house, the lower garner, with free egress and regress for horse, coach or carriage through the gates. Some of the terms require explanation. The boulting house was probably used for sifting and storing flour. The kiln was doubtless the malt kiln, in which the barley that had germinated in the malt lofts was roasted prior to brewing in the brew house. The hack house was presumably for horses used in agriculture and for drawing carts and carriages, whereas the horses for riding would have been kept in the stable. The lower garner must have been a granary ('lower' to distinguish it from the nearer barn?).

The Randle Holme sketch (fig. 17) shows a series of buildings around the courtyard. The main range of the house and the gatehouse on the north of the building with a projecting angular front on the south can all be identified with buildings shown on the 1727 Buck brothers' engraving (fig. 18). One building to the south of the angular building is labelled 'arched' – perhaps this was the 'dairy vault'. Immediately north of the gatehouse is apparently a long buttressed wall, alongside which several buildings stand. Reference to the J.E. 1757 map clarified the position of these. In fact they were situated further north than the sketch indicates – the spacing has been compressed to fit the outer buildings on to the sheet. One of the outer buildings shown on the sketch has the appearance of a gatehouse. This identification is supported by an account of the 'remarkable echo at Norton' which described a double echo that could be heard when a flute was played in front of the house. The explanation of the echo was that the sound was reflected by the *two* gatehouses of the mansion (Leigh 1700). The other buildings mentioned in the IPM must have been distributed around the courtyard and between the inner gatehouse and the northern boundary wall. The two areas are probably those referred to in the 1545 sale agreement as the higher and lower courts.

The church, the claustral ranges, the service buildings to the west and the other buildings to the north alongside the Halton–Moore–Warrington road together formed an impressive collection of structures. Surrounding them were the elements that made up an integrated system of water management. Documentary research and excavation have provided a considerable amount of information about the extent and use of the system, the principal features of which were moats to the south, east and on part of the northern side of the priory, and a large millpond to the west.

Water management

The existence of the moats and millpond was unknown until research associated with the excavation started, but the knowledge that the monastic precinct was almost

Fig. 19. The point of junction between the moat system and the monastic drain. Here water was diverted into the drain, the masonry lining of which has been largely robbed out (compare with masonry in fig. 55).

entirely surrounded by water explains the otherwise obscure reference in Sir Piers Dutton's letter to Sir Thomas Audley, the lord chancellor, of 12 October 1536 (*Letters and Patents* 10, 516). Dutton's account of his suppression of the riot that took place when the king's commissioners visited Norton states that when disturbed the rioters 'took to the pools and water'. Also explained is a feature on the Randle Holme sketch (fig. 17) to the west of the courtyard, which is labelled 'pools' – this must represent the mill pond.

The existence of a moat system was realised when the J.E. 1757 map came to light, for the system of water-courses is shown on it (fig. 13). Prior to the construction of playing fields in 1974 to the east of the priory site, fifteen trenches were machine excavated across the suspected line of moats, following a geophysical survey. The moats were found to be 8 to 10 metres wide, and on average 2 metres deep. That they were medieval in origin was proved when the junction with the main monastic drain was examined (fig. 19). The moat fed water into the monastic drain, the level in the moat being maintained by a 'stanks' system: a dam comprising a pair of masonry abutments into which removable beams of timber were slotted. The drain was contemporary with the moat; as the former was constructed in the thirteenth century the moats must be at least as early as that.

Water from springs at the south east corner of the moats was brought to the point where it could flow down the monastic drain by an additional part of the system. This isolated a rectangular area which was reached by a bridge which crossed the moat at the stanks. A horizontal timber with mortice holes was set in the base of the moat between the masonry abutments: it must have provided the base for the central supports for the bridge. A crossing of the moat at this point is shown on the J.E. 1757 map (fig. 13).

The flow of water along the monastic drain through the rere dorter was regulated by a wooden sluice. Part of the timber frame to hold the sluice gate was excavated (fig. 20). Water, having flowed through the rere dorter, was supplemented by roof water and waste from the kitchens before flowing out to the mill pond on the west side of the priory. The moats endured until the middle of the eighteenth century.

The mill pond was formed by damming the Banner-stich brook. Water from another spring to the south of the priory, which was also utilised in the medieval period and later for a piped supply to the kitchens and other parts of the buildings, fed the mill pond, as well as the water from the drain. The pond is shown on the J.E. 1757 map. The northern outflow is shown to be constricted, passing under the Halton–Moore road. A building is shown standing alongside. That this building was a water mill is confirmed by an ink and watercolour perspective executed in about 1770 (Mellon collection, RIBA library) (fig. 21).

The water mill has an undershot wheel. The mill pond had by this date assumed an additional function, that of a landscape lake. Within a few years however, the lake and moats had been filled following the construction of the canal. Unfortunately, no trace of the mill now exists. All remains must have been removed when a large road cutting was dug to the north of the priory in 1970, before any archaeologist was employed in the area. The cutting is also likely to have removed any traces of the boundary wall, outer gatehouse and buildings alongside it.

The water mill was one of the properties listed by the Augmentation Office commissioners in 1536, and must have been a valuable asset throughout the medieval period. It was listed amongst Norton's properties in 1279 (*Pope Nicholas Taxation*, Record Office 1802, 259).

The construction of the water system must have required a considerable investment of labour. The moats had a total length of about 1,100 metres, and were on average 2 metres deep and 9 metres wide. The volume of boulder clay removed must have totalled about 19,800 cubic metres. Clay with an average water content has a density of 2,050 kilos per cubic metre, so the total weight moved must have been in the order of forty thousand tonnes. A tonne constitutes about forty wheel barrow loads – a hard day's work for one man. At this rate of work the digging of the moats would take a team of forty labourers about three years to complete. In addition, the construction of the mill pool dam would have been a sub-stantial undertaking.

Although construction required a high initial investment of labour, the system thereafter would only have needed occasional maintenance. In return, the priory gained a defined, secure boundary; the means of draining the area encompassed by the moats; a source of water to clean the rere dorter; a means of removing roof water and kitchen waste; and a source of energy used to grind the priory's cereals. In addition, the large volumes of water were no doubt used as fishponds. It is a mark of the elegance and efficiency of the system that it endured, apparently little altered, from the thirteenth to the eighteenth century. The fact that two different springs and the Bannerstich brook could all be utilised for the water system was a result of the siting of the priory in 1134, which clearly demanded a shrewd evaluation of the topography of the manor.

There is no direct evidence of the use to which the large areas bounded by the moats to the east and south of the priory were put, apart from the small area immediately east of the church that was used as the canons' burial ground. Three items listed in the 1545 grant to Sir Richard Brooke were however probably within the moats. The 'fermery orchard' was presumably situated near the monastic infirmary. Although the infirmary has not yet been excavated, it is probable that it was built in the con-ventional position to the south east of the claustral

Norton Priory 36

Fig. 20. Wooden frame of sluice gate situated where water flowed beneath the monastic latrines. The sluice would be used periodically to send large volumes of water through the drain, thereby cleaning it. The channel for the gate can be seen on the vertical timber. The mortice hole for a pegged tenon is visible on the horizontal timber.

buildings. The large rectangular moated area may have defined the infirmary orchard – certainly, orchards were frequently moated in the medieval period. The 'great garden' probably lay to the south of the monastic buildings where it would have been conveniently placed to supply vegetables and culinary herbs to the kitchens and medicinal herbs to the infirmary. The 'smith's orchard' may have been situated near the outer courtyard, where it is probable that a smith would have had a forge.

The area outside the moats

The 1536 Augmentations Office Commissioners' accounts recorded some of the names by which different parts of the demesne were known, and in a number of cases it is possible to identify where they were situated from later evidence. Church Fields, for example, was the name given to the large area (centred on SJ 551 827) lying to the south of the priory, and rising up to Windmill Hill; the name was still being used in the nineteenth century

(Tithe Map 1843; Dunn 1811). Sely Lowe in 1536 had become Sillylow by 1811; meaning 'little mounds' the field is centred on SJ 555 832 to the north east of the priory. The Saundersfield of 1536 can be identified with two large fields to the south west of the priory named as Sanders Heys in 1811 (centred SJ 545 825). The Abbey Park mentioned in 1536 is difficult to identify – it may have been the area to the south east of the priory that was still partly wooded in 1757. No name occurs on either of the nineteenth-century maps that can be identified with the 1545 reference to the Mayden's Crime or Great Crime, though it may be the same as the Chanoncrymbre ('the canons' bit of land') recorded in 1353 (Dodgson 1970, 175). Fortunately, there is a map, apparently made for the duke of Bridgewater to counter the arguments of the Brookes over the route of the canal, and therefore dating to about 1770, that labels the area to the west of the priory and its millpond 'The Crime'. It is centred SJ 545 830. The location of these names is shown on fig. 24.

Other field names that were specified in the 1545 sale agreement but which cannot now be placed are nonetheless of interest. The Great Orchard Field, the Shepe House, the Fowle Acre and the Hemp Yards all derive their names from their use. Dame Savage Meadow was presumably given to the canons by a person of that name or to provide money for memorial prayer. The Savage

Fig. 21. Perspective watercolour and ink drawing of 'Norton Hall' and its parkland made *c.* 1770 as evidence against the duke of Bridgewater's intention of moving the line of his canal from F to H. The mill and millpond (being used for boating) can be seen, as well as stables, dovecot and walled garden.

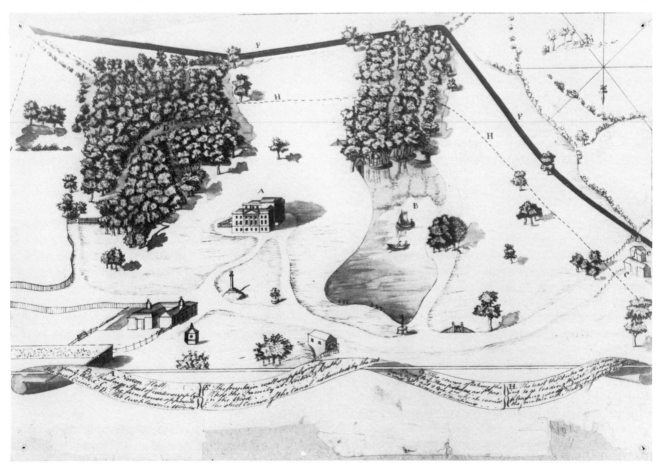

family were resident at Clifton Manor (later given the grandiose name of Rock Savage) in the late medieval period. The Cellarer's Meadow must have been named because of some connection with the monastic cellarer. The origin of the 'Trentham Trental' is obscure, but a trental is a set of 30 successive daily masses for the dead, so the land may have been given to finance such masses on an annual basis.

On the two nineteenth-century maps the name Coneygreaves applied to a number of fields to the north east of the priory. It is a common field name which means a rabbit warren ('Coningre': Dodgson 1970, 175).

The early vegetation of the site of the priory

Knowledge of the medieval landscape of the Norton demesne is largely derived from sixteenth-century documents and by a process of regression from later documents, maps and field survey. It can be assumed to describe only the landscape as it existed in the years before the Dissolution; knowledge of the changes which had occurred in the previous four centuries is very limited. However, there is information about the vegetational landscape of the priory site itself. Changes in the flora are apparent through an examination of the pollen grains present in the pre-priory turfline and subsoil (Department of Environment, Ancient Monuments Laboratory, R. Macphail and H. C. M. Keeley). The subsoil sample appeared to represent a wet, base-rich wood scrub environment of alder and hazel, with a ground cover of ferns such as bracken. The soil, at its junction with the subsoil, showed a more varied environment with significantly more wooded conditions of alder, birch and lime, with a compensating decrease in hazel. Bracken was still important, but the ground cover may have been more open and affected by grasses, cereals, and Compositae (daisy, thistle, dandelion etc.). The sample above showed another episode of hazel scrub growth, with a decline in alder but a presence of oak. The under-flora was again dominated by ferns, with little grass.

Above this, alder and other trees continued to decline in favour of hazel, but the under-flora of bracken was enriched by a number of herbs and grasses. Towards the top of this layer, a revival of the woodland of alder, oak and birch produced a decrease in hazel, and a large number of herbs were present in the under-flora.

In summary, it appears that the environment of the pre-priory soil comprised sequences of hazel scrub or tree dominance. The soil was buried under a layer of crushed sandstone, laid down at an early stage of construction of the church, probably to provide a compact dry surface from which to work. The sandstone was found to contain similar quantities of alder and hazel to the soil beneath, but less bracken (13% cf. 18–20% in the buried soil). There were increments of grasses and herbs (Compositae) which may suggest disturbance of bracken in favour of these plants. Perhaps this resulted from the clearance of

scrub and woodland as part of the process of colonisation by the canons of what was clearly a marginal area that had not been used for cultivation.

Windmill Hill

Outside the demesne, 1.1 km (0.7 miles) south east of the priory, was Norton village. The two were separated by the sandstone ridge known still as Windmill Hill. The ridge formed the boundary between the demesne land on the west, and the village land on the east.

The manorial windmill was situated on the hill. The earliest map to name the hill Windmill Hill was Dunn 1811, although Burdett places a symbol indicating a windmill here on his map in 1777. However, it is doubtful whether the windmill did in fact still exist at that date. It is not shown on the J.E. 1757 estate map, the comprehensiveness and standards of accuracy of which are very high. The use of Windmill Hill as the site for the manorial windmill can be traced back to the medieval period. It is mentioned in the charter of sale to Sir Richard Brooke in 1545 (Beamont 1873, 200) and was listed by the commissioners in 1536 (Augmentations Office). A settlement of 1607 included the windmill among the properties listed (Cheshire Record Office, Brooke papers, DBN/B/1/12).

The probable site of the windmill has been located by fieldwork. On the crest of the hill is a low mound, about 20 m in diameter and about 2 m high, situated at SJ 5523 8824. A few fragments of seventeenth-century pottery have been found there in the topsoil. No excavation has been undertaken, but the siting is perfect to obtain the maximum benefit of winds blowing across the hill. Leading to the base of the outcrop on which the mound stands is an abandoned hollow-way track, which forks with one branch leading towards the priory and the other towards Stockham. The latter intersects Norton Lane, which leads to Norton village. These tracks could thus have given access for those taking their grain to be milled, and collecting their flour.

The hill had an additional function. The limit of agriculture on the west and east coincides with the outcropping of the red sandstone which forms the ridge. It appears that this sandstone was exploited during the medieval period and later. Field survey has shown that the whole of the sandstone outcrop is pockmarked with quarry pits. Some are quite small and most have become partially filled. None has been excavated, but it seems likely that many date from the medieval period, and were probably the source of stone for building the priory. Within some of the quarries traces of tooling on the sandstone is visible; it consists of horizontal bands of diagonal marks. The techniques used to quarry sandstone are discussed later.

Norton village

Norton village is situated in the lee of Windmill Hill, on the gentle slope that runs from the crest of the hill (Ordnance Datum 60 metres – 200 feet) down to the valley through which Keckwick Brook flows (O.D. 9 metres – 30 feet). By the middle of the nineteenth century the village had contracted to a handful of farms and houses, but cartographic, documentary and archaeological evidence all

Fig. 22. Norton village in 1757, based on the J.E. estate map. Each parcel of land is identified by a letter to show of which tenancy it formed part. The ponds originated as marl pits.

prove that the village was once much more populous, and had experienced a steady decline in size over several centuries.

The starting point for a discussion of the history of the village is the J.E. 1757 estate map (figs. 13 and 22) – indeed it was the evidence of the map that prompted excavation in 1974. The two nineteenth-century maps (Dunn 1811, Tithe Map 1843) recorded a situation which

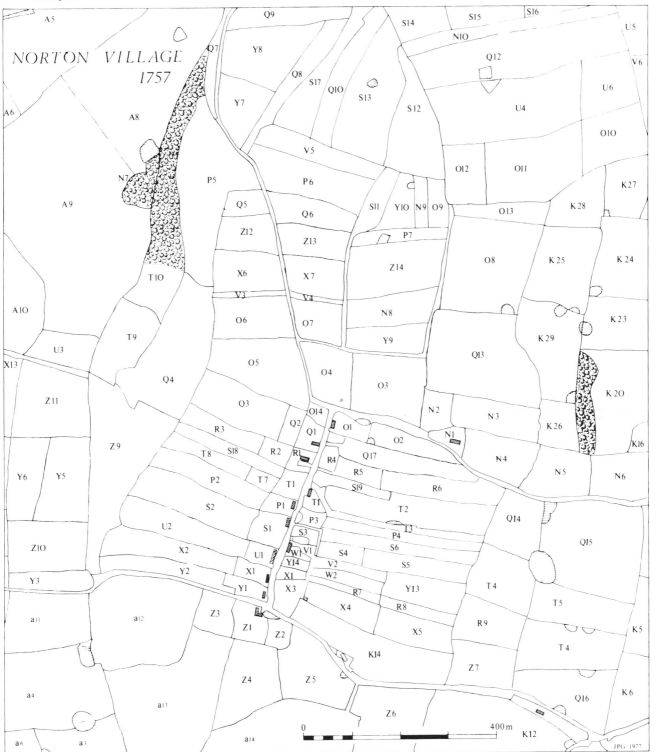

Fig. 23. Norton village in 1843, based on the Tithe Map. The radical changes in the landscape (including the construction of the Bridgewater Canal) can be seen by comparing with the situation 86 years earlier in fig. 22.

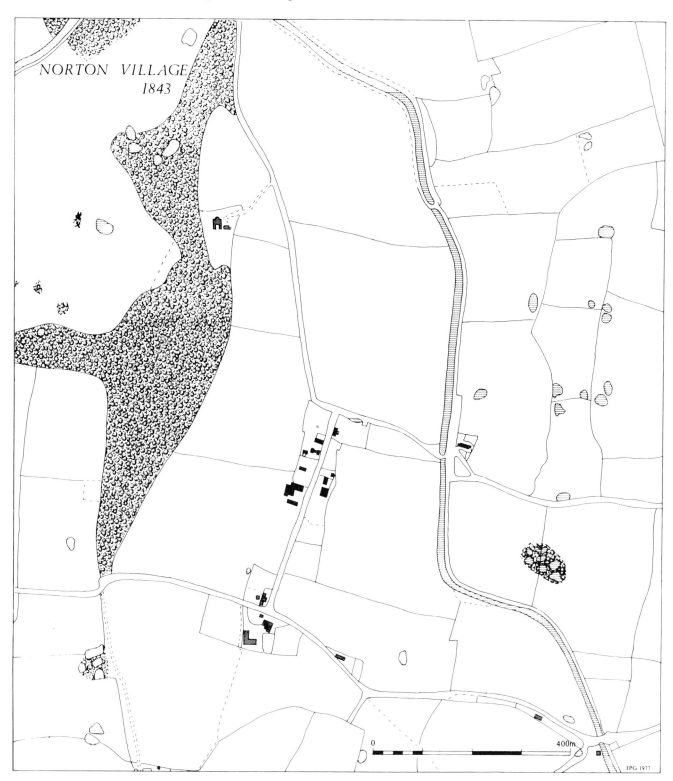

NORTON VILLAGE
1843

0   400m

JPG 1977

had radically altered (fig. 23) and which obscured the important evidence for the origins of the village that can be gleaned from the earlier map. The eighteenth-century village consisted of an axial street, alongside which were plots of land, some with buildings and others that were vacant. Behind these tofts, on each side of the village, was a lane, beyond which were long narrow fields. The form of the village in 1757 suggests that it was the product of an earlier, probably medieval, arrangement of tofts of equal size which fronted the street.

To test this theory, and to investigate the settlement history of the village, an excavation was organised on an area that had been designated for house building (the results are described in Greene and Hough 1977).

The excavation produced evidence of several kinds:
(1) It confirmed the layout that was suggested by map evidence (J.E. 1757) i.e. tofts alongside the road, separated by boundaries (that in two cases were accompanied by access tracks) with a back lane behind.
(2) Buildings were erected near the road, leaving the rear of the toft free for other activities.
(3) Finds of objects suggested occupation going back at least to the thirteenth–fourteenth centuries and continuing until the late eighteenth century.
(4) There was evidence for abandonment of one toft in the sixteenth century and another in the eighteenth century. This accords with cartographic and documentary evidence.
(5) The digging of a well was one means used for obtaining water.
(6) The axial street had developed into a hollow way.

The ultimate origin of the village remains obscure. The earliest finds (apart from Neolithic pottery and flints) can be no earlier than the thirteenth century. This need occasion no surprise however. The excavation of Norton Priory, whose social standing would have been reflected in a relatively high material culture, has produced only a small amount of twelfth-century pottery, compared to very large quantities of thirteenth-century and later pottery. At Norton village the total quantity of medieval finds is fairly small, a characteristic shared by many village sites. The absence of early finds cannot therefore be taken as evidence that there was no occupation before the thirteenth century. Indeed it is likely that the village has its origins in the pre-Conquest period.

The earliest reference to the manor of Norton is in the Domesday survey of 1086, but information on the village as distinct from the manor is non-existent throughout the medieval period. However, the plan of the village as shown on the J.E. 1757 estate map (fig. 14) and confirmed by excavation does provide a basis for comparison with villages elsewhere, and thus for suggestions about its origins. Norton's plan, comprising an axial street lined with regularly placed tofts, with a back lane and fields beyond on both sides of the village, is a type which occurs widely throughout England and has been given the generic name of 'street village'. Two examples that have been discussed in print are Braunston in Northamptonshire and Chelmorton in Derbyshire (Beresford and St Joseph 1979, 63 and 99).

It has been suggested that the regular form of the street village is likely to have arisen as a result of planning, probably by the owner of an estate engaged in reorganisation (Roberts 1972). In Durham, Roberts suggests that the allotment of estates following the Conquest might have been the occasion for reorganisation, partially necessitated by the wasting to which much of Durham had been subjected by the Conqueror's army (*ibid.*, 52; Roberts 1977, 141). The same reasoning could be applied to Norton. In Domesday, Cheshire had a greater proportion of waste manors than any area apart from Yorkshire (Tait 1916, 7–8). Norton itself was described in 1086 as having been waste, and it still had a diminished value compared to its pre-Conquest rating. It seems equally possible however that the assumption of ownership by the canons in 1134 was followed by a reorganisation of the estate, including the re-establishment of the village on a planned pattern.

The first evidence (after Domesday) for the size of the population of Norton is provided by the 1545 sale agreement. Cheshire's separate administration in the medieval period resulted in the exemption of the earldom from most forms of taxation that were exacted by the central government (Booth 1976) and which for many counties are useful indicators of population trends.

In 1545, 29 people were listed by name as being in possession of tenancies in Norton township (Beamont 1873, 204–5). In 1632, an *inquisition post mortem* of Sir Richard Brooke listed fourteen tenants in Norton, as well as Norton Hall itself and three dwellings probably nearby (Stewart-Brown 1934, 82–3). If this is the total of substantial tenancies at that date, it represents a considerable reduction since 1545. A process of amalgamation may have occurred, and there is no doubt that one of the buildings excavated was abandoned in that period. The Brookes may have pursued a policy of encouraging the aggregation of individual holdings in the interest of efficiency.

The pattern of gradual amalgamation of holdings and long drawn out decline in population that occurred in Norton is probably far more typical of the changes taking place nationally than the picture presented by those villages that became completely deserted, and which have received more attention. In the late eighteenth and nineteenth centuries the trend reflects closely the widespread movement of population from rural areas to industrial towns. In the case of Norton, it was Runcorn that grew rapidly in size as a result of the construction of the Bridgewater canal. It was the canal also that was the reason for the construction of the new houses at Preston Brook, which to a certain extent balanced the decline elsewhere in the township. The establishment of farms away from the settlement centre and within blocks of tenanted land was also a widespread post-medieval phenomenon.

The pattern of fields

The J.E. 1757 estate map (figs. 14, 22) recorded an extensive area surrounding Norton village that was divided up into fields. The information provided by the shapes and pattern of the fields in the mid-eighteenth century is of great value in investigating the earlier agricultural exploitation of this part of the manor. There were two main elements in the 1757 field pattern – blocks of long narrow 'linear' fields, and other fields that were elongated but broader in shape (rectangular or irregular). The former type existed close to the village. On the west the gently sloping hillside between the village and the outcropping sandstone of Windmill Hill was covered with linear fields. On the east the narrow fields ran down the hillside to the edge of the wetter ground of the wide valley. Blocks of linear fields also covered the north eastern slopes of the higher ground to the north of the village. None were drawn on the J.E. 1757 map to the south of the village.

To the east of the village and the blocks of linear fields was a broad sweep of land with fields of a quite different type. In most cases these fields were broader, shorter, and were rectangular or irregular in shape. They occurred on the wetter land of the Keckwick Brook valley and also to the south of the village and west of Windmill Hill.

The other element in the 1757 landscape was the network of roads, lanes or tracks that linked all the parts of the manor (fig. 14). The axial street of Norton village at its southern end made a T-junction with a lane leading from Halton to Daresbury. At the northern end of the village was another T-junction, with the eastern arm leading to Wharford, and the other running westwards for a short distance before turning north west to join eventually the Halton–Moore road near Norton Priory. The abandoned lane still exists in Big Wood (SJ 553 832) where it can be traced in the form of an earthwork, which must represent a substantial causeway flanked by ditches. Part of the route of this track on the map was shown to cut obliquely across a block of linear fields to the north of the village. This suggests that it was part of a later development, superimposed on the existing field system and perhaps growing from a short cut footpath. Other lanes to the north of the village were an integral part of the field system, providing a means of access through the fields. The back lanes to the west and east of the village similarly provided access to the two areas of fields there.

The reordering of the landscape which had occurred by 1811 must have involved complicated arrangements with the holders of the fields. On the 1757 map the presence of letters denoting the tenancy of each field de-

monstrates the scattered nature of individual holdings. The two large fields that were shown on the 1811 map to the west of the village had replaced thirteen fields held by nine different people. One part of the process was the creation of miles of new hedges. An order to the nurserymen, Caldwells of Knutsford, for 7,500 thorns was sent by Thomas Brooke in 1797; no doubt they were intended for hedge planting (Caldwells Ledgers, Cheshire Record Office, DDX 363/7). Indeed the ubiquity of hawthorn hedges throughout the manor today shows that not only were new hedges planted with thorns, but existing hedges were also replanted in the same material. By 1811, the landscape was indistinguishable from enclosure field patterns elsewhere in England – only the field name The Butts hinted at the earlier linear fields to the west of the village.

The origin of the fields

The narrow fields with their curving sides to the west, east and north of the village are of a type which has many parallels elsewhere. It is now generally accepted that such groups of linear fields with curved sides were once part of open fields, arising from the piecemeal enclosure of one or more strips whose curving shape was the product of ploughing with large medieval plough teams (Baker and Butlin 1973, 32). Map evidence of the enclosure of strips of common field to produce an enclosed field system very similar to that of Norton in the eighteenth century has been published for many places. One north western example is Hayton in Cumberland (G. Elliott, in Baker and Butlin 1973, fig. 2.1, 44) where enclosure took place in the seventeenth century. In contrast, enclosure might produce a much more drastic change to the landscape. At Ilmington in Gloucestershire (Beresford and St Joseph 1979, 26–9) enclosure in 1788 involved the wholesale substitution of large rectangular straight hedged fields for a multitude of strips, with the new boundaries paying little heed to the edges of strips or furlongs of the open field. By the early nineteenth century, both Ilmington and Norton possessed a very similar field system – large rectangular fields with straight hedges of thorn bushes. The difference between them was the nature and pace of change – at Ilmington abrupt, at Norton gradual, taking place by a number of steps which included the enclosure of groups of strips as at Hayton.

The area of linear fields to the north of the village also has the appearance of open field that has been enclosed. Most of the tenancies in the village are also represented by holdings in this area, though there is no indication of allotment on a regular basis. The probable extent of medieval open field is shown on fig. 24.

Beyond the village and the areas of linear field, the J.E. 1757 map recorded fields that were broader and shorter – some rectangular in shape, others irregular. They occupied areas that were less well drained than the

Fig. 24. The manor of Norton towards the end of the
medieval period, based on the topographical information
from the sources described in the text.

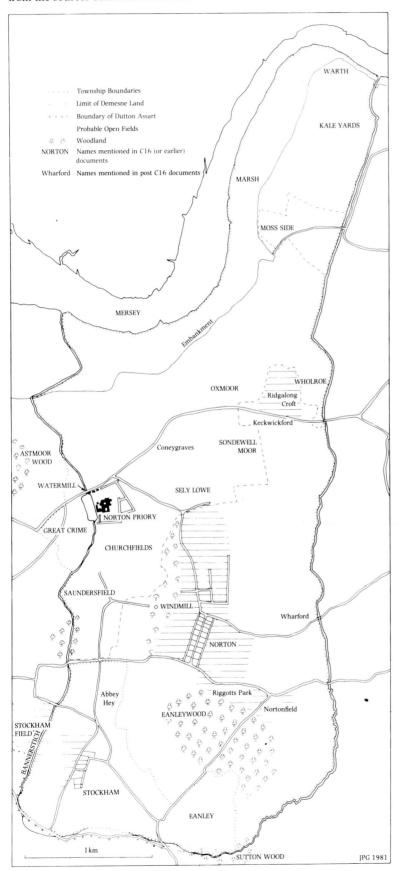

. . . . . .	Township Boundaries
— · — · —	Limit of Demesne Land
· · · ·	Boundary of Dutton Assart
	Probable Open Fields
♧ ♧	Woodland
NORTON	Names mentioned in C16 (or earlier) documents
Wharford	Names mentioned in post C16 documents

WARTH

KALE YARDS

MARSH

MOSS SIDE

MERSEY

Embankment

OXMOOR

WHOLROE

Ridgalong
Croft

Keckwickford

Coneygraves

SONDEWELL
MOOR

ASTMOOR
WOOD

SELY LOWE

WATERMILL

NORTON PRIORY

GREAT CRIME

CHURCHFIELDS

SAUNDERSFIELD

○ WINDMILL

Wharford

NORTON

Abbey
Hey

Riggotts Park

Nortonfield

EANLEYWOOD ♧

STOCKHAM
FIELD

BANNERSTICH

STOCKHAM

EANLEY

1 km

SUTTON WOOD

JPG 1981

eastern slopes of Windmill Hill, such as the broad valley through which Keckwick Brook flows, and the flattish land to the south of the village and west of the southern part of Windmill Hill. The distinction between the two zones is particularly clear on the 1843 Tithe Map (fig. 12) where numerous water-filled marl pits can be seen on the wetter land, but very few occupy the drier land.

The wetter land was probably used for pasture and meadow. To the east of the village, some of the field names recorded in 1843 convey the character of the land – Brook Meadow, Denton's Meadow, Churner and Great Moss, for example. There are two names at the south eastern end of the village however that raise the possibility that open field was at one stage present there as well – Riggotts Parks and Norton Field. Both occur on sloping (and therefore better drained) land between the road from Halton and Norton Village to Daresbury.

That the linear fields around the village originated as medieval open fields is supported by two further pieces of evidence. One is the name of the bridge that was built by the duke of Bridgewater to take the road leading north west from the village to Norton Priory. The canal skirts the northern edge of the postulated open field; the bridge was given the name Norton Townfield Bridge. In the north west of England 'Townfield' was used in the eighteenth and nineteenth centuries to denote a small surviving area of common field arable which remained after the rest of the township's common fields had been enclosed (Elliott, in Baker and Butlin 1973, 46). The second piece of evidence is the faint traces of ridge and furrow which (until house building covered the area) could be seen to the west of the village in low sun.

The two large areas of linear fields in 1757 apparently represent two extensive areas of open field. They could each be regarded as a very large furlong, or an individual open field – the terms field and furlong were in any case often interchangeable in medieval documents (Elliott, in Baker and Butlin 1973, 45). These two areas would seem to be the primary arable of the village. How the holdings of the villagers of Norton were distributed through the open field cannot be known. However, if the layout of the village was the result of deliberate seignorial planning in the late eleventh or in the twelfth century then it seems equally likely that the impetus for clearance or re-occupation of land abandoned in 1070 and the method of distribution of the arable amongst the villagers also came from the lord of the manor. The linear fields to the north of the village were grouped in five or possibly six furlongs of greatly varying size. They could represent units of conversion of waste to arable, extending gradually northwards from the village within the limits imposed by Windmill Hill on the west and the wetter ground on the east.

The appearance of three main areas of open field to the west, east and north of the village on the J.E. 1757 map

might suggest three-field rotation. However, there was insufficient evidence for Dorothy Sylvester to demonstrate the presence of a genuine three-field system when she examined the county of Cheshire (Sylvester 1958). It has now been widely demonstrated that the unit of rotation was often not the field but the furlong, making it immaterial from the point of view of actual farming practice whether a village had two or three fields (Baker and Butlin 1973, cf. Darby 1973, 81–6). There is good evidence from the records of the royal manor of Frodsham that furlong rotation took place in the demesne furlongs of the reclaimed marsh in the fourteenth century. Individual furlongs were being rested every third year, or as an alternative a third of a furlong might lie fallow each year (Booth and Dodd 1979, 41).

It is not known how the pasture and meadow of Norton were managed. Presumably at an early stage in the development of the village it was surrounded by extensive waste that might be grazed by beasts in common, the only exceptions being the areas of open field, Eanley Wood to the south, and that land set aside for meadow. Meadow would have had to be protected from wandering animals by permanent hedges or temporary fences. Meadow had the highest value per acre of the land in the demesne at the Dissolution and it was no doubt valued highly by the villagers also – the hay was essential to permit the overwintering of cows, sheep and horses. It was probably cropped by the villagers in strips – an annual reapportionment of meadows by lot was customary in many English villages (Baker and Butlin 1973, 651). Unlike arable farming, which affected the structure of the surface of the landscape, hay-making had no physical impact and therefore perpetuation in field boundaries and other features is unlikely, unless enclosure took place on the basis of traditional allotment. It is possible that an area to the north east of the village, where a series of parallel hedge lines were shown on the J.E. 1757 map (demarcating Q12, U4, O10, O11 and O12), represents enclosure of meadow on this basis and is not enclosed open field.

Two separate enclosure processes can be recognised in the area of pasture-meadow. One is the establishment of farms and smallholdings in the waste, which seem to have acted as nuclei for enclosure in the form of irregularly shaped fields. A notable example is Wharford.

The second enclosure process is quite different. Instead of occurring in compact blocks, the remainder of the waste is characterised by very scattered holdings. The conclusion to be drawn from this is that enclosure of the waste started from the nuclei with their small irregular fields, and then by agreement or seignorial direction the remaining waste was enclosed, with portions being allotted to all those who had an interest in it – every villager, and the three nuclear farms. Abbey Hey, immediately north of Riding (from 'ryding', meaning 'clearing', Smith 1956, pt 2, 90), provides a clue to the date of enclosure. As the religious house achieved abbey status in 1391, and was dissolved in 1536, and was known as Norton Abbey only during that period, it is likely that it was during the fifteenth century or early sixteenth century that the process was under way, though the possibility of a name change cannot be ignored.

Unfortunately it is not possible to obtain information about the date of enclosure from hedge dating. The application of this technique involves the counting of the number of different species of flowering shrubs in a thirty-metre length of hedge; the number of species has been found to be an indication of the age of the hedge (Moore, Hooper, and Davis 1967). In Norton, estate improvement in the late eighteenth and early nineteenth centuries included a thorough replanting of all hedges.

It has been suggested above that the enclosure of the waste was taking place in the fifteenth or early sixteenth centuries, and was still occurring in the late eighteenth century. A long drawn out process of this kind, starting in the later part of the medieval period, would be consistent with the general picture of piecemeal consolidation and enclosure in Cheshire.

Stockham

The township of Stockham lies to the south west of the township of Norton but has as its western and southern boundaries Keckwick Brook and Bannerstich Brook and so forms a natural part of the manor of Norton. Its absence from the Domesday survey, but nonetheless likely existence in the eleventh century, have already been discussed. The earliest recorded spelling of the place name is Stoccum, in a charter which was probably drawn up during the period 1199–1203 (Barraclough 1957, 24). This name is derived from the dative plural *stoccum* meaning 'at the tree stocks', which in later forms becomes confused with *cumb*, 'a hollow' and *ham* 'a homestead' (Dodgson 1970, 180). It seems likely therefore that the name was adopted when the place was characterised by the stumps of cleared woodland. The clearance to which the place name refers must have taken place long before the period of the charter, by which time the occupants had extended their arable into Halton township (see below).

The township is roughly triangular in shape with a bulge to include Eanley in the south east (fig. 24). The fields alongside the Halton–Stockham–Sutton Weaver road form the north eastern boundary. The western side is marked by the Bannerstich Brook, and the south by the rising of Keckwick Brook, and another road which follows a direct route from Halton to Sutton Weaver. The western and southern boundaries would seem to be identical to those described in the charter of 1199–1203, which granted Adam de Dutton the land he had cleared nearby:

> From the hedge between the field of Stockham and the land in question as far as the Banalsiche and along the Banalsiche to the road running from

Halton towards Sutton, and along that road to the Henedelake and from the Henedelake across through the wood of Sutton to Sutton Heath, and from the heath the marsh contained within the boundaries of the land aforesaid, as far as the ditch previously mentioned, which is the division between the field of Stockham and the land in question.

The topographical information provided by the charter was briefly discussed by Barraclough, but it is possible to enlarge on his comments in the light of additional information. The crucial piece of knowledge which is essential to understand the boundaries is that the 'field of Stockham' did not lie within the boundaries of the township, but was in fact part of Halton township, lying to the west of the 'Banalsiche'. With this information, it is possible to follow the boundary on the Tithe Map and J.E. 1757 estate map. The latter is important in showing the Halton–Sutton road on what was probably the same route as it followed at the time of the charter – by the mid-nineteenth century the creation of the turnpike had altered the line of the road. Barraclough did not discuss the name of the 'Henedelake', but thought he could identify a pond to which the name might have applied. Dodgson suggested that the name might mean 'duck stream' (*ened, lacu*) (Dodgson 1970, 182). However, an alternative derivation can be suggested. 'Henedelake' in 1199–1203 is similar to 'Hendeleia' in the grant of Eanley to Norton Priory in the time of King John (Ormerod 1882, 1, 680). As Eanley was situated in this vicinity (see page 29) it seems possible that Henedelake refers to Eanley, either directly or by reference to a lake with a prefix common to both place names. The boundary through Sutton wood, across Sutton heath and round the marsh to Stockham field cannot be precisely defined, but the area can be suggested on the basis of the existing lie of the land (marked on fig. 24).

Within the township, information on the earlier structure of the landscape can be gleaned from the J.E. 1757 estate map. In 1757 the Halton–Stockham–Sutton Weaver road swung around a group of six dwellings that formed the settlement of Stockham (fig. 14). The buildings were positioned between two parallel lanes leading off the road. The western of the two lanes continued as a straight field boundary line, which suggests that the lane had previously joined the direct Halton–Sutton Weaver road on the south side of the township. A short lane linked the two parallel lanes. In the township were two other dwellings in 1757 – one in the extreme south eastern corner, which has the appearance of a roadside allotment or squat, the other a farm (now known as Woodfalls Farm) to the east of the main group of dwellings. It was probably established at a relatively late date. The six dwellings between the parallel lanes are likely to have occupied earlier sites, for in the available records (which are those that have been used in the case of Norton) the number of tenancies or houses remained remarkably stable. The grant of the manor of Norton to Sir Richard Brooke in 1545 mentioned seven messuages and lands in Stockham, and names those in possession of them (Beamont 1873, 202). Stockham had seven or eight tenancies from 1545 until at least 1811. It would seem to have been a hamlet of a type that appears to have been common in Cheshire, comprising a single row of houses with lanes and fields.

The occupants of the hamlet must have had access to what the Dutton charter refers to as Stockham Field. A map in Dunn's 1811 book provides a location for Stockham Field. Three fields adjoining the township but within Halton were situated to the west of the Bannerstich Brook, named First, Second and Third Stockham Field. They were all long fields with long edges that curved in a manner that suggests enclosure of ridge and furrow strips. There is thus evidence of open field arable farming being practised here at least as early as the twelfth century. Another probable area of previous open field is that between the hamlet and the Bannerstich Brook, where in 1757 there were more long narrow curving fields. The rest of the township in 1757 was occupied by many relatively small irregularly shaped fields.

Eanley

It has already been established that the Enlelei of Domesday became an integral part of the manor of Norton when Richard fitz Gilbert de Aston gave it to the canons. It remains to attempt to define the bounds of Eanley. Once again, the 1757 Estate Map provides crucial evidence (fig. 14). The map shows a straight road (named on later maps as Wood Lane) running in a north easterly direction from the south east corner of Stockham to Sutton. The straight course of the road is disrupted by a small dog-leg, and from this bend the Stockham–Norton township boundary can be traced on the map. The boundary (shown on fig. 24) follows an irregular course eastwards and then south, where it terminates at Keckwick Brook, which rises a short distance to the west. On the 1757 map the field boundaries in this area are all clearly later than the irregular boundary; they all terminate at it. The field names provide evidence which permits the identification of the area encompassed by the boundary, the straight road and the brook with Eanley. Within these limits thirteen fields are shown; all but one (Stone Delf Field) have 'Ainley' as part of the name. Of the seven fields east of the boundary that are named on the 1757 map, none includes the word Ainley in its name.

Woodland as an element in the manor of Norton

During the medieval period woodland was an important resource. It provided materials for construction and other uses, was a renewable fuel source, and in the form of parks could be used for harbouring game animals and agisting swine (i.e. allowing pigs to feed on acorns, mast etc). There can be no doubt that the manor of Norton possessed its own woodland, or access to woodland elsewhere, which was managed in such a way as to fulfill some of these functions.

Writers such as Oliver Rackham have stated that, contrary to views commonly held until recently, considerable tracts of open land existed by the end of the Iron Age, which were expanded further in the Roman period. There is also evidence that the end of the Roman period did not result in large-scale afforestation. Thus by the time of the Norman Conquest, England already had a cleared landscape. It has been calculated, on the basis of Domesday and other evidence, that an average of only 7% of the English landscape was covered by woodland in the late eleventh century, and that in some counties it was much less (3.4% of Lincolnshire for example) (Rackham 1976). Wildwood must have been converted to grazed or coppiced wood practically everywhere by the thirteenth century.

What we do not know is how and when the process of clearance occurred in Cheshire. It may well be that it took place more slowly than is the case for most of England. The reason for supposing this to be so is the paucity of known prehistoric and Roman period occupation sites in the county. The result may have been to leave medieval Cheshire with a relatively high proportion of its area wooded compared to the average for England, though the total area would still have been small in comparison with that utilised for arable and pasture. None is likely to have been wildwood.

In the case of the manor of Norton, there is some evidence for those areas that were still wooded in the medieval period. Domesday recorded, in addition to the six ploughlands, three acres of meadow, four acres of wood and two hays (usually interpreted as woodland clearance). Unfortunately, the proportion of the manor that was wooded cannot be calculated from the Domesday entry, for the size of the acre is unknown (Darby and Maxwell 1962, 356). No woodland is mentioned in the Eanley entry – only half a ploughland. Eanley Wood is therefore likely to have been in Norton near Eanley itself. The situation of Eanley Wood is suggested by field names containing a 'wood' element.

It is unfortunate that only on the southernmost part of the J.E. 1757 map were field names marked. However, the Dunn 1811 map and 1843 Tithe Map between them, in spite of the reduction in the number of fields and therefore of names, provide valuable evidence of the earlier extent of woodland. On the J.E. 1757 map, three fields contained the 'wood' element to the north east of the suggested boundary of Eanley (Great Longwood, Higher Longwood and Lower Wood). The straight boundaries to those fields may indicate enclosure, possibly involving clearance of woodland, at a relatively late date compared to other enclosure in the manor, which is characterised by irregular field boundaries. The area retained 'wood' field names in 1843 (Farther Wood, Fletchers Wood and Leadbeaters Wood, and two fields called Nearer Wood).

On the opposite side of the significantly named Wood Lane, but effectively continuous with the area of wood names that have been described, the two later maps show a compact block of wood names (Little Wood and Hough; Big Wood; Higher Wood, Middle Woods and Withers Wood, Withers Little Wood; and Baxters Wood; plus Cockshot and Wood Hatch). The field names, and lines of field boundaries, provide a basis for defining the wood (fig. 24) which to judge by the name of the farm immediately north west (Eanleywood Farm, SJ 553 814) and the farm to the east (Lower Eanleywood Farm SJ 564 813) was known as Eanley Wood. Beyond the suggested edge of the wood, the field names are indicative of pasture or probable enclosed pasture (Big, Lower and Little Meadow; Outlet; Rushy Field; Square, Further, Lower Wood and Higher Wood Intake form a band on the west). To the east was the suggested open field (Riggots Parks and Norton Field); to the south west was Eanley.

On the south side of the manor was the 'wood of Sutton' mentioned in Adam de Dutton's charter of 1199–1203. This wood, later becoming known as Murdishaw Wood, still exists. It lies mainly to the south of the boundary of Norton where it meets the boundaries of Aston, Preston, Stockham and Sutton. It has been suggested that the wood was a suitable place for local assemblies, hence the name *motere sceaga*, 'spokesman's wood' (Dodgson 1970, 181). It is worth recalling that Adam de Dutton's activity was not clearance of woodland, but of open land. The assumption that the process of assarting was clearance of woodland to establish fields has been shown to be incorrect in other parts of England, and of twelve examples in Cheshire quoted by Hewitt for the late thirteenth/early fourteenth century, only two appear to have affected woodland (Hewitt 1967, 15). Like Adam de Dutton's earlier clearance, they involved ploughing up heath and 'waste' (both of which were terms for rough grazing).

It is most unlikely that any woodland existed in Stockham, particularly in view of the fact that its open fields extended beyond its boundaries into Halton. Stockham had lost its tree stumps at a much earlier date.

Apart from Eanley Wood in the southern part of Norton, and Sutton (Murdishaw) Wood beyond, there can have been relatively little woodland in the manor in the medieval period. It seems probably that Windmill Hill, where the outcropping sandstone made agriculture impossible, was wooded at least on the sides. The only other wood was apparently beyond the north west boundary of the manor, in Astmoor. The confirmation charter of Roger de Lacy made in about 1200 referred to 'one parcel of land which is called Roger's Croft, which is

between the fishpool of the canons and the wood which is called Estmor' (Beamont 1873, 163). The fishpool was probably the dammed stream that flowed past the priory which had already become, or was about to become, the millpond. Astmoor Wood started beyond the boundary of Norton, and it still exists in fragments although cut by new roads and Astmoor Industrial Estate. Its probable location is shown on fig. 24.

In the mid-eighteenth century, the lack of woodland is demonstrated clearly by the J.E. 1757 Estate Map (fig. 14). This shows a narrow strip of woodland along part of the boundary with Sutton (Sutton or Murdishaw Wood) and a strip along part of the western boundary where Bannerstich Brook flows through a steep sided clough, which is still wooded. The northern part of Windmill Hill is shown wooded, and two woods were drawn near Norton Priory, one to the south, the other to the east.

No other woodland is marked, and there is no reason to think that it existed. As the eighteenth-century landscape reflected the medieval landscape to an extent, the lack of woodland in 1757 provides some confirmation that the impression of a medieval manor with little woodland is correct.

It is possible that the woodland shown on the 1757 map to the east and south of Norton Priory (fig. 13) represents the 'park' which is referred to, for example, in the Dissolution documents (Beamont 1873, 201). Much of that woodland was destroyed following the construction of the Bridgewater Canal (fig. 21). The part of the wood south of the priory, retained as the gardens of the country house, produces an annual flowering of bluebells, whereas the areas known to be later do not. Bluebells are regarded as an indicator of woodland of some antiquity, and this would certainly seem to be the case here. The southern part of the wood was cut off by the canal and was cleared. Its position has appeared on aerial photographs, though, as the outline of a large ditch which may have served as a park boundary.

In the extent of woodland, as in other matters, comparison between maps drawn in 1757 and 1843 shows considerable change. By 1843, when the Tithe Map was drawn, much more woodland existed (fig. 12). The new areas are often described as 'plantation', indicating deliberate planting of trees by the Brookes. Other areas are described as cover. The reasons were twofold – the planting of trees for aesthetic motives, and the provision of cover for game. Foxhunting and shooting became fashionable pursuits for the landed gentry in the second half of the eighteenth century, and the encouragement of earths and coverts was a widespread reason for planting. Mary Brooke's journal, written between 1829 and 1831, makes many references to foxhunting on the estate where it was clearly a popular pastime.

Summary

Limited deductions about the landscape of the manor of Norton in the medieval period can be made from evidence that is mainly post-medieval in date. However, the foregoing account has shown that it is possible to draw a series of conclusions about the topography of the area in the late medieval period (fig. 24):

1. The boundaries of the manor were natural features – the River Mersey, Keckwick Brook and Bannerstich Brook. Within the boundaries were three distinct parcels – the townships of Norton and Stockham, and Eanley.

2. The northern part of the manor consisted of reclaimed marsh, protected by an embankment, which on at least two occasions was overwhelmed by floods (in 1332 and 1429). The marsh was part of the priory demesne, and its uses are known to include the pasturing of cattle, and the cutting of turf.

3. Norton Priory was itself an extensive topographical feature, comprising the church and other claustral buildings, the buildings around the outer courtyard, the system of moats, drains, millpond and the mill itself, orchards and gardens, and the priory park.

4. The priory demesne was extensive, occupying more than half of Norton township, and in the early sixteenth century was being used for pasture (50%), arable (34%) and meadow (16%). The location of many of the fields whose names are known has been suggested.

5. The sandstone ridge of Windmill Hill formed a spine along the central axis of the manor. On the hill was the medieval windmill, the position of which has been identified. The hill was used for quarrying.

6. On the eastern slope of Windmill Hill was the village of Norton, which comprised an axial street lined by crofts on both sides, with back lanes beyond. The ordered arrangement of the village may be the result of post-Conquest planning. Excavation has confirmed the evidence of maps for the layout of the village.

7. To the west, east and north, and possibly also to the south east, were areas of open field that utilised sloping better-drained land. Wetter land in the valley was probably used for pasture and meadow. Enclosure and reorganisation of the open field may have occurred as early as the sixteenth century; enclosure of pasture may also have begun by this date.

8. The south western part of the manor was occupied by the township of Stockham, which, although not mentioned in Domesday, was almost certainly in existence by then. Stockham, a hamlet of seven dwellings in the sixteenth century, possessed open field within the township and also in Halton township.

9. The other part of the manor, in the south, was Eanley. It was a distinct (although small and waste) entity in Domesday, but became an integral part of Norton in the early thirteenth century.

10. Woodland was present in Norton in 1086, but its extent at that date is unknown. By the late medieval period, the only substantial wood seems to have been Eanley Wood, the position of which has been identified. There were some small woods on the fringes of the manor.

11. The network of roads and tracks that existed in the eighteenth century probably perpetuated the medieval pattern. As well as roads to Halton, Moore, Daresbury and Sutton, tracks led to the windmill and provided access to the fields.

3

Products and resources of the manor

In the absence of Norton Priory's own manorial records, insights into the products of the manor and surrounding land must be obtained from other sources. These are of two types: the evidence provided by excavation, and the evidence from documents of various kinds. The latter may only mention products of the estate incidentally. In the following account, the two classes of evidence are combined to provide as full a picture as possible of the potential resources of the manor – of which the canons will have taken advantage to a varying extent at different periods.

The waters of the Mersey

The northern edge of the manor of Norton is bounded by the River Mersey (fig. 24). The estuary, referred to as 'the area of sea called the Mersey' in 1332 (*Cal. Papal Reg. 2*, 379) has a large tidal rise and fall. When the foundation charter of 1134 granted the canons the manor of Norton 'with all its appurtenances in wood, with forests and warren and in plain, with lands pastures and waters . . .', William fitz William was following a formula, but in this case the waters were a substantial asset. Their value as a source of fish had been noticed 48 years earlier, when Domesday listed a fisherman as one of the inhabitants of the manor. Not only those waters which formed part of the manor were given, however; also granted was 'one fishery, called Pulceorpe which belongs to the church of Runcorn . . . half of all the fisheries which belong to Halton . . . half of my whole fishery of Thelwall . . . and the fisherman there'. The priory thus had a string of fisheries extending up the Mersey from Runcorn to Thelwall. Such extensive rights did not prevent problems arising however. In 1367, Walter, prior of Norton, was fined for encroaching on the fishery known as Charneth. The offence was not an uncommon one; at the same court held

at Thelwall seventeen other people were fined for similar offences at a number of different fisheries (Beamont 1879, 30). In 1388 the prior of Norton was charged with making two fishyards which obstructed the passage of the lord's eight-oared boat. In view of their illegality, their names are ironic: Gracedieu and Charity. In 1393 the abbot of Norton (called such under his newly acquired title) was mentioned in connection with an identical offence at the same fishyards (Beamont 1879, 32). Obstruction of the river to navigation was an offence perpetrated by many time and again as the court records show; in the late seventeenth century it was still occurring.

The fish weirs were doubtless similar to those investigated on old courses of the River Trent at Colwick in Nottinghamshire (Losco-Bradley and Salisbury 1979; also Salisbury 1980). A Saxon weir, carbon-dated to the ninth century, was 38 metres long and was built of posts, wattles and boulders. It ran obliquely across the river, and seems to have functioned as a funnel down which fish were directed into a net. A twelfth-century weir consisted of six rows of oak and holly posts which supported wattle panels. It formed a 'V' pointing downstream; presumably nets were placed at the angle of the weir. One arm of the weir was 30 metres long, the other was estimated as 'up to 100 metres'. The Mersey weirs were probably of similar size and construction, so it is not surprising that a conflict arose between the use of the river for fishing and for navigation.

Salmon were an important catch. They are referred to as being taken in nets and at the weir in Thelwall fishery in 1367. During the same year a sturgeon was caught in the Mersey (Beamont 1879, 31) which was one of the privileges claimed by the Baron of Halton. The fish weirs, like those on the Trent, were timber structures. When a fishery called Tolfy was leased out in 1369 the lord was to find and carry timber and the tenant at the end of his term was to leave the fishery in repair (*ibid.*, 32). At the Halton court held at Thelwall on 19 March 1513, twenty-three persons were fined for taking young salmon and salmon that had spawned, and for using unlawful nets (*ibid.*, 33). In 1516 another twenty persons were fined at Thelwall for a similar offence (*ibid.*, 34). Apart from salmon, and the solitary sturgeon, no other fish are mentioned in the court rolls as being caught in the Mersey. Pollution has now all but eliminated salmon in the river – there are only five records this century (Merseyside County Museum survey).

Fishbones recovered at Norton Priory were few in number, due presumably to smallness making recognition during excavation difficult, and a greater tendency than most animal bones to decay. However, those identified extend the knowledge of fish caught and consumed locally. Of the total of twenty-three bones, eleven were from pre-Dissolution layers and twelve from post-Dissolution layers. All but two of the total were bones of cod. Although commonly thought of as a sea fish, cod do in fact occur frequently in estuarine conditions, and were probably plentiful in the Mersey. Cod was one of the fish cooked in the kitchen of St Werburgh's Abbey, Chester as well as salmon, bass, conger eels, and ray (Burne 1962). With the waters of the Dee and Mersey rich in fish, and imports of herring, white fish and ling through Chester (Driver 1971, 96) both monks and canons could enjoy a varied fish diet.

Occurring in both pre- and post-Dissolution contexts were large numbers of oyster shells, and smaller quantities of mussels and cockles. Before modern pollution, the extensive mud and sandbanks that are revealed every low tide would have provided a suitable habitat for oysters and cockles in profusion. Mussels require rock or other firm surfaces for adhesion, and might have been found particularly at those points where sandstone outcropped, such as Runcorn Gap.

An unexpected find was one bone from a porpoise (the centrum from a vertebra) from a thirteenth-century context. Marine mammals still occasionally find their way into the Mersey. In 1960, for example, about forty whales came up the river as far as Runcorn. It may well be that the porpoise was washed up on the shore or caught in the nets or weirs of local fishermen. Porpoise was apparently regarded as a delicacy in the medieval period (Hartley and Elliot – 14th century – 1925, 29).

It is clear that the River Mersey was a rich source of fish and shellfish which the canons and their lessees exploited fully. It is also probable that the large volumes of water that formed the moats that bounded the priory on the south, east, and partly on the north, and the millpond on the west, were used as fishponds. The 'canons' fishpool' is referred to in a grant to the priory of land 'between the fishpool and Astmoor wood'. The fishpool was formed by damming the Bannerstich Brook so that it also functioned as the pool for the water mill. Fresh fish would have been a much more easily obtained element in the diet of the canons of Norton than in that of many inland monasteries, where the fishponds and stores of salted fish would have had to suffice.

Birds

The estuary of the Mersey is an important gathering area for many varieties of migrating birds. The land of the manor of Norton would also have provided habitats for many birds that featured in the extensive medieval diet. A variety of birds has been recognised from bones recovered in the excavation. A large number of individual bones (30) were those of geese, which in the view of the specialist who identified them (D. Bramwell) were probably all domestic birds. There was evidence of butchering to remove feet, and charring of three examples of distal tibiotarsus, which in cooking are exposed as 'drumsticks'. A larger number of bones of fowl (40) were identified, some of which showed evidence of butchering. Both geese and fowl were probably kept at the priory; certainly in the post-Dissolution period

this was so, for in the 1632 *inquisition post mortem* of Sir Richard Brooke III one of the outbuildings mentioned was for 'pullen' (Stewart-Brown 1934, 82–5).

In 1522, when a special episcopal inquisition was carried out at Norton (transcribed in Heath 1973, 90–5), it was mentioned in passing that a servant of the abbey, one William the joiner, 'fattens also the geese and capons of the monastery for which he receives a portion of food suitable for this'.

Other bird bones were present in small numbers. Mallard duck may have been domestic as they were sometimes hatched under domestic fowls and reared; they may however have been caught on the Mersey marshes. Teal would have been common in the marshes as well. Three birds that were probably also eaten favour a habitat of woodland verging on agricultural land: wood pigeon, rook and jackdaw. Another bird that was eaten at Norton was woodcock.

It is interesting to compare the post-Dissolution birds with those consumed during the monastic period. Of the birds of sixteenth- and seventeenth-century date, fowl with 86 bone fragments was again the most common, followed similarly by goose (82). Turkey and peafowl are two species not represented in the medieval period that occur later, but mallard, teal, rook and woodcock were eaten in both periods. Other species not found in medieval deposits but occurring later were partridge, curlew, redshank, snipe, red kite, buzzard, dove, crane, heron and mute swan. Bones of sparrowhawk may have come from a bird used for hawking. The larger variety of post-medieval birds may be purely a result of the larger total bone sample produced by the excavation of the later deposits. The mid-eighteenth-century perspective engraving of the Georgian country house (fig. 21) shows a dovecote in the foreground – no doubt doves were kept for their meat and their eggs for some time before this.

Mammals

Of a total of 12,436 animal bones collected and subsequently examined by Judi Caton, 6,556 (53%) were assigned to species. The remainder consisted of 3,389 small chips and 2,491 rib fragments which were not positively identified. Excluding fish and birds, the total of pre-Dissolution fragments identified was 1,263, the total of post-Dissolution (*i.e.* later sixteenth-century and seventeenth-century) 4,846. The preponderance of post-medieval bones is explained by the fact that a rich source was the cloister, which became a rubbish dump for the Tudor mansion, until the construction of the Georgian house in about 1740 was accompanied by the laying out of a garden over that area. In contrast medieval deposits of rubbish resulted apparently from casual disposal in a great variety of places – disused drains, cisterns etc., and simple squalor. The main areas where medieval rubbish was dumped have yet to be found.

To have samples of animal bones from the medieval

priory and from the Tudor mansion is of great value, for as the estates that were run from Norton were little different in extent, a valid comparison may be made between the two groups of data. The numbers of fragments do not however provide a basis for detecting changes of diet with time over shorter periods.

Of the mammals, cattle, sheep and pigs were the most commonly occurring animals in both periods. The numbers can be expressed in terms of total number of fragments (excluding rib, skull and vertebra fragments) or the minimum number of individuals (based on the best represented part of the bone present). Both are given in the table below.

The Augustinian order always had a comparatively relaxed attitude to the consumption of meat. There were strict Cistercian ordinances against meat; these became steadily less rigid and in the mainly fifteenth-century kitchen rubbish deposits at Kirkstall Abbey, Yorkshire, there were many animal bones (Ryder 1959). These were studied in several groups, but none produced figures of less than 75% for cattle, and none more than 14% for sheep and 5% for pigs based on the 'total fragments' method of counting. A small sample from Pontefract Priory (Ryder 1965) ranging in date from the twelfth to the sixteenth centuries produced figures of 30% for cattle, 45% for sheep and 20% for pigs counted on the same basis, much more similar to the Norton figures. Pontefract was a Cluniac house where abstinence from meat would not have been practised with the fervour of the early Cistercians.

Sheep

The contrast in the proportions of cattle and sheep between Kirkstall and Norton is not what might be reasonably predicted from documentary evidence. In 1301 the tally of animals kept on the Kirkstall land was 4,500 sheep and 618 cattle (88%:12%). This is somewhat earlier than the date of the excavated sample but although changes may have occurred in stock rearing, in the

fifteenth century, sheep must have still outnumbered cattle to a considerable extent. Although the importance of sheep was to a great degree due to the production of wool and fleece, their relative abundance might also lead one to expect a predominance as a source of meat. In contrast, Cheshire appears to have supported a small sheep population. In the fourteenth century there is no evidence of large-scale sheep farming on monastic manors in the country, indeed 'we are not aware of there being any sheep on the manors of the religious houses of Norton, Birkenhead or even Chester till, in the last decade of the fourteenth century, some sheep were stolen from the abbot of Chester' (Hewitt 1967, 36). Records of wool exports from the county confirm its unimportant role in wool production. So we have the surprising situation of the monks of Kirkstall, in a county where sheep dominated, apparently eating less mutton than the canons of Norton in cattle-favouring Cheshire. It seems very likely that some sheep were reared on the Norton estate, although no documents have survived which mention sheep farming. They would have been a source of meat and wool (a medieval spindle whorl from Norton village is one indication of its use in the peasant community). One of the names of the fields conveyed to Sir Richard Brooke in 1545 was the 'Shepe House', and local wool production at that date was sufficiently great to justify a fulling mill in the manor of Norton (Beamont 1873). Pre- and post-Dissolution samples of sheep bones revealed a very similar pattern of age structure, with the majority being eaten at two to three years, and a smaller number at maturity. A few lambs were eaten in the medieval period. The large numbers of sheep tibiae and humeri may indicate a preference for legs of mutton and lamb.

Cattle

Cattle farming was an important element in Cheshire's pastoral economy, providing not only meat but also hides. As draught animals, in agriculture and haulage, cattle played an important role. In the manor at Halton in 1304–5 there was a stock of 125 beasts; on the royal manor of Macclesfield in 1356–7 there were 542 cattle and many were driven to London each year for the royal households (Hewitt 1967, 31). However it seems likely that on most manors the number of cattle was much more modest. Indeed it is probable that historians have overemphasised the pastoral, cattle-farming side of Cheshire's economy in the past, and have underestimated the importance of arable farming.

One area of Norton's demesne that was used for cattle raising was the reclaimed marsh by the Mersey; in 1522 an inquisition was told that one Thomas Ruttour 'has supervision of oxen, horses and other cattle there, taking for his labour the increment of 4 cows and the profit of one cow of the oxen of the abbot' (Heath 1973, 92).

Cattle were a important element in the diet of the

	Total fragments			
	Pre-Dissolution		Post-Dissolution	
	Number	%	Number	%
Cattle	577	47	3528	85
Sheep	380	31	328	8
Pigs	280	22	255	7

	Minimum number of individuals			
	Pre-Dissolution		Post-Dissolution	
	Number	%	Number	%
Cattle	13	30	87	70
Sheep	20	47	22	17
Pigs	10	23	17	13

canons as the 'Total Fragments' tables show (p. 51). When the numbers are adjusted to take account of the greater meat yield of a cow compared to a sheep or pig, the importance is emphasised further.

One question that is raised by comparison between the two groups of figures above is whether in the post-Dissolution period cattle gained a greater dominance than previously in the agricultural economy of the county. Of course, the tastes of the canons and the Brooke household need not reflect a wider situation, but there is little evidence of dairy farming being the dominant form of agriculture in Cheshire before the Dissolution. Cheshire cheese appears rarely in documents before the fifteenth century. It seems possible that enclosure from the late medieval period onwards was connected with cattle farming, including an increasing role for dairying. Cheshire's agriculture may have been much more mixed than has generally been assumed.

A study of the proportions of bones present in both samples of cattle has shown a similar pattern, with the main meat yielding bones well represented, while the extremities are not. Shoulder, fore-leg, rump and hind leg cuts were consumed in larger quantities, or more often, than the inferior joints. Very little skull or upper jaw material was present in the medieval sample, and no horn cores, so it is impossible to determine how the head was removed from the carcass. Cuts on the mandibles indicated that the jaws were removed from the skulls by chopping away the coronoid process. There were many and varied cuts on the humeri, but the indications are that the proximal ends were cut through to separate the humeri and the scapulae, and the distal ends were removed in the separation of the humeri and radii. It is likely that the hind limb was treated in the same way, with the heads of the femora being removed with the pelves, and the distal epiphyses severed with the tibiae.

It is not known whether there was a slaughter house at the priory, but it seems quite likely that one would have been situated on the outer courtyard. It is not surprising then that extremities were not found in the excavated deposits, most of which must have originated in the kitchens where cooking of already partly prepared meat would have taken place. A slaughter house certainly figured in the 1632 *inquisition post mortem* of Sir Richard Brooke III (Stewart-Brown 1934, 82–5). It may have been the successor of a pre-Dissolution slaughter house.

Proportions of species present after adjustment for meat yield

	Pre-Dissolution	Post-Dissolution
Cattle	68%	93%
Sheep	17.5%	3%
Pigs	14.5%	4%

The ageing of cattle was assessed by Judi Caton on the basis of fusion of the long bones and eruption stages of the mandibular teeth. The results show that about 20% of the bones were from animals killed when aged 2 to $2\frac{1}{2}$ years, and 20% from those aged $3\frac{1}{2}$ to 4 years. The majority, however, were eaten in maturity, at 4 years and over. There appears to be a continuity of practice between monastic and lay establishments, since the age structures of the two groups were very similar. The explanation of this is not that draught animals were slaughtered when they became feeble. A study of the diseased and abnormal animal bones from Norton Priory has been carried out by John Baker of the Department of Veterinary Medicine, University of Liverpool. His findings show a remarkably low level of disease in the cattle population with a complete absence of severe arthritic lesions. Draught animals in contrast would be expected to show signs of their use having affected their bones, with levels of up to 30% of severe arthritis, occurring as chronic damage to the joint, being found on most sites. Cattle bones from medieval villages do tend to include some older animals that were probably used for draught; most village cattle were, however, killed at two years (Beresford and Hurst 1971, 138).

The explanation of the preponderance of mature cattle may be dairying. It is possible that there was a dairy herd both before and after the Dissolution which was managed in such a way as to provide meat from animals that had passed their peak milk yield. Alternatively, meat was provided by prime beef cattle. Certainly, as the results previously described show, the inhabitants in both periods could well afford to eat the best cuts of meat. Dairying at Norton was certainly being practised in the post-Dissolution period. The *inquisition post mortem* of 1632 lists the dairy house and the dairy vault, as well as the cow house (Stewart-Brown 1934, 82–5). Like the slaughter house previously mentioned, these buildings may continue a practice started in the monastic period. Another indicator of continuity is the presence of minor congenital defects occurring in cattle in the articular surfaces of the first and second phalanges, observed by John Baker. The defects, which are of unknown etiology and which would not have caused clinical symptoms, were observed in samples ranging in date from the fifteenth century to the seventeenth century. The prevalence was 13.2%, the highest seen by Dr Baker in any sample from the British Isles, the next highest being 7% in a Scottish sixth–seventh century site. 3% of modern dairy cattle are affected by these minor congenital variations.

Pigs

On the basis of the excavated bones, pigs were the third most commonly eaten animal at Norton Priory before and after the Dissolution. Analysis for age revealed a different structure to that of cattle and sheep. More pigs were killed in their first and second years and few in maturity, in both periods. Another marked difference was that pig mandibles occurred in a much higher proportion than those of cattle and sheep. Caution must be exercised due to problems of retrieval, identification and differential survival which may bias a relatively small sample. However, it would seem that the canons and their Tudor successors favoured young and sucking pigs.

The rearing of pigs on Norton's demesne is suggested by one of the field names, the Lower Swine Park, listed in the Augmentation Office valuation (Beamont 1873, 204). Outbuildings for swine were among the features of the Tudor mansion listed in 1632 (Stewart-Brown 1934, 82–5). Roger de Lacy (Baron of Halton, 1190–1211) provided the canons of Norton with a confirmation of their charter. Of particular interest is the grant that 'all their demesne swine may be with my demesne swine in all my woods, and wherever else I may have mast for the same' (Beamont 1873, 163). This grant was valuable in that it provided the right to agist pigs without the payment in money or in kind (or both) that operated in Cheshire's royal forests and other woodland. Most owners had to pay, but a few were exempt in certain woods on a parallel with Norton Priory's rights in Halton. For example, the abbot of Chester had the right to have fifty pigs in the woods of Bebington without payment, and the abbot of Dieulacres (Staffs.) claimed freedom from payment of pannage for all his swine in all woods in Cheshire belonging to the earl (Hewitt 1967, 28). Pigs were a feature of rural life throughout medieval England, but Cheshire with plentiful supplies of salt was in a good position to preserve the meat in the form of bacon. The consumption of bacon at Norton Priory will have left no trace in the kitchen debris, and so the proportion of pig meat eaten may be under represented by the excavated animal bones.

Deer

In addition to the right of free pannage granted by Roger de Lacy, another new privilege formed part of the confirmatory charter: 'I grant also, to the before named canons every year, for ever, at the Assumption of the Blessed Mary, two deer from my park at Halton' (Beamont 1873, 163). Some deer bones have been identified, though in small numbers. From medieval deposits four fallow deer bones and eight red deer bones have been counted. Post-medieval deposits have yielded ten and two respectively – Halton continued to have a park, in which King James I hunted and killed a buck on 1 August 1617. However, despite the proximity of the baron's park, the evidence from the excavated animal bones suggests that venison was relatively rarely eaten at Norton before or after the Dissolution.

Horses

Only three bones from medieval deposits were identified as being from horses. The eating of horse flesh in medieval England was unusual, at least on sites belonging to the higher social classes. On village sites, much higher levels have been recorded, as much as 20% in some contexts at Wharram Percy (Beresford and Hurst 1971, 140). However, the feeding of horse flesh to dogs must also be considered: the presence of horse bones need not necessarily imply human consumption.

Horses must have been important animals at Norton for draught and riding. Three horseshoes, and numerous horseshoe nails, were found embedded into the cobbled entrance track to the outer courtyard of the priory at a point where the track had subsided into the softer fill of twelfth-century drains.

Another piece of archaeological evidence for the use of draught horses at Norton dates from the sixteenth century. In a post-Dissolution destruction layer of rubble covering the north east chapels, a small spherical bronze bell was found. This type of bell is usually described as a packhorse bell, and it may have been lost from a horse being used for taking stone or other materials from the demolished church. Horses were widely used in Cheshire for drawing cartloads of stone, for example during the construction of Vale Royal Abbey, when 35,448 loads were transported in three years (Hewitt 1967, 56). In the autumn of 1282, at a time of royal commandeering of transport in preparation for a campaign against the Welsh following David ap Gruffydd's revolt, the prior of Norton was specifically excluded from having to supply goods, horses or carts. This was revoked in December when Edward I ordered the heads of all the religious houses in Cheshire to send all their horses and carts to Chester for transport (*ibid.*, 45).

Stabling of the riding horses of the priory was one of the conditions of the Aston corrody (Beamont 1873, 173). It is probable that they were accommodated in a stable which would also have housed horses used by the prior or abbot and those obedientiaries whose duties took them outside the bounds of the priory. When Sir Geoffrey Warburton made his will on 1 September 1448 one of his bequests was that of his best horse to the abbot of Norton (Beamont 1873, 180). In 1392, Sir Lawrence de Dutton left his black horse to the convent of Norton (Ormerod 1882, 1, 648).

Horses were mentioned as being grazed at the Mershe (Mersey fringe) in 1522 (Heath 1973, 92), and the Ministers' Accounts at the time of the Dissolution name one of the demesne fields as 'Horselownes'.

Dogs

Another condition of the Aston corrody was that a brace of greyhounds was to be kept at the priory. Relatively few dog bones (seven) have been identified from medieval deposits, but a large number (396) have come from post-Dissolution layers. The difference is probably due to the different nature of the rubbish of the two periods. The medieval bones are largely food debris. The later bones however are from the cloister, which seems to have been a general dump for the Tudor mansion. This rubbish included dead dogs. The fact that the dog bones found were more often than not complete supports the view that they represent discarded carcasses, that may have belonged to hunting or guard dogs. Some of the post-Dissolution dogs have been shown by John Baker to have been suffering from rickets.

Cats

Only three cat bones were found in medieval layers, but fifty-four in post-Dissolution deposits. The same factors that give a false impression of scarcity of dogs at the Priory in the medieval period probably operate to underestimate the cat population. In both periods it is likely that cats will have been kept for their rodent catching qualities. Their efficacy is perhaps illustrated by the small numbers of mice bones found – none in the medieval deposits, and only seven of post-Dissolution date.

Rabbits and hares

A surprising aspect of the animal bone analysis is that only one medieval and three post-Dissolution rabbit bones, and only one post-Dissolution hare bone were identified. It is true that rabbit bones are relatively small, and might

therefore be more likely to be missed during excavation. However, as over 400 equally small bird bones were recovered, failure of recovery cannot be the reason, as survival factors should be similar. It is also difficult to conceive of any method of butchery that would provide boneless carcasses for consumption – rabbits were either jointed and boiled or roasted whole on a spit. The conclusion must be drawn that rabbits and hares were not a significant part of the diet of the medieval or later occupants of Norton – another instance of continuity in meat-eating habits. This is in spite of the fact that the presence of rabbits in the medieval period gave the name Coney Graves to a number of fields to the north of the priory (fig. 24).

Arable agriculture

Information about the crops that were grown in the manor of Norton is slight. Only a few documentary references are available, and little archaeological evidence. The record of the Augmentations Office commissioner, Thomas Combes, drawn up in 1536, provides a general picture of the way in which the demesne land was being used at that date. The account is given below, in full (summarised in Beamont 1873, 204 and checked in the original PRO SC6/Henry VIII/410 26259).

Meadow
First 64 acres of meadow lying about the abbey;
   price the acre, 4s

     £12 16s 0d

Pasture
Item, 72 acres lying about the abbey; price the acre, 2s
   (an error – see page 55)

     104s

Item, 6 acres lying in Middleton; price the acre, 18d
   (an error – see page 55)

     12s

Item, Barlowe and Mosse Moor worth by the year   33s 4d
Item, the Oxmoor with the appurtenances is worth by the year   40s
Item, a pasture called Sondewall Moor, by the year   33s 4d
Item, the Park is worth by the year to be letten   13s 4d
Item, the Lower Swyne Park is worth by the year   2s 8d
Item, the yards at the Sheephouse be worth by the year   5s

     £12 3s 8d

Ley
Item, 24 acres in Saundersfield; price the acre, 8d   16s
Item, 16 acres in Cropfield; price the acre, 8d   10s 8d

     £ 1 6s 8d

Arable Land
Item, 10 acres lying in Horselownes; price the acre, 2s   20s
Item, the Cryme 6 acres; price the acre, 2s   12s
Item, 16 acres lying in two orchard fields; price the acre, 22d   29s 4d
Item, 5 acres lying in Morley crofts; price the acre, 20d   8s 4d
Item, 7 acres in Churchfield; price the acre, 18d   10s 6d
Item, 17 acres lying in Middleton; price the acre, 8d   34s
   (an error – see page 55)

Item, 10 acres in Radford field; price the acre, 8d   6s   8d
item, 14 acres in the Weldmare Flatts; price the acre, 8d   9s   4d
Item, 13 acres of barley stubble; price the acre, 18d   19s   6d
                                                                                                          ───────────────
                                                                                                          £ 7   9s   8d

Item, the site of the monastery there by year   20s
Item, the water mill there by year   20s
Item, the windmill there by year   20s
Item, the herbage of the Warth and the Moss, where the
    tenants get their turf is worth by the year   100s
Item, the fishing in the Mersey is worth by the year   20s
                                                                                                          ───────────────
                                                                                                          £ 9   0s   0d

                                                                                                          Sum
                                                                                                £42   16s   0d
                                                                                                ═══════════════════════

By Thomas Combes, Auditor

Thomas Combes made a mistake with three items on the list. Errors in arithmetic are a common feature of suppression commissioners' accounts.

It should be asked whether Combes was using the standard acre or the Cheshire acre. As he was no doubt referring to the abbey's own documents, or verbal information from the bailiff, it is more likely that local measurement was used. The Cheshire acre was larger than the standard acre by a factor of 2.1, being based on the Cheshire rod which was 24 feet in length (compared to the standard rod of 16 feet). An indication of which acre was being used is provided by a comparison of the tithe-free land in 1843 (shown on fig. 24) with the total demesne acreage recorded in 1536.

Unfortunately, no acreage for six of the areas of pasture is provided – these are mainly the areas of reclaimed marsh, and if a value of one shilling per acre for these is assumed, the total acreage amounts to 412 acres, assuming five acres for the sites of the monastery and mills. To this must be added the land listed in the 1536 Augmentation Office Account of Norton's revenues in the demesne but let out to farm. This amounted to £3 12s 0d compared to the £42 16s 0d value of the rest of the demesne. If the total is adjusted in proportion, it amounts to 442 acres. The comparison between this and the 1843 figure of 1,193 acres provides a factor of 2.7. However, in the tithe assessment most of the woodland and plantations in the township were exempt, and were therefore included in the total of 1,193 acres. In most cases, the 1536 commissioners ignored woodland in their assessment of monastic income (Knowles 1959, 305) and therefore woodland areas in the demesne, particularly in the park, do not appear in the total. Thus, the factor must have been near the 2.1 value, which supports the view that it was the Cheshire acre that provided the basis for Combes' account.

To summarise, 16% of the demesne land was being used for meadow, 50% for pasture and 34% for arable cultivation. However, as 13% of pasture was land lying fallow (ley) the land that formed part of the arable cycle was 47%, a substantial proportion. This is consistent with the results of archaeological and historical research throughout Cheshire, in which evidence is accumulating to suggest that arable farming was much more important than has been assumed in the past. Manorial records (for example those of the royal manors), and the extent of ridge and furrow that aerial survey has revealed, both indicate that Cheshire agriculture, at least in part of the medieval period, had a substantial arable content. Hewitt's view that 'a good deal of the surface of Cheshire at that period (the end of the thirteenth century) was ill adapted for arable cultivation' (Hewitt 1967, 23) is not supported by the growing evidence.

It would be interesting to know what was being grown on the arable demesne in 1536. Only the mention of thirteen (Cheshire) acres of barley stubble provides any information. In the previous century, some evidence is provided by the mention in a court case of wheat, barley, peas and oats which had been sold by the abbot to William Starkey of Northwich, who had not paid the price of 16s 8d (Driver 1971, 93). On the royal demesne of Frodsham in the mid-fourteenth century, wheat occupied 22.4% of the total cropland, oats 32.4%, barley 3.5% and pulses 12.8% (Booth and Dodd 1979, 45).

Orchards near the priory are known from Dissolution records, which also mention fields named Hemp Yards. Wheat and barley would have been needed at the priory for the production of bread and ale, two staple ingredients of monastic diet. In the 1522 episcopal inquisition (Heath 1973, 90–5), the wife of William the joiner was described as 'alewife to the abbot', while William is said to have baked fortnightly a quarter part of a measure of corn for the abbot. The discovery in the kitchens of part of one of the stones of a handmill with lead setting for the pivot, and fragments of a second near the kitchens, indicates that some grain was ground at the priory. However, most grain produced on the demesne and by tenants would have been processed at the priory water mill or at the mill on Windmill Hill. The bakehouse and brewhouse were probably situated on the outer courtyard where they certainly existed in 1632 according to the *inquisition post mortem* of Sir Richard Brooke III.

Woodland products

There are two sources of information about the use of timber in the manor in the medieval period. There are a few documentary references; these are complemented by information derived from the excavation.

The most impressive evidence consists of the stumps of posts of twelfth-century buildings (fig. 25). These were preserved by the exclusion of air. Most of the timbers were dressed to a square or rectangular section. The largest was judged by Liverpool Polytechnic Department of Botany to have an age of more than two centuries when felled (fig. 26). All the structural timbers examined were identified as oak, which is consistent with the national picture of oak everywhere being the commonest *timber* tree in medieval woods (Rackham 1976). Oak was not the only timber

Fig. 25. Post pit with a stump of the carefully squared timber post of a twelfth-century temporary building. The near half of the pit has been fully excavated; the outline and mixed clay and soil filling of the remainder can also be seen.

used in the twelfth-century buildings, however. A ditch running through the kitchen area was contemporary with the phase one timber buildings, from which roof water drained into it. When the buildings were demolished the ditch was partially filled with the debris of wattle and daub walls. Some wattles were recovered from the water-logged bottom of the ditch in the excavation and were submitted to Dr J. F. Hughes of the Commonwealth Forestry Institute. The larger wattles were identified as wood hazel (*Corylus avellana*) and the smaller were Salix species, probably willow (*Salix alba*). These are the species that might have been predicted: hazel rods would have been produced by coppicing, and willow by pollarding. It was clearly important that substantial quantities of wattles were available for the construction of the large buildings in the twelfth century, and substantial managed coppice woodland must have existed in the priory park or elsewhere in the vicinity. Oak was also used in the construction of wooden coffins. A number of these were found in the (lay) cemetery to the north of the church. They consisted of planks bound together at the corners. Identification by Carole Keepax of the Ancient Monuments Laboratory (series/number 91/75) proved the planks to be of oak. The binding material was found to be hazel. Charcoal from the bell pit found in 1976 was identified by Mrs Keepax as being from fairly large timbers of alder, oak and hazel (AML 767849). The presence of oak and hazel is not surprising. Both grew readily on boulder clay; indeed oak is the climax woodland on it.

Wooden vessels have been found at Norton Priory in water-logged deposits, ranging in date from the thirteenth to the sixteenth century. They comprise eleven wooden bowls and two wooden platters, all of which appear to

Fig. 26. Post pit with surviving timber; it proved to have been from an oak tree two centuries old when felled.

have been made of alder, turned on a lathe. From the sixteenth-century rubbish deposits in the cloister came a core from lathe turning, which suggests that wooden bowls were being made at Norton. Another wooden object to have been discovered in a sixteenth-century layer is a substantial fragment of a wooden comb.

To summarise, the types of wood known to have been utilised by the medieval inhabitants of Norton Priory are oak, hazel, willow and alder. These trees, as well as birch are the species that have been identified from pollen grains present in the pre-Priory turfline and subsoil.

There are a number of documentary references to the use of timber in the manor and surrounding area. Grants of timber occur occasionally. For example, one of the items specified in the charter of licence issued by Edward III in 1329 was 'timber from the wood of Keckwick to repair the mill of Keckwick' granted by Hugh de Dutton (Beamont 1873, 171). Nothing else is known of this mill. It may have been a water mill built on Keckwick Brook, but is more likely to have been a windmill standing on Keckwick Hill.

Norton was entitled, or seems to have thought itself entitled, to a tithe of timber in Halton. In 1393, when a large wood of the lord's was felled, Richard Wyche, recently elevated to abbot, claimed and took ten of the trees. However, he seems to have had doubts about the entitlement, and gave the steward an undertaking to return them if the law should be against him (Beamont 1879, 14). From this it is clear that wood was not so plentiful on the estate that the chance of acquiring further stocks could be ignored. Another example of wood being imported into the manor is provided by a document of early sixteenth-century date. During the abbacy of William Merton, a request was directed to Henry VIII for permission to take thirty oaks from Delamere Forest, for repair for fire damage. The oaks were to be used for boards and shingles, and the grant was made (Cheshire Record Office, DSR/G/50/1). The need to acquire wood at this date is consistent with the picture presented by the study of the landscape of a very small amount of woodland extant in the early sixteenth century (fig. 24). It is also consistent with the entry in the Augmentation Office survey of income from sale of wood and underwood, recorded as nil during that year and the period of account (PRO SC6/Henry VIII/410 26259).

The use of wood at Norton Priory must have been much more extensive than the archaeological and historical evidence alone can reveal. The need for structural timbers, wattles and shingles has been mentioned already, but the construction of masonry buildings required large quantities as well. During building operations there was the need for timber scaffolding, planks and centering for vaults and arches. Considerable quantities of timber will have gone into the buildings as part of their structures. The roofs of all the buildings would have been of timber, with a covering of sandstone slabs, lead in some cases, some slate, or shingles (the last probably on subsidiary buildings of the outer courtyard). Floorboards would have been needed on the first floors on east, west and south ranges – an extensive area.

The canons' choir stalls were probably elaborately carved in wood, perhaps of as high a quality as those at St Werburgh's Abbey, Chester or Nantwich St Mary parish church. Certainly, high quality woodcarving was carried out in the area; the appropriated churches at Runcorn and Daresbury had fine screens. Only fragments of the Runcorn screen have survived. It was similar to the superbly carved Perpendicular screen at Daresbury (illustrated in Pevsner and Hubbard 1971, plate 30).

The post-Dissolution mansion was partly timber framed. The Buck engraving of 1727 (fig. 18) shows the southern part of the the main range with a timber framed upper storey; the windows suggest a post-Dissolution construction date for this part. A sixteenth-century saw-pit was excavated on the north-west side of the outer courtyard (figs. 27, 28). It may have been used during the conversion of the monastic buildings into the secular mansion. On the bottom of the pit, used to stand on, were five timbers. Two broad plank-like timbers, with peg holes, had been part of a roof. A third may have supported a bell, or been part of mill machinery.

Turf

A number of references reveal that turf was dug and used for fuel. In 1376 the prior of Norton was paid twelve pence for a cart load of turf sent from the priory at Halton Castle (Beamont 1879, 12). In 1512, some men were presented at the Halton Court for using bows and arrows to drive a man off some land where he was digging turf (*ibid.*, 27). The turf (peat) must have been dug on the lower lying areas along the Mersey. In the seventeenth century, land transactions in Halton Village often specified rights of turbary in Halton Marsh as one of the privileges that burgesses possessed (Brooke papers, Cheshire Record Office). The site of a turbary – broad, shallow trenches now filled with water – can still be seen on Halton Marsh.

Stone

There are no documentary references to quarrying in the manor during the medieval period, but it is very likely that stone was dug on Windmill Hill for the construction of the priory buildings. The hill, about one kilometre from the priory, was a convenient source. Evidence is provided by the multitude of small quarry pits that pockmark the top and sides of the hill. There is no proof that they are medieval in date, but it is very likely. Norton Priory was fortunate in having a source of high quality sandstone so near. The builders of Vale Royal were faced with the laborious task of carting all their stone from quarries at Eddisbury, a distance of about 9 kilometres (6 miles).

Fig. 27. Saw pit with bed of sawdust and offcuts of wood. It was probably used during the conversion of the monastic buildings into the Tudor mansion.

Fig. 28. Planks laid on the bottom of the saw pit for the lower sawyer to stand on while working as part of a two man sawing team.

There is information on how sandstone was quarried from a site, Rock Farm in Halton Village, that was excavated by the writer in 1973. Small-scale quarrying had taken place to the rear of the farmhouse. A long, roughly rectangular quarry pit was excavated, measuring 13 m by 2 m and with a maximum depth of 1.1 m. There was clear evidence of the techniques that had been used to remove the stone, which, because the pit was back-filled soon after quarrying ceased, had been protected from weathering. Channels had been cut into the stone with metal tools (masons' picks or perhaps points) which left diagonal marks on the sides of the channels, which were V-shaped in section. The stone must have been split along its bedding plane by driving metal wedges horizontally into the rock face. In this way, a face could be worked back, resulting in the rectangular shape of the quarry pit. Pottery found in the bottom of the pit indicated that it went out of use in the late fifteenth or early sixteenth century. It is probable that it was the source of stone for the foundation walls of the timber framed farmhouse.

At Windmill Hill, the outcrops of sandstone provided ready made faces to work back. The hill continued to be used as a source of stone in the eighteenth and nineteenth centuries – one large quarry that operated in the nineteenth century is still visible. The same type of diagonal tooling can be seen. Similar techniques appear to have been used for cutting the inner ward ditch at Beeston Castle (Hough 1978).

Clay

The discovery of the tile kiln provided evidence for the use of the local boulder clay for making the tiles that formed the mosaic floor. The subsequent discovery of large clay pits near the kiln confirmed the source. Analysis of the tile fabrics by Dr D. F. Williams of Southampton University provided additional evidence. The later relief decorated tiles may also have been made at Norton. However, as boulder clay is so widespread over Cheshire, tiles made elsewhere in the county would be virtually indistinguishable by fabric alone. Similar considerations apply to 'Norton Priory Type Ware' – the great majority of jugs are made of the ware, characterised by good quality finish and simple rouletted decoration (it is illustrated and described in Greene and Noake 1977). Fabric analysis has revealed a similar composition to that of the tiles made at Norton, but although a local kiln is very likely it has not been found. Experiments, making replica tiles at Norton, have confirmed that the local clay is entirely suitable, and requires a minimum of preparation (Greene and Johnston 1978, 30–41). In the post-medieval period the boulder clay was used for brick making as the number of 'Brick Kiln Field' names show, particularly in the Wharford Farm area of the Keckwick valley.

Marl

The surface of the manor is pockmarked with marl pits, the majority of which are probably post-medieval (see figs. 12 and 14). Some, however, were probably dug in the medieval period. The use of marl was already widespread in Cheshire in the thirteenth century (Hewitt 1967, 16). Although it is frequently stated that marl was dug for its lime content (which in some areas of England was indeed the case) in Cheshire its value seems to have been through its general fertilising mineral content and its sandy nature which would have helped make the heavy clay soils more workable.

Sand

Although the priory and its immediate environs are on boulder clay, and sandstone outcrops to the south (Windmill Hill), there is an area to the north which the Geological Survey (sheet 97 Drift edition) shows as fluvio-glacial sand and gravel. Here there is considerable depth of sand at the highest point, which is suitable for use as building sand. Some sand pits are visible in this area and are known to have been used in the last century. It seems probable that the enormous quantities of sand required for the construction of the priory, used in mortar for wall cores, bedding and pointing, was obtained within the manor.

Water

The system of water management has been described. A spring rising to the south of the priory was utilised as a source of drinking and washing water, being carried by lead pipe to the priory buildings. Another spring to the south east filled the moat system with water, which was partially diverted down the monastic drain to clean the rere-dorter. The Bannerstich Brook to the west of the priory was dammed to provide a fishpool that also held the water that drove the canons' water mill. The use of water in these various but complementary ways demonstrates how carefully the priory was situated and how well this resource was harnessed (figs. 13, 19, 20, 21).

The extent to which the canons' possessions could provide for their needs

There are two main aspects of Norton Priory's potential to meet its needs from the products and resources of its possessions. The first concerns the day to day running of the priory, which involved providing for the requirements of the brethren, their servants, and their guests. The second aspect is the degree to which materials required for capital works, particularly building campaigns, could be supplied locally.

Requirements of the brethren

As has been described, the manor had considerable resources to provide for the most basic needs of the priory's dependants, food and drink. Excavated food debris has on analysis shown that meat of prime animals in excellent health was consumed at Norton, with beef being the most popular, followed by sheep meat and pig meat. A small amount of venison was also eaten. All four types of animals were raised locally, cows, sheep and pigs on the priory demesne and deer in the neighbouring hunting park. Fish was particularly important on fast days and during Lent. Salmon were caught at the priory's weirs on the Mersey, and cod is testified to by the evidence of surviving food bones. The fishponds would have extended the range of fresh fish available to include carp, tench and bream. The variety of shellfish, including oysters, mussels and cockles, would have been collected on the sandbanks and rocks of the Mersey estuary. An extensive range of birds was eaten including geese and fowl that were kept at the priory – mallard and teal from the Mersey marshes, and wood pigeon, rook and jackdaw from inland. Rabbits and hares did not form part of the diet of the occupants of either the priory or the Tudor house. They might however have been utilised for their fur which was used in clothing.

Most of the religious houses in Cheshire had an interest in one or more salthouses in the salt towns – Norton owned one in Northwich. The availability of salt will have been of advantage in preserving meat and fish. A Cheshire salthouse has recently been excavated (McNeil 1983).

Vegetable products were also available from the monastic demesne, which at the Dissolution was divided equally between pasture and arable. Wheat, barley, peas and oats are all known to have been grown on the canons' land. Wheat and barley were essential for two of the staple ingredients of the monastic diet, beer and bread. There are numerous references to them in the Barnwell Observances, lists of instructions that were observed at the Augustinian priory of Barnwell in Cambridgeshire in addition to the Rule (Clark 1897). Norton is likely to have had a similar set of observances. The fraterer was instructed to 'fetch bread from the cellar that was clean and not burnt, nor gnawed by mice'. Drink was to be poured into jugs in the presence of the fraterer after High Mass; after dinner two jugs of beer were to be available to the convent and guests, one drawn freshly from the barrel, the other filled with liquor left in other jugs (153–5). The daily entitlement of a canon was one loaf of bread and a gallon of beer (217). The almoner was to provide bread and beer, as well as peas and beans, for the poor (179). The sub-cellarer's duties included preventing the bakers or servants at the mill or the oven stealing bread, beer, flour, bran or malt; he also had care of the barrels of beer (185). On feast days the cellarer was to provide beer of extra strength and bread of superior quality (187). Wine however had to be imported. The discovery of a wooden cask, identified as being for French wine and dated from its context, testified to its import in the thirteenth century.

Bread would have been baked in the bakehouse which probably stood on the outer courtyard, after the wheat had been ground to flour in either the water mill or the windmill. Beer would have been made by sprouting barley in the malt loft, heating it in the malt kiln, and completing the process in the brewhouse. All three buildings were listed, along with a bakehouse and granary, in the 1632 *inquisition post mortem*. The cellarer had to attend to everything to do with food, drink and firing for the bakery, the brewhouse or the kitchen (181). Another use of wheat was in the preparation of hosts – the sacrist had to make sure it was pure and free from spots (71).

Another commodity mentioned in the Barnwell Observances is fruit. For example, 'when fruit is soft, or has been cooked, it ought to be served in bowls to prevent the table cloth from being stained' (163). Unfortunately, the type of fruit is not specified. It is possible that wooden bowls found in the excavation were used for this purpose. Orchards near the priory (the Infirmary Orchard and the Smith's Orchard) will probably have supplied the canons with apples and pears.

There is likely to have been a herb garden at the priory, probably situated to the south of the refectory, where it could have been convenient for both the kitchens and the infirmary. Again, the Barnwell Observances include a number of references to herbs. The master of the infirmary was to be ready to tend canons who were to be bled, with sage and parsley washed with salt water (203). The fraterer was to ensure that there were mats and rushes for the floor of the refectory, and that flowers, mint and fennel were thrown in the air to make a sweet odour (155).

Two other products of the monastic demesne are likely to have been hemp (a field is called Hemp Yards at the Dissolution) and flax (there is a post-Dissolution references to one John Leftwich of Norton, linen webster – *Cheshire Sheaf*, 25, 1928, 23). Sisal or rope could have been made from hemp, and linen could have been made from flax. Woollen cloth may also have been made locally. The canons may however have obtained the cloth required for their dress in local markets, where for example dyed woollen cloth for copes (which were lined with lambskin in winter), and fine linen for surplices or rochets and breeches may have been more readily available. It is uncertain whether leather was prepared at the priory. Leather was required not only in the form of shoes (numerous examples of which have been found in the excavation) but also as legging boots mentioned in the Barnwell Observances (Clark 1897, lxxx).

The wooden bowls (referred to earlier) and platters,

turned on a lathe, may have been made at Norton in the medieval period. Knives and spoons were used at the table, and are referred to in the Barnwell Observances (*ibid.*, 153, 155). Knives were an article of dress, and were used in violent brawls which occurred on occasions at Norton (Heath 1973). No medieval knives have been found at Norton, but numerous whetstones. The pendant variety were also frequently carried on the person in addition to a knife. They are made from schist, mudstone and sandstone, all non-local stones. It is likely that knives, spoons and whetstones were obtained at the local markets (Halton, Frodsham or possibly Warrington or Chester). One of the duties of the fraterer was to keep the whetstone and sand always ready beside the lavatorium for the brethren to clean and sharpen their knives (155).

Medieval pottery from Norton Priory is dominated by jugs. Jugs feature in the Observances in the instructions about the refectory tables referred to earlier – drink was to be poured into them and they were to be washed inside and out once a week (153). The great majority of the jugs are Norton Priory type ware (Greene and Noake 1977). The small amounts of non-local pottery at Norton are likely to have found their way to Cheshire as adjuncts of some other activity. Thus Saintonge ware probably accompanied wine imports, and Stamford ware may have been brought back as a result of visits to Norton's Lincolnshire properties.

Wax and tallow candles were used extensively. The fraterer was to supply wax candles to be used in the refectory in winter (Clark 1897, 155). The sacrist was responsible for tapers, candles and lamps in the church. Although tallow might have been prepared at the priory, wax and oil might have been more easily obtained at fairs – the sacrist is instructed not to go to fairs to buy lead, glass, wax or oil without leave from the prelate (*ibid.*, 73).

Construction materials

Timber was an essential material not only for the construction of the early temporary buildings at Norton but also as a component of masonry buildings. In the earlier part of Norton's development as a religious house there can be little doubt that the manor could have supplied the timber that was required, including oak from standard trees and hazel and willow from coppiced and pollarded trees. However, in the later period there are signs that woodland resources had declined.

The presence of an excellent building stone within the manor was a considerable asset. Windmill Hill was a convenient source of stone – blocks of sandstone extracted from quarries there could be carried in carts down the hillside to the priory just one kilometre away. The stone was not only suitable for ashlar masonry and rubble for wall cores, it could also be used (from certain beds) for roof and paving slabs. As a result, 99% of the stone used at Norton was the local sandstone. The only non-local stone was North Wales slate, a small amount of which was used in the late medieval period.

Another building material required in large quantities was sand. It could be obtained at a number of places in the manor, and would have been used primarily as the principal ingredient of mortar. The lime to mix with it would however have had to have been imported, possibly from North Wales.

In the case of the tiles for the floor of the church, the raw material for their manufacture formed the subsoil upon which the priory was constructed – boulder clay. Clay pits were found to the north of the church alongside the kiln in which the tiles were fired.

Most materials needed for building the priory could therefore be found within a short distance on land owned by the canons. The exceptions of lime, and on a lesser scale slate, have been mentioned, with North Wales suggested as a source. The same area may have supplied lead, which was required for gutters, flashing, window lead, pipes; some roofs probably had a lead covering. The glaze for pottery and tiles also required lead – a hearth for burning lead to make oxide was found near the tile kiln. Iron also needed to be brought in, but the process of converting the ore to the metal used in nails and fittings such as hinges was carried out at Norton. Furness is the most likely source.

Three other resources present in the manor had an economic importance. Turf was dug for use as a fuel, no doubt supplementing wood. Coal does not seem to have be used at Norton in the medieval period, but it does occur in sixteenth- and seventeenth-century post-Dissolution deposits. It is obtainable from the South Lancashire coalfield where it was certainly dug in bell pit mines in the St Helens area in the sixteenth century. Marl was spread on fields to increase their productivity. Springs and streams provided fresh drinking water for the priory, filled the moat, were utilised for the sanitation system and powered the water mill.

The resources of the manor were such that, potentially, all the major requirements of daily life, and of construction, could be met from within its bounds. However, self-sufficiency was not a monastic objective, and the priory is likely to have engaged in a much more complex pattern of exchange using local markets and fairs. Norton's strength was the capacity to meet many of its own needs when circumstances demanded it, and to generate surpluses for exchange.

4

The canons and the community

The primary function of the brethren of a medieval religious house was the worship of God. 'Before all things, dearest brethren, let God be loved' are the opening words of the Rule of St Augustine, which the Barnwell Observances describe as 'the divine plan for the salvation of the human race' (Clark 1897, 321). From the standpoint of the founder, the priorities of the canons were seen in a different light – although the worship of God is acknowledged as a principal activity in the foundation charter, great stress is placed on the obligation of the canons to pray for the salvation of the souls of the founder and his family (Tait 1939, 22). This relationship with the benefactors, which resulted in the steady growth of Norton's properties during the first two centuries of its existence, has been described. There were, however, other activities in which the brethren of a religious house inevitably became involved. Two principal social duties were demanded by the Rule, charity and hospitality. In addition, the head of a religious house would be called upon to give counsel to his secular peers and superiors, and to carry out tasks on behalf of the Church, the Crown and local administration.

The role of the prior

In the absence of Norton's own records, the social and political role of successive priors can be only imperfectly understood. Nonetheless, it is clear that priors did play an active part in the life of the locality. The impression given by the records is one of increasing involvement in matters beyond the cloister. No doubt this varied according to the personal qualities of those elected to the office, but the raising in status of the prelate from prior to abbot at the end of the fourteenth century is the climax of a process of increasing importance of the house, reflected also in its properties and the size and extent of its buildings.

The heads of religious houses were often expected to

attend the court of their patron and other prominent benefactors. This was certainly the case with priors of Norton and their patrons, the barons of Halton. The Duttons also received priors of Norton at their manor houses. The evidence for this is provided by charters in which the list of witnesses includes one of the priors. One example is the prior acting as a witness to a charter of a baron of Halton in which Richard of Moore (one of the baron's tenants) quit-claimed to John, constable of Chester, the site of Stanlow Abbey, which John was in the process of founding, in exchange for four bovates in Runcorn (Barraclough 1957, 6–7). The list of witnesses is headed by Robert, abbot of Chester, whose name is followed by that of Henry, prior of Norton. Other familiar personages are Hugh of Dutton and Hugh and Adam of Dutton, his sons. There are numerous other examples of the priors witnessing agreements – notably land transactions.

Henry, who was prior from before 1175 to about 1195 (Knowles, Brooke and London 1972, 178), had a prominent role in the foundation of another Augustinian house, at Burscough in Lancashire, in about 1189. He was present at, and witnessed, the foundation by Robert son of Henry of Lathom (Webb 1970, 19). He also witnessed the bishop of Lichfield and Coventry's confirmation of the grant (*ibid.*, 158). It is likely that the original canons of Burscough were drawn from Norton which was the first, and until the foundation of Burscough the only, Augustinian house in the north west. In 1232 the prior of Norton witnessed the bishop's confirmation of Burscough's possessions (*ibid.*, 153). Two other confirmation charters of the possessions of Burscough were made during the periods 1228 to 1236 and 1229 to 1231, with the prior of Norton as witness.

It is necessary to dispose of the myth that the prior of Norton occupied a seat in the earl of Chester's parliament (stated, for example, by Beamont 1873, 152). The existence of a palatinate parliament is a theory based on no solid fact which has gained acceptance through repetition. The original account of the parliament was published in the mid-seventeenth century, in the *Vale Royall of England* (King 1656). This included a Hollar engraving showing the earl of Chester flanked by the heads of the religious houses of Cheshire, each one identifiable by the arms of his house. The engraving is thought to be based on an illuminated pedigree of the earls of Chester, produced sometime before 1603, which is illustrated with a representation of the 'parliament', for which no contemporary evidence exists.

Expansion that had started in the late twelfth century continued with building operations in the early part of the thirteenth century (fig. 42). A mark of the strength of the priory was the swift recovery from the fire of 1236 – the quality of the rebuilt cloister arcade (fig. 50) is a measure of the confidence and the financial resources of Norton. The century came to a close with the notable events associated with a miracle-working cross and the construction of a large eastern chapel (figs. 79, 80). Priors of Norton continued to be involved in matters beyond the cloister. In 1288 for example, concord was reached in the court of Chester concerning repairs of the Dee bridge. The case was heard before the justice of Chester and the priors of Norton and Birkenhead (*Cheshire Sheaf*, 21, 1924, 33). In the following year Roger prior of Norton is described as one of the king's 'fideles', assisting the judge in the court of Chester (*Cheshire Sheaf*, 27, 1920, 25). An interesting piece of evidence for the activity of Norton Priory on a wider scale is recorded for 1289. On 20 November, safe conduct was granted 'for men of the prior of Norton going with a ship to Ireland for victualls and other things' (*Cal. Patent Rolls*, Edward I, 1281, 82, 334). Runcorn was a small port on the Mersey estuary and doubtless the boat left from there – to purchase food at a time of local shortages?

Financial management

For much of the fourteenth century Norton Priory suffered misfortunes and mismanagement. Only towards the end of the century was there a resurgence in the financial standing of the priory.

In 1310 the prior was accused of wasting the goods of the priory and Bishop Walter Langton ordered a reform in the administration of the house (*VCH Chester*, 3, 166). By 1315 a dispute had broken out with one of the benefactor families. The priory and convent were cited by Sir Hugh de Dutton before two commissaries of the bishop. They were accused of not providing a chaplain and a lamp for Poolsey chapel under the agreement for which Sir Hugh had the evidence of a charter. Prior Olton confessed the charge, and was ordered to cease neglecting his duties (Beamont 1873, 170). In 1329 Norton's affairs again attracted episcopal attention. The election of Robert Bernard was declared invalid by the bishop, but after the petition of the sub-prior and convent, he confirmed their choice (Lichfield Joint Record Office B/A/1/2 f104).

In 1331 a natural disaster was claimed to have damaged the priory's finances. In a petition to the pope, the canons claimed that 'high tides and flooding had diminished the fruits of the land'. Pope John XXII therefore issued a mandate to the bishop of Lincoln authorising the appropriation of Castle Donnington church (*Cal. Papal Reg.* 2, 379); the appropriation was licensed by Edward III (*Cal. Patent Rolls*, Edward III, 88–9).

It is not clear what direct effect the Black Death had on Norton Priory. In 1349 Thomas de Fraunkevylle was elected prior, possibly because of the death of a prior in the Black Death. However, that prior cannot have been Robert Bernard, for he was still a member of the house c. 1357 (*VCH Chester*, 3, 170).

In the 1350s further problems beset Norton. In May

1354 the prior complained that the spiritualities of his house had been assessed when in fact they should have been free of tax, in connection with the fine of 5,000 marks that had been granted to the Black Prince (*Black Prince's Register*, 165, f.87).

By 1354 more disputes had broken out with benefactors. The Aston family required confirmation of the particularly onerous corrody which had probably been granted to the family at the time that it gave Eanley to the canons. Under the terms of the corrody Sir Richard Aston, knight, Hugh and Richard his sons, and also Sir Robert Aston, knight (father of Richard Aston) each had the finding of a yeoman and a page, with three horses, a brace of greyhounds and a goshawk according to their estate, with their chambers and such easements as belonged to their degree, in the priory (Beamont 1873, 173). The canons were evidently trying to escape these unwelcome commitments, but in this they were unsuccessful.

The year 1354 was not only marked by disputes with the Aston family. On 4 January the Black Prince ordered John de Delves, his lieutenant of justice in Chester, to investigate the claim of Thomas de Dutton against the prior of Norton concerning a parcel of land which his ancestors had given to the house. The prior was said to be likely to lose the case by default of his attorney, and Delves was instructed to urge Dutton to adjourn the process of the claim without prejudice while investigations proceeded (*Black Prince's Register*, 3, 139, f.74d).

The crisis came to a head in the years after 1354. Bishop Norbury issued injunctions to the prior of Norton stating that the house had been beggared by indiscreet undertakings (Hobhouse 1880, 282). This was followed in 1357 by an admonition that the prior of Norton abstain from the illegal and rash contracts which were ruining his house (*ibid.*, 285). In answer to the admonition, the prior and brethren asked for permission to sell the advowson of the church of Radcliffe on Soar to a 'magnus reverendus' to relieve the house of debt – permission was granted with limits in 1357 (*ibid.*. 286). On 1 December 1358 a royal licence was granted for John of Winwick, treasurer of York Minster, to grant the canon forty shillings a year in rent from the land in Burgh in Lonsdale (*Cal. Patent Rolls*, Edward III, 1358–61, 122). The grant was made in return for the church of Radcliffe on Soar. The church was subsequently given to Burscough Priory – the gift was confirmed in 1410 (*Cal. Close Rolls*, Henry IV, 4, 182).

Religious houses frequently resorted to the sale of corrodies as a short-term solution to the problems of debt. The longer-term commitments, frequently limited only by the length of the corrodian's life, presented problems for the future. Norton was no exception. At Easter 1358, at the height of the financial crisis, Prior Walter of Weaverham granted a corrody to John son of John de Hallam of Newton, and Katherine his wife, for the term of his life. The corrody was to be supplied by the cellarer of Norton – 16 white loaves of full weight, 16 gallons of beer and 16 black loaves weekly, and half the said quantities to Katherine if she survived him (*Cat. Ancient Deeds*, PRO, 4, A9847).

Despite the problems, disputes and debts that the priors had to deal with in the first sixty years of the fourteenth century, there were other matters which required their attention beyond the cloister. One was attendance at the triennial general chapters of the English Augustinian houses. These had been established following the Lateran Council of 1215; the first general chapter in England was held at Leicester in November 1216 (Knowles 1948, 28). In 1337, in the chapter held at St Frideswide's, Oxford, the prior of Norton was a diffinitor – one of the officers charged with examining visitations, and drawing up rules for their conduct (Salter 1922). At Northampton in 1350, the prior was appointed visitor for the for the diocese of Coventry and Lichfield. Priors of Norton doubtless regularly attended the chapter – an experience which would have brought them into contact with their fellow prelates from many parts of England. Occasionally other duties were carried out for the Church. In 1346, for example, Prior Robert was appointed in a letter of Pope Clement VI as the examiner concerning the conferring of the office of notary on a clerk (*Cal. Papal Registers*, 3, 233).

Recovery, and elevation to the status of abbey

In about 1366 a new prior's name appears – Richard Wyche. He was to remain the head of Norton for the following thirty-four years (*VCH Chester*, 3, 170). His vigorous leadership brought about a revival of the fortunes of the house, and made him a respected figure beyond the cloister. It is possible to bring together more information on his career than for any other heads of Norton. His activities demonstrate the extent to which the head of Norton could play a role in the outside world.

Prior Richard was an active participant in the Augustinian Chapter. At the meeting held at Newstead in 1371 he was appointed a visitor for the diocese of Coventry and Lichfield. In 1380 and 1383, at Northampton and Newstead respectively, he was made a diffinitor (Salter 1922).

Richard shouldered a particularly onerous duty in 1379. In that year he was appointed assessor and collector of clerical poll-tax for the archdeaconry of Chester (Bennett 1972). Richard's assessment survives in an unusually complete form, listing the liability of clergy to contribute to the 'subsidy granted to the king by the prelates and clergy of Canterbury province'. The archdeaconry comprised Cheshire, and that part of Lancashire south of the Ribble. The assessment is a useful guide to the size of Norton in relation to other religious houses in the area. The largest was St Werburgh's Abbey in Chester which had twenty-seven monks. Whalley Abbey had twenty-four monks, Vale Royal had eighteen monks, and

Norton had fifteen canons. Consequently, Norton's assessment for poll-tax was fourth highest of the eleven religious houses on the list. The fact that Norton had fifteen canons in 1379 suggested to Knowles and Hadcock (1971, 168) that the priory's complement of canons had been doubled from an original twelve or thirteen. This view has subsequently been confirmed by the results of the excavation.

Another fact that emerges from a study of the clergy listed in the poll-tax assessment is the role of Norton Priory as a sponsor in the ordination of priests. Norton seems to have given titles to clerks in the northern part of Cheshire, while Combermere Abbey provided a similar service in the south of the county (Bennett 1972, 15).

On 13 November 1379, when Sir Thomas Dutton, a member of the family who were benefactors of Norton, founded a perpetual chantry in the Augustinian friary at Warrington, Prior Richard was one of those present (Beamont 1873, 175). In January 1387, he appeared as a witness for Sir Robert de Grosvenor in one of the hearings to decide the heraldic dispute with Sir Richard le Scrope concerning the right to the shield *azure a bend or* (Morris 1894, 171).

In 1391 Richard Wyche succeeded in obtaining for Norton the distinction of elevation to the status of mitred abbey. Three successive grants were made by Pope Boniface IX in that year. The first consented to the elevation of Norton to an abbey, with Prior Richard as abbot, at the petition of John, duke of Lancaster, the patron, and the prior and convent of the Augustinian priory of St Mary's, Norton (*Cal. Papal Reg.* 4, 405). The next communication from Rome was a faculty to Abbot Richard to receive benedictions from any catholic bishop of his choice in communion with the apostolic see (*ibid.*, 4, 408). The third letter, addressed to Abbot Richard, was an indult to him and his successors to use the mitre, ring, pontifical staff and other pontifical insignia, and to give solemn benediction in the monastery after mass, vespers and matins, provided no bishop be present (*ibid.*, 4, 411). Thus Norton became the only mitred abbey in Cheshire apart from St Werburgh's, Chester.

The circumstances of the elevation of Norton have been discussed by the writer elsewhere (Greene 1979). Abbey status was rare for Augustinian houses. Apart from Arrouasian and Victorine establishments, only seven Augustinian houses were abbeys from their foundation to the Dissolution. Four more were made abbeys relatively soon after their foundation in the twelfth century, and one (North Creake) in 1231. For 160 years there were no further elevations until that of Norton in 1391. There was then another gap until the elevation of Kenilworth in the mid-fifteenth century. Finally, Bruton Priory in Somerset was elevated in 1511. With the exception of short-lived cases, but including Arrouasian and Victorine members, there were twenty-eight Augustinian abbeys out of a total of about two hundred Augustinian houses in England and Wales. Of these, seven, including Norton, became mitred – four priors were also entitled to wear the mitre. Richard therefore achieved an unusual distinction for himself and his house.

It might be argued that Norton was able to gain its enhanced status by taking advantage of Boniface IX's undoubted financial problems, caused by the Great Schism. Boniface sold papal privileges on a large scale (Binns 1934, 168). In many cases this practice worked to the disadvantage of Augustinian houses by releasing many canons from their vows (Knowles 1955, 170–4). However, if abbey status was to be obtained solely by payment, it seems likely that many ambitious priors would have taken advantage of the opportunity of aggrandisement. However, Norton is the only Augustinian elevation during Boniface's papacy, and indeed in the period from 1231 to about 1448. The use of pontifical insignia was a different matter. A number of Augustinian abbeys and priories followed Norton's example during Boniface's papacy – St Osyth's (Essex), Bristol, Southwark, Bridlington and St Frideswide's (Oxford).

Two criteria must have been size and financial standing. Norton, despite its problems in the mid-fourteenth century, had a substantial endowment which improved management later in the century could utilise. There is no evidence of problems with finance following Richard Wyche's election. The size of the community is known from the poll-tax returns. In 1379 and 1381 there were fifteen brethren (Bennett 1972, 22); in 1401 there were sixteen, making it over twice the size of the larger Augustinian houses in neighbouring Staffordshire (*VCH Chester*, 3, 167). There are about one hundred Augustinian houses for which numbers of canons at this period are known. About twenty-five are of a similar size or larger, seventy-five smaller. In the context of the north west part of England, Norton's size is more unusual. There were eighteen Augustinian houses in Shropshire, Staffordshire, Cheshire, Lancashire and Cumbria. Norton was at this date the largest, with more canons than Carlisle, Haughmond, Lilleshall and the rest (data from Robinson 1980, 399–403). Norton could therefore justify its petition for elevation on grounds of size and endowment.

The support of an influential patron was another important factor. John of Gaunt, duke of Lancaster, lent his weight to the canons' petition. His connection with Norton derived from the original foundation by the barons of Halton. By a succession of marriages, the hereditary title of baron of Halton and office of constable of Chester passed to the Lacys of Pontefract and subsequently to the earls of Lincoln. The earldom in turn became part of the duchy of Lancaster, so when John of Gaunt acted as petitioner with the priory it was as the fourteenth baron of Halton. It was therefore particularly appropriate that John's son, the new King Henry IV, in whom the barony now resided, set the

final seal on the elevation. He granted a licence, dated 22 December in the second year of his reign, for the prior and convent of Norton to elect an abbot – presumably Richard's successor (PRO, Duchy of Lancaster Misc. Books, 15, 140).

The buildings at Norton had expanded greatly, the church almost doubling in length to 87 metres. A new larger chapter house had been constructed, the dormitory had been enlarged, and the south and west ranges had been totally rebuilt on a larger scale. The structures had been embellished with stonemasonry and tiled floors of the highest quality. The buildings were therefore of a size and quality that were consistent with abbey status (figs. 63, 82, 100).

The size of other Augustinian churches in north west England can be compared to Norton. The total length of the church at Carlisle was greater (about 100 metres), but all the others for which the size is known were smaller – Burscough 57 metres, Cartmel 52 metres, Conishead 43 metres, Haughmond 62 metres, Lanercost 58 metres and Lilleshall 73 metres (figures derived from Robinson 1980, 397–8). In addition to its size, Norton could claim to be one of the oldest foundations in the region (1115); only Haughmond, which may have been founded as early as 1110 (Knowles and Hadcock 1971, 159), could claim to be older.

Norton therefore had several grounds for justifying its enhanced status – its physical size, the size of community, the early foundation date, the backing of a prominent patron and a substantial endowment. Above all, there was the vigorous leadership of Richard, which had been exemplified by his role as poll-tax assessor and by his work on behalf of the Augustinian chapter. Four years after he had assumed the mitre, Abbot Richard was elected President of the chapter of Augustinian houses of the province of Canterbury held in Northampton in 1395 (Salter 1922, 77). He is the only head of Norton to have enjoyed this distinction, and it is a mark of the respect he commanded amongst his peers.

The elevation was followed by the adoption of new arms which demonstrated possession of the mitre. To Norton's original arms *gules, a pale fusilly or* was added *a bordure azure thereon eight mitres of the second* (Woodward 1894, 380). It is also possible that the association of St Christopher with Norton coincided with the elevation – perhaps his adoption as an additional patron saint. The giant statue of St Christopher (fig. 72) has been dated to the late fourteenth century (Thompson 1967, 67). The west tower of Great Budworth church can be cited in support of this theory. The church was one of those owned by Norton, and when a new tower was erected in about 1500, niches were incorporated in the north and south sides. That on the north contains a figure of the Virgin and Child, and on the south is St Christopher and the infant Christ – both are references to the saints associated with the mother abbey. Above the door are carved the arms of Norton, and those of benefactor families. St Christopher was an appropriate patron saint in view of Norton's proximity to the Mersey, and the hospitality given to travellers who had to cross it. The saint might also have been regarded as a protector against a repeat of the floods of 1331.

Only a few years after abbey status had been achieved, Norton sought a further privilege from Boniface IX. In 1399 he issued an indult to the abbot and convent of Norton to enable their churches at Great Budworth, Runcorn, Castle Donnington, Burton on Stather and Pirton to be served by the canons as priests (*Cal. Papal Reg.* 5, 186). The practice of appointing canons and monks to the livings of appropriated churches was disapproved of by the English state. Only four years later, an act of Henry IV specified that 'the vicar of every church should be a secular person, and not a member of a religious house; that he should be vicar perpetual and not removable at the caprice of the monastery'. This followed a rash of similar grants to abbeys and priories during the pontificate of Boniface IX; he eventually stopped making grants and cancelled those that had not been used.

Despite official disapproval of the practice, Norton exercised the right it had acquired. At the two nearest churches, Runcorn and Great Budworth, canons of Norton acted as vicars until the Dissolution. At Pirton, a canon of Norton was presented as vicar in 1417, and a later vicar was Henry Terfoot (1436–47), also a canon (*VCH Oxfordshire*, 8, 170). At the Dissolution Richard Wright, recently canon of Norton and vicar of Burton on Stather, was given the dispensation to continue to wear the habit of his order beneath that of a secular priest (Chambers 1966, 98). The right was challenged in the mid-fifteenth century. In 1455 a special episcopal commission was assembled to investigate the right which Norton claimed to appoint canons to livings. The incumbents of Davenham, Rostherne, Runcorn and Frodsham, together with six chaplains, were summoned to Great Budworth church. They found that the abbot and convent of Norton were the true patrons and that they possessed the right, by virtue of a papal dispensation, to present one of their brethren whenever the vicarage should fall vacant (Lichfield Diocesan Registry, B/A/1/11, Reg. Boulers, f.39v).

It seems likely that the churches mentioned in Boniface's grant possessed copies of the document, which could be produced on occasions such as the visit of the special commission to Great Budworth. This would explain the discovery of a papal bulla in the churchyard of All Saints Parish Church in Runcorn in 1910. The bulla, after conservation, was identified as one issued by Pope Boniface IX (illustrated Greene 1979, pls. 1 and 2). At the Dissolution, the privilege obtained by Abbot Richard was still recognised. Two canons of Norton, William Hardware and Thomas Fletcher, were vicars of Great Budworth and Runcorn respectively; they were denounced for their sins committed while acting in this capacity (PRO, State Papers, Domestic, SP/1/91). Cromwell's agent reported that the canons served as vicars 'under a general capacity from the bishop of Rome' (*Letters and Papers Henry VIII*, 4, 2010).

There can be little doubt that Abbot Richard's motive in seeking the dispensation for Norton's canons to act as vicars in the appropriated churches was financial. At Pirton the value of the vicar's entitlements in 1281 was £5 6s 0d, a sum well worth appropriating. By the Dissolution these entitlements had risen to the considerable sum of £17 9s 4½d, which compares with the £22 value of Pirton rectory: together they made a sizeable contribution to the abbey's budget (*VCH Oxfordshire*, 8, 170). At Burton on Stather the value of the vicarage was substantial: £10 in 1291, when the rectory was worth £26 13s 4d (Jarvis 1922, 31).

It seems probable that the exploitation by Norton of this additional source of revenue was the result of the ambitions of the abbey in its new status. In the case of other abbeys that were given mitred status by Boniface IX, similar grants followed their elevation.

Richard Wyche's rule of Norton, over a period of more than three decades, must be seen as one of the most successful episodes in its history. Through him Norton gained in prestige and influence, and although none of his successors seems to have been of such calibre, the status of mitred abbey that he had achieved endured until the Dissolution.

The enhanced status of the head of Norton required extra accommodation. This is probably the explanation for the large tower house projecting westwards into the outer courtyard from the west range, shown on the Buck engraving (fig. 18). The style of the tower house (fig. 29) and details of the corbels and vault ribs suggest a fifteenth-century date for its construction, so it was probably erected by one of Richard's successors.

Richard Wyche died in 1400 and his prior John Shrewsbury was appointed abbot by Archbishop Arundel during his metropolitan visitation in 1401. He was still abbot in 1426 (*VCH Chester*, 3, 170). In contrast to his predecessor, he has left little mark of his abbacy. He does seem to have followed in Richard's footsteps as a collector of royal taxes in the archdeaconry of Chester in 1404 (*Cal. Close Rolls*, Henry IV, 2, 414).

By 1429, troubles had returned to Norton. In that year the church and buildings were described as ruinous, and frequent floodings of the Mersey were said to have diminished the revenues of the house so that they hardly sufficed to meet the costs of hospitality. A papal indulgence for ten years was offered to those who contributed to the repair of Norton (*Cal. Papal Reg.* 8, 169–70). Such petitions can never be taken fully at face value for there is usually an element of exaggeration; nonetheless it is clear that the abbey was again experiencing financial difficulties. When so much depended upon the management skills of the abbot, it is hardly surprising that the fortunes of a religious house could fluctuate so greatly.

Problems with Norton's commitments to benefactors' chapels recur in the fifteenth century. In June 1425 Richard, son of Sir Robert Aston, complained that the chapel at Aston was out of repair and services in it were intermittent, except on Sundays, and had been so for years. The archdeacon of Chester upheld the complaint and on 25 August he ordered the abbot and convent immediately to redress the wrong (Beamont 1873, 177). By 1452 the same complaints about the repair of the chapel and irregularity of the services were again being made. After arbitration, the abbot undertook to arrange the repair of the chapel and to perform the stipulated services (*ibid.*, 181).

The internal order of the house suffered a breakdown in 1441. Following the death of Abbot John Sutton, the election of Thomas Westbury was disputed. He was accused, with two alleged conspirators, of poisoning Sutton, but all three were acquitted (*VCH Chester*, 3, 167).

Financial difficulties must explain the decision by

Robert Leftwich, abbot of Norton from 1451 until he resigned in 1460 (*VCH Chester*, 3, 170), to sell the advowson (the right to appoint the vicar) of both Kneesall and Grappenhall churches. In 1459 the abbot and convent quit-claimed to John Southwell, parson of Kneesall, a yearly rent of four marks which they claimed as rectors of the church, and all claim or interest in the church. The advowson and patronage were granted to various men at the same time (*Cal. Close Rolls*, Henry VI, 6, 373). In the following year Robert granted to Henry, John and Thomas Byrom, their heirs and assigns, the advowson of Grappenhall with the reservation of a pension of 12 pence to the abbot (*Deputy Keeper's Report*, 37, 445–6). Neither church had been fully appropriated, and neither was covered by Boniface IX's dispensation for canons to act as vicars. As the least productive churches, Kneesall and Grappenhall were clearly the two that could be disposed of without a major loss of income.

Despite the various problems, the abbots and some of the canons continued to play a part in the world beyond the cloister. One example is that of Adam Olton, a canon of Norton, who became master of the hospital of St Anthony of Vienne in London (*VCH Chester*, 3, 167). He was pardoned by Henry V for 'all treasons' (*Cal. Patent Rolls*, Henry V 1416–22, 340). Abbots of Norton attended the Augustinian Chapter, but none appears to have been elected to any of the offices. At the chapter held at Oseney

Fig. 29. Model showing the probable appearance of the fifteenth-century abbot's tower house, with west range beyond.

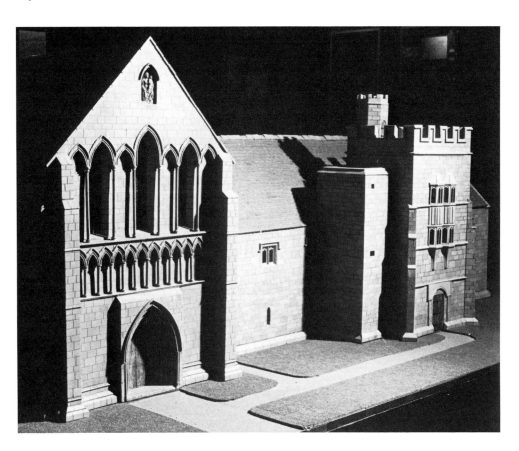

Abbey in 1443 the abbot explained that the problems over his election had resulted in no student from Norton being sent to university (Salter 1922, 100).

In 1417 Pope Martin V instructed the abbot to dissolve a marriage that was within the degrees of kinship, absolve the couple from excommunication, and then permit them to contract the marriage anew. The abbot was asked to act as Bishop John was at the Roman court (*Cal. Papal Reg.* 7, 41). Similarly, Eugenius IV issued a mandate in 1431 to the abbot to confirm a divorce by papal authority (*ibid.*, 8, 331–2).

On occasions the abbot might be called upon as an arbiter in a dispute. One example is the conflict between Sir Geoffrey Warburton and Thomas Venables about claims to a property, which John Sutton was called upon to settle in 1441 (Beamont 1873, 179).

Disputes, and Dissolution

In the early years of the sixteenth century, Norton Abbey was again charged with debt. In 1511 the obligation of William Merton to the king was recorded (*Letters and Papers Henry VIII*, 2, 1484). In 1512 he was listed as not paying his debts (*ibid.*, 1, 1493). In 1515, 25 marks were said to be due to the king (*ibid.*, 2, 1364).

Visitation records become available for Norton only from 1496. By that year, the number of canons had fallen from the sixteen recorded in 1401 to just nine. In 1518 there were seven, in 1521 there were eight, and in 1524 there were seven brethren (Heath 1973). The abbot was asked to increase the number of canons but reported in 1518 that he had been unable to find any suitable recruits (*ibid.*, 51). No serious transgressions are recorded in 1518 and 1521, although the accounts were not being kept as they should have been; there was also an injunction issued in 1518 against visiting alehouses. By 1522, however, there had been a collapse in the order and morale of the house. Bishop Blythe himself held two inquisitions in April and May of that year (*ibid.*, 90–5, 107–9; *VCH Chester*, 3, 168). The prior (William Hardware) had libelled the abbot (William Merton, who was elected in 1507) in letters to the 'prior' of Lees, a cell of Rocester Abbey. The abbot was accused of a catalogue of misdeeds when the inquisition took place – relations with women over many years, wasting the resources of the house, favouring his relatives, entertaining strangers at the expense of the house, etc. The prior in turn was accused of (and confessed to) fornication and lapses in the observance of the Rule. In the interval between the inquisitions, more trouble had broken out. The prior and others had threatened the abbot with a knife; the prior had subsequently gone to Halton.

In the enclosed world of a religious house, disputes tended to assume a greater intensity than those outside. They might also be short-lived. By 1524 the animosity that had reached such serious proportions two years previously seems to have been forgotten. In the visitations carried out in that year, William Hardware the prior praised William Merton the abbot in all things. All the canons, when questioned, agreed that there was good order and that the Rule was being observed; there were, however, still no inventory or accounts.

The physical state of the abbey buildings had also deteriorated by the early sixteenth century. William Merton had to request thirty oaks from Delamere Forest from Henry VIII to repair fire damage (Cheshire Record Office DAR/G/50/1). In 1524 the visitation had to be held in the abbot's oratory as the chapter house was dilapidated. Repairs were ordered within the resources of the house (Heath 1973, 126–7). However, there is archaeological evidence that the thirteenth-century cloister was demolished and replaced with a new, probably fenestrated, cloister (fig. 98).

In the sixteenth century the abbot of Norton was still expected to become involved in the world beyond the cloister. In 1515, for example, the abbot was made a member of a commission for the duchy of Lancaster enquiring into a case of Thomas Boteler *v.* Sir Thomas Bernard, knight, and others concerning an assault at a cock fight (Fishwick 1896). In 1529 the abbot of Norton is listed as being present at the convocation at Canterbury (*Letters and Papers Henry VIII*, 4, 2700). The convocation was called to consider the legality of Henry VIII's marriage to his brother Arthur's widow, Katherine.

The events that surrounded the dissolution of Norton provide some guidance as to the standing of the abbey in the locality, and relations with various personalities in the politics of the county. There have been a variety of interpretations of the evidence. All differ in their description of what happened. They include Beamont 1873, 191–200; Ormerod 1882, 1, 502; Gasquet 1902, 2, 85–9; Cook 1965, 120–3, Chesters 1962, 45–7, etc.; Knowles and Hadcock 1971, 168; and most recently (1980) *VCH Chester*, 3, 168–9. Of these, the fullest account is that by Chesters, who attempted to put the events at Norton into the wider context of the politics of Tudor Cheshire.

The dependence of Norton Abbey upon the goodwill of local men of importance is amply demonstrated by the dissolution and the events that led up to it. The two men who determined the fate of Norton and its inmates were Sir Piers Dutton and Sir William Brereton of Brereton. Sir Piers was a neighbour of the canons, with his manor house at Dutton. He was a member, although not a direct descendant, of the family who had been benefactors of Norton ever since its foundation, and whose dead had been buried within the church. He had obtained the Dutton inheritance after a protracted and bitter legal dispute with the family of Sir Lawrence de Dutton, who had been buried at Norton in 1527.

Dutton was undoubtedly a ruthless man, and as one of the largest landowners in Cheshire, a powerful one. In

1504–5 he had been imprisoned on a number of counts, including murder, by Sir Randolph Brereton of Malpas, the chamberlain of Cheshire from 1504 to 1530 (Chesters, 1962). Sir Randolph was father of Sir William Brereton, Groom to the Privy Chamber, who was executed in 1536 for criminal intercourse with the Queen. The William Brereton who became Dutton's principal enemy was from the branch of the family whose seat was in Brereton parish, not to be confused with the Malpas Breretons. This animosity was of long standing; Norton Abbey became one of the battlegrounds upon which their rivalry could be expressed. The conflict was fought on two fronts – alleged counterfeiting of money at Norton, and rebellion by the abbot. Both were treasonable offences.

Dutton probably coveted the extensive landholdings of the canons which adjoined his principal manors, and which had in many cases been given to Norton by holders of the title that he had inherited. He is noticeably absent from the list of office holders of the abbey in the *Valor*; Sir William Brereton was listed as steward with an annual fee of sixty shillings. Dutton's first move against the abbey was made in 1535, when he arrested the abbot of Norton and several other people – Robert Jannyns (the bailiff of the abbey), two of the abbot's servants, Randal Brereton, baron of the King's Exchequer at Chester, John Hale of Chester, merchant, and 'the stranger, a cunning smith'. He reported the arrests in a letter to Thomas Cromwell on 3 August 1535 (*Letters and Papers Henry VIII*, 7, 1037 p. 405, where it is incorrectly dated 1534). The previous month, two servants of the abbot of Norton, Thomas Holfe and Robert Jannyns, were listed as prisoners in Beauchamp Tower within the Tower of London on charges of coining (*ibid.*, 8, 1001). On 26 August 1535, evidence was taken from one Henry Broke, gentleman, about coining at Norton. He alleged that Robert Jannyns and James Pate, a canon of Norton, had tried to change forged coins in his presence in 1534. It was stated that John Heysam, the abbot of Norton's smith, had fled. Broke, on the prompting of Dutton's deputy sheriff, Ralph Manning, repeated hearsay evidence that the abbot had asked Thomas Berlow, one of the abbot's tenants and also a smith, whether Thomas Holfe was a 'cunning workman'. Berlow had replied that Holfe had worked in the Mint in the Tower, whereupon the abbot had taken him into his service (*ibid.*, 9, 183, p. 57–8). This would seem to have been the evidence upon which the arrests reported on 6 July and 3 August had been made.

Dutton's case against the abbot was weak, consisting only of the circumstantial evidence of Thomas Holfe's employment at Norton. The abbot was taken to London and a hearing took place in the King's Council in which the abbot was accused of coining. At this stage Dutton attempted to gain a conviction by using a perjured witness, one Piers Felday. Felday was himself a convicted forger who was promised his freedom if he would implicate

Dutton's enemies in receiving or uttering forged coins. In the event, the 'evidence' of Felday was insufficient and the abbot was released. Felday eventually came into the hands of Sir William Brereton, before whom he made a full confession which Brereton sent to Cromwell on 8 June 1537 (*ibid.*, 12 vol. 2, 58, p. 20). He admitted having been procured by Dutton to accuse Dutton's enemies, who he named and who correspond largely to those arrested in 1535. He gave full details of the methods used by Dutton and his servants, and the mixture of threats and inducements used against Felday. Dutton had already tried to prevent Felday falling into Brereton's hands – Audley had written on 26 May to Cromwell urging him to send Felday to Dutton, not to Brereton, 'who wishes to save him as he saved the abbot of Norton' (see below) (*ibid.*, 12 vol. 1, 1282, p. 585). As long as he lived, Felday was a threat to Dutton – the more so in the hands of his enemy Brereton. On 28 August 1537 Brereton wrote to Cromwell reporting that Dutton had forcibly taken Felday from Brereton's custody at Chester gaol. Felday had been taken to Boughton to be executed on 4 August. On the scaffold he had denounced the knights, esquires and gentlemen for their duplicity, and when he went on to say that there were three pairs of coining irons in the county, and in the possession of persons listening to him, servants of Sir Piers Dutton quickly despatched him before he could say more. Brereton also stated that friends of Sir Piers 'openly report that he can do as he likes in this county' (*ibid.*, 12, vol. 2, 597, pp. 221–2).

Dutton's attempt to convict and depose the abbot of Norton in 1535 failed. However, another opportunity quickly presented itself. In 1535 Cromwell had started to gather information to the discredit of persons in Cheshire, including the religious. His agent was Adam Becanshaw, who wrote to him 'in obedience to his commission to set forth such offences as require correction in Cheshire, and hopes Cromwell will not credit evil reports of himself' (*ibid.*, 8, 496, p. 290–2). He reported that William Hardware, vicar of Great Budworth, 'keeps in his house a single woman named Margaret Kynderdale, by whom he has had several children; Thomas Fletcher, vicar of Runcorn, has had ten or twelve by Agnes Habram'. Both were canons of Norton. Ironically, Becanshaw went on to criticise in extreme terms the character of Piers Dutton. Cromwell could be selective in choosing those who required correction.

In February 1536, Doctors Layton and Legh gathered further information to the discredit of the religious houses on their visitation of the area. At Norton two canons were reported to be sodomites, and two had broken their vows of chastity (one with five women). The house was said to have an income of £260 and a debt of £200 (*ibid.*, 10, 364, p. 141). The figure for the income was presumably based on that obtained by the *Valor* commissioners the previous year, who recorded a total of £258

11s 8d. Expenses, pensions and alms reduced this figure to £180 7s 7d, bringing Norton within the net of those monasteries with an income of less than £200 that were caught by the suppression.

The disparity between the figure for income in 1535 and the total recorded the following year by the Augmentation Office commissioner Thomas Bolles (£343 13s 7¼d) has been discussed. Whether the understatement in 1535 was a deliberate attempt by the *Valor* commissioners, who in Frodsham deanery were led by Sir Piers Dutton, to bring about the closure of Norton Priory is open to question. Knowles and Hadcock (1971, 168) thought it was: 'As at Hexham, the income appears to have been falsified to bring it below £200, so that Norton could be suppressed in 1536.' Whether or not this was the case depends upon the interpretation of the intention of the 1535 commissions. They were set up on the 30 January 1535 with the objective of assessing ecclesiastical incomes as a basis for the new tax of one-tenth of spiritualities which was to be levied by the Crown (Knowles, 1959, 242). At what stage it was decided to use the results as the basis for a quite different purpose, the selection of monasteries for closure, is unclear. If Dutton wished to falsify the accounts in an effort to bring down the abbot of Norton and to acquire the possessions of the abbey through its suppression, he had to have known of the £200 deciding figure. He may have been sufficiently close to Cromwell to have learnt about the ulterior motive for the survey. Alternatively, the abbot of Norton may have wished to reduce his tax liability by understating the spiritual income of the house (that is the main area of discrepancy). Sir Piers, however, seems an unlikely person to have been the victim of deception by someone he clearly regarded as an enemy.

At the beginning of October 1536 the opportunity arose for Dutton to finally dispose of the abbot of Norton. When the commissioners Combes and Bolles attempted to close the abbey, trouble broke out – at least according to Sir Piers it did. He claimed in a letter to Sir Thomas Audley sent on 12 October 1536 that after the commissioners had packed up 'such jewels and other stuff as they had there' they intended to leave the abbey the following day. The abbot gathered a great crowd (two or three hundred according to Sir Piers) and the commissioners, in fear for their lives, were forced to take to a tower. They sent a letter to Dutton which arrived at about nine o'clock, asserting the danger they were in and asking him to assist. He arrived with a company of 'lovers and tenants' and found fires lit inside and outside the gates. The abbot had arranged for an ox to be roasted and other victuals prepared. Dutton says that he came suddenly upon the crowd, which fled, with the fugitives taking to the pools and water. As it was dark, Dutton could arrest only the abbot and four canons, whom he took to Halton Castle. His letter ends with some self-congratulation and a request for advice as to what to do next (*Letters and Papers Henry VIII*, 2, 681, p. 265).

On 19 October the answer came, in a letter from the King at Windsor which was addressed jointly to Sir Piers Dutton and Sir William Brereton, his two principal officers in Cheshire. He stated that if it was true that the abbot and canons had behaved in a traitorous manner, then without further delay they should be hanged in such places that would provide a terrible example to others. 'Herein fail ye not – travail with such dexterity so as this matter may be finished with all possible diligence' (*ibid.*, 11, 768, p. 306–7).

This letter was unambiguous, but on 20 October another letter was sent to Dutton by the earl of Derby informing him that the rebels in Yorkshire had been scattered, and ordering him to do no hurt or molestation to the commons 'as you will answer to the King's highness at your peril' (reproduced in full in Beamont 1873, 197). This letter served to stay Dutton's hand, and while Brereton obstructed the execution of the abbot by refusing contact with Dutton, Sir Thomas Boteler made representations on behalf of the canons. Boteler, the lord of Warrington, wrote to Cromwell saying that he would not have interceded if he believed them guilty: 'the common fame of the county imputes no fault to them'. He begged Cromwell's interference as he feared that Dutton would have them executed without examination. The letter was sent on 8 November (*Letters and Papers Henry VIII*, 11, 1019, p. 413).

On 30 November Dutton, evidently frustrated by Brereton's obstructionism but not daring to proceed with the executions himself, wrote to Cromwell for further guidance (*ibid.*, 11, 1212, p. 487). Brereton's delaying tactics were effective, and in a letter to Cromwell on 18 January 1537 he turned the tables by asserting that it was Dutton who would not meet him to discuss the 'supposed insurrection' at Norton. He suggested that a commission of worshipful men should be sent to the shire (*ibid.*, 12 vol. 1, 130, p. 61). Twelve days later a privy seal was issued at Greenwich authorising the examination of the abbot and canons of Norton. Eventually the abbot and canons were discharged having given sureties, as Brereton reported to Cromwell on 29 August 1537 (*ibid.*, 12 vol. 2, 597, pp. 221–2). On 7 November, Abbot Thomas Birkenhead was awarded a pension of £24 per annum (*ibid.*, 13, part 1, 583). On 20 December, Birkenhead, described as a priest, recently abbot of Norton, was given a dispensation to become a secular priest with or without the cure of souls (Chambers 1966, 177). A final irony is that after all Dutton's efforts to expel and execute him, thus leaving the monastery lands vacant for Dutton's acquisition, Birkenhead came into the ownership of some of the Norton lands. In a will of 1543, one William Reed of St John's in Middlesex left to Thomas Birkenhead, clerk, a burgage and gardens at Astmoor, and also the lease of a parcel of land called the Cryme and Little Meadow and a pasture called Venables Moor, within the lordship of Norton 'belonging to the late abbey of Norton' (*Cheshire Sheaf*, 19, 1922, 3). In contrast, for all Dutton's efforts he received none of Norton's land, which was retained in crown hands until sold to Sir Richard Brooke in 1545.

Dutton continued to feud with Brereton after the release of the abbot. Brereton tried to acquire the stewardship of Halton Castle, which Dutton protested about to Cromwell. Dutton said that Brereton was offering 100 marks for it, although it was only worth 100 shillings a year. He pointed out that his manor and house were within the circuit of the said office – the thought of Brereton having jurisdiction over him was clearly intolerable (*Letters and Papers Henry VIII*, 12 vol. 2, 1215, p. 428). Cromwell acceded to Dutton's request and made him deputy to Sir Edward Neville, steward of Halton. Predictably, this led to trouble, with a complaint by Thomas Aston, Dutton's neighbour but an ally of Brereton, who was King's Attorney at Halton. He claimed that Dutton was interfering with the courts by appointing his servants to them, fixing charges, falsely imprisoning innocent people, and with his servants causing riots in Halton, Eanley and Norton (*ibid.*, 13, 1114, p. 407–8).

The canons of Norton, having escaped execution, were, like the abbot, awarded pensions. On 27 June 1537 William Hardware and Henry Barnes were given dispensations to hold benefices and for a change of habit (Chambers 1966, 59). On 20 September, John Penketh and Roger (Thomas?) Fletcher were similarly released (*ibid.*, 72). On 30 May 1537 Richard Wright, priest, recently a canon of Norton and still vicar of Burton on Stather, was given a dispensation to wear the habit of the order beneath that of a secular priest (*ibid.*, 98). James Pate received his dispensation on 20 December (*ibid.*, 117). Richard Walton was dispensed from his vows in the same year (*ibid.*, 86). There were therefore at least seven canons in 1536 in addition to the abbot.

It is interesting to note that despite the reports of immorality against William Hardware and Thomas Fletcher by Adam Becansaw, and despite the allegations of forgery and treason against their abbey, they continued to work as vicars of Great Budworth and Runcorn respectively. Indeed, Hardware also became vicar of Weaverham.

The events of the Dissolution show that even in the face of a ruthless and implacable enemy, there was sufficient goodwill towards the brethren of Norton for support to be forthcoming from persons of influence such as Sir William Brereton and Sir Thomas Boteler.

5
Building the priory

Introduction

The excavation of the site of Norton Priory has revealed a considerable amount of information about the structures of the twelfth-century priory, and the way in which the original buildings were modified in succeeding centuries. The development sequence is shown on fig. 4. There are three types of evidence which contribute to an understanding of the buildings:

1. The remains of walls and foundations

The site was heavily robbed after the sale to the Brookes in 1545; demolition seems to have been organised in a systematic manner over the following two centuries. As a result most walls are represented at best by one or two courses of ashlar masonry; more often only the foundations have survived (fig. 35). The two exceptions are the south wall of the nave, which acted as the foundation of the eighteenth-century mansion and which survives to a height of four courses of ashlar, and the west range undercroft (fig. 43). The incorporation of the latter into the eighteenth-century house fortunately resulted in its survival. It has been possible to study the nature of the excavated walls and foundations, and their relationships, to provide a source of information about the development of the priory and the techniques of construction.

2. Other stratigraphical information

In addition to the relationships between walls and foundations, which are themselves part of the stratigraphical sequence, it has been possible to examine the relationships of other layers, pits, robber trenches, graves, construction trenches, ditches, drains etc., to the remains of the structures. This has provided additional information about the sequence and methods of construction, dating of phases of building, methods of building, activities carried on in different parts of the priory, nature of floor surfaces, and much else. The intensity of eighteenth- and nineteenth-century disturbance, particularly gardening, has however reduced the amount of stratigraphical information severely, so knowledge of the later phases in the history of the priory and of post-Dissolution developments is limited.

3. Surviving architectural decoration

The severity of robbing and later disturbance resulted in the absence of architecturally decorative, and therefore diagnostic, features from all except the medieval undercroft. Despite this, a substantial amount of moulded and carved stonework survived to be recovered in the excavation. Much of it had been incorporated as rubble in foundations of various dates from the thirteenth century to the eighteenth century. Architectural details can provide information about the structure and appearance of demolished buildings, their date and occasionally the origins of the masons who constructed them. The quality of workmanship is an indication of the financial standing of the priory.

Other sources are of more marginal importance, though nonetheless valuable when available. For example, references in medieval documents to the structures are few in number, but very useful when they do occur.

Temporary buildings

A group of temporary buildings was constructed of timber in the twelfth century. They are interpreted as quarters for the canons and their resident servants during the period in which the masonry buildings were being erected. Norton Priory is one of very few sites to have produced evidence of temporary quarters, so the information that has been obtained about them is of particular importance.

There are a number of documentary references to temporary accommodation being established as a first step in the foundation of a religious house. When the first monks of Fountains arrived in Skelldale in 1132 they are reputed to have sheltered under rocks, and then in a hut beneath a large elm tree. They constructed a wattle chapel, and in 1133 they began to erect timber buildings under the direction of Geoffrey d'Ainai, who had been sent from Clairvaux. In 1134 there were carpenters on site, presumably erecting temporary quarters; a start on the permanent stone buildings was made in about 1136 (Gilyard-Beer and Coppack 1986). In 1281 carpenters at Vale Royal were erecting timber lodges for the workmen and the monks – 12,800 boards were cut from trees in Delamere Forest, and laths and clay were also used (Crossley 1949, 86). At Meaux a great house with mud walls (wattle and daub?) and a chapel with a dorter underneath served as temporary quarters for the monks; it was ten years after the foundation before the construction of masonry buildings was started (Brakspear 1905, 8).

It was universal practice to begin construction of a monastic complex with the church. It was there that the bulk of the monastic day was spent. Patrons and benefactors also had a strong motive to see the church complete, for within its walls they might expect to be buried and to have prayers offered for their souls. The time taken to bring a church to the state in which it was suitable for worship varied – a point discussed later – but before this stage was reached it is unlikely that resources of manpower would be available to work on the domestic buildings. Temporary quarters for the brethren (and their servants and the team of masons) would therefore be required.

Despite the number of religious houses that have been the subject of an excavation of some kind, very little archaeological information is available about temporary quarters. This must be partly the result of the process of 'clearance' to which so many monastic sites have been subjected. The removal of material with no regard paid to stratigraphy is unlikely to result in the recognition of timber structures even when their remains are as substantial as those at Norton. The scale of good-quality excavation has been insufficient to encounter temporary buildings in all but a few cases. The discovery of a pair of timber buildings at Fountains beneath the church demon-

strates the potential on even an apparently well-known site (Gilyard-Beer and Coppack 1986).

Timber buildings have been found in three areas at Norton. To the north of the priory church two large post holes were found, which belong to a building lying mainly outside the area excavated. Their date is uncertain as a result of attenuated stratigraphy.

Due west of the west end of the church a timber building was found, lying partly beneath the metalling of the entrance track to the priory. It consisted of earth-fast posts erected within post pits (fig. 30). The posts were approximately 0.25 by 0.15 m scantling, and the pits were dug 0.5 m into the boulder clay from the original pre-priory ground surface. There can be no doubt that they are primary features in the stratigraphical sequence. It may be postulated that this building was a lodge regulating entrance to the outer courtyard of the priory, replaced later by a gatehouse of masonry.

The building measured about 6.8 m wide by at least 7.8 m long, with the roof support timbers integral with the walls (i.e. not aisled as some of the other temporary buildings were). To the north east a very large post pit 1.6 m in diameter and 0.7 m deep was found. Within the pit was a post pipe 0.58 m by 0.46 m in plan, with some wood surviving in the base. It is possible that this was one of a pair of gate posts – if so its twin must lie beneath the current entrance track to the museum. The timber building must have been demolished by the early thirteenth century, by which date a drainage ditch had been dug through its site, and the first metalling of the entrance track had been laid (fig. 93).

Fig. 30. Post pits of the temporary timber building that probably served as an entrance lodge. In the thirteenth century an open drainage ditch was dug through the site. Later in the century the stone drain was set within the ditch; it carried water from the cloister.

Fig. 31. Twelfth-century post pits and drainage ditches. The positions of the timbers, where known, are shown in black. The cross hatching shows the minimum extent of one of the first phase buildings, and two of the second phase buildings. The subsequent position of the late twelfth-century undercroft is shown at the top of the plan.

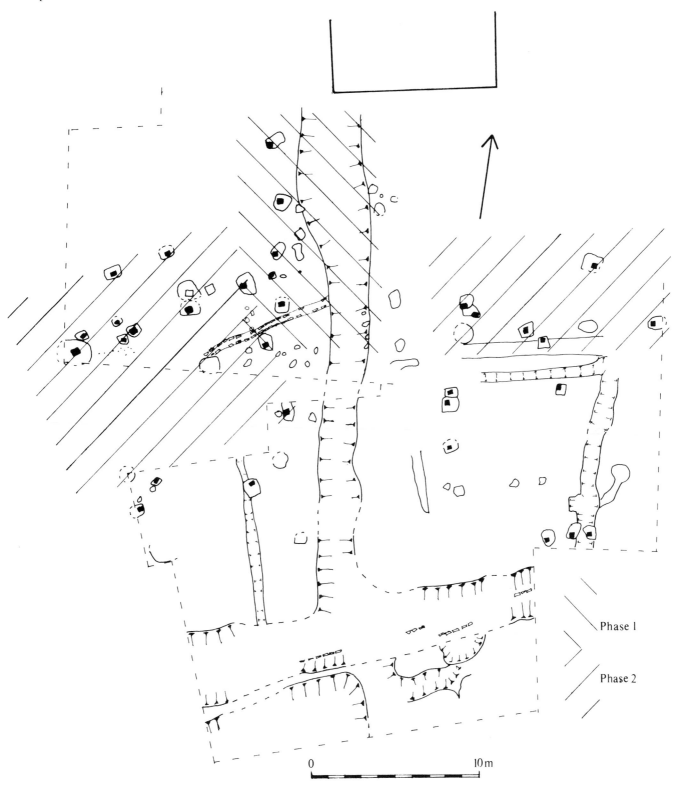

Phase 1

Phase 2

0   10 m

By far the largest group of timber features was discovered in the south western part of the site (figs. 31, 32). Their interpretation has been hindered by five factors: damage by nineteenth-century gardening which in places penetrated no less than 0.8 m from the current ground surface; many eighteenth- and nineteenth-century drain and pipe trenches; eighteenth- and nineteenth-century walls of the country house; Victorian terracing; and medieval walls and ditches cutting the earliest layers and features. In addition the need to preserve existing trees partly restricted the area available for investigation.

Despite the problems, it is possible to draw some conclusions about the temporary buildings. Two phases have been identified. One row of posts running south from the later masonry undercroft may be a set of aisle posts, the second set of which will have been removed by the main west wall of the Georgian house. Smaller post holes on the south and east may have held wall timbers. The building was at least 12 m long (N–S) and was either burnt

Fig. 32. Post pits of the large aisled hall (the western-most of the two second phase buildings shown on fig. 31). The ranging rods are set at the centres of the post pits of the northern alignment of aisle posts. The difficulties of recovering a complete plan are illustrated by the drain trenches and structures of the eighteenth-century house that cut through the early features.

down or deliberately demolished. It was replaced by a new aisled building of larger size. The destruction or demolition of the first building was represented by an extensive area of charcoal and burnt daub, overlying the fill of the original post pits, cut by the succeeding post pits, and overlain by the clay floor of the second building. A large drainage ditch was cut through the site of the first building, and a small stone drain serving the second building fed into it. The drainage ditch is part of the early system of water management – it ran south to form a junction with the original main monastic drain, itself also an open ditch.

The new building was 11.0 m wide by at least 14 m long (its western limit has not been located). It consisted of two rows of aisle posts set in large post pits up to 0.6 m deep, and over 1 m in diameter (figs. 32, 26). The side walls had post pits situated opposite each of the pairs of aisle posts – of smaller scale (about 0.6 m diameter) but nonetheless substantial. The aisle posts and wall posts were respectively of 0.30 m by 0.40 m and 0.22 m by 0.18 m scantling. The building had a thick clay floor, and a central stone built hearth (fig. 33). The latter was surrounded by many stake holes, which may have been associated with a spit or screen, or (less likely) a fire hood. The presence of the hearth indicates that the building was of one storey, unlike the Meaux building.

The end of the building's life can be associated with

the construction of masonry buildings. The soil layer which overlay the floor of the building also filled the ditch; one of the buttresses of the west wall of the masonry kitchens, and also the west range undercroft (built *c.* 1190) overlay the ditch fill.

To the east of the drainage ditch, more timber features were found. Here also two phases can be identified. The plan of the first building is difficult to discern but it was constructed of earth-fast timbers. It was replaced by another aisled building; the southern row of aisle posts were excavated. The northern row was largely obscured by later medieval masonry walls but one of the posts was located in a gap in the masonry. On the south was a trench which probably represents the wall line, and running parallel to it a drainage gulley which fed into yet another open ditch which emptied into the main monastic drain ditch. Interestingly, the southern row of aisle posts must have rotted where they emerged from the ground, for a trench had been dug along their line, removing the upper part of the pits and post pipes, to accommodate a masonry support which had itself been substantially robbed later. The stumps of the posts were preserved (fig. 25). The building measured at least 12 m long by about 6 m wide; the spacing between the posts was 3.8 m.

Eventually the site of this timber building and the area to the south were occupied by the monastic kitchens which went through a number of phases, starting with earth-fast timbers and eventually with timber framed

walls set on masonry dwarf walls, with some roof supports on pad stones.

Although few sites have produced evidence of temporary buildings, there are numerous references to such structures particularly in the case of the Cistercian order (Fergusson 1983). The Cistercian charters of about 1119 contain a specification of the essential elements that must be present: 'No abbot shall be sent to a new place without at least twelve monks and . . . without the prior construction of such places as an oratory, a refectory, a dormitory, a guest house, and a gate-keeper's cell, so the monks may immediately serve God and live in religious discipline' (*ibid.*, 75). The canons who moved from Runcorn to Norton were not bound by the strictures of Citeaux, but their requirements were probably very similar. The temporary structures found at Norton could be identified with some of those in the Cistercian document. The structure near the entrance track is likely to be a lodge for the gate-keeper. Masonry foundations (fig. 34) to the north west of the masonry church could be part of the 'oratory' or temporary church.

A distinction must be drawn between temporary buildings, and buildings erected in the monastic precinct such as barns and stables for which timber was often the appropriate material throughout the medieval period.

The construction of the timber buildings

The excavation revealed many interesting details of the constructional techniques of the carpenters. The post pits were large in all cases, and the posts were rarely placed in the centre of the pit. Although the post pits were far from regular, the centres of the posts were very precisely placed.

Fig. 33. A stone lined hearth set in the clay floor of the large aisled hall; the near side was destroyed by a drainage trench.

In some cases the posts had been chocked up on short lengths of plank placed horizontally on the base of the pit. These details suggest that the posts were set upright and their position adjusted in the pits to create the basic framework of the building. In the case of the aisled buildings, this could have consisted of each row of aisle posts attached to purlins, with principal rafters providing rigidity across the building. Once these elements had been assembled, and the post pits packed with clay, a framework existed which could then be provided with a roof, walls and floor.

Not all the posts survived in the post pits. In every case, however, a post pipe announced its presence to the excavators in the form of a post void. By careful excavation, it was possible to show that the posts had been neatly cut square or rectangular.

The building to the north west of the church had a different form of construction altogether. A trench 1.4 m broad had been dug into the early ground surface, and packed with rough lumps of sandstone (fig. 34). In the middle of each trench the sandstone had once been packed against horizontal timbers 0.16 m square. Although the timbers had rotted, their position was quite clear as strips of grey clayey soil. At the corner the timbers had never

joined, and were on slightly different levels. This suggests that the timbers were not connected with the superstructure of the building, but were laid as a device to prevent subsidence. The technique of using horizontal timbers to provide stability within foundations is found widely across a considerable time range, from Roman masonry fort walls to medieval churches (Wilcox 1982). The building's construction is known to predate the extended west end of the church, which must date to about 1200 (see below), and it may have been a temporary church. It could have been retained as a mortuary chapel after the consecration of the permanent church. Only further excavation can clarify its function. Temporary chapels are very rare – one of the few that is known is the chapel of St John the Baptist at Finchale in Durham, which was eventually enclosed by the choir of the priory church. A suite of temporary buildings constructed of stone also exists at Finchale (Peers n.d.a.).

There is no documentary evidence for the source of the large timbers used in the temporary quarters, but it is likely that the substantial areas of woodland in the manor of Norton were capable of supplying the timber at this early date. The walls of the early buildings were composed of wattle and daub. Quantities of daub were associated with the demolition deposits of all the timber buildings, through being partially burnt. The wattles left impressions

Fig. 34. Foundations of the possible temporary church.

in the daub in the form of cylindrical voids. A sample of sixty-five pieces of daub were measured to reveal a range of wattle diameters from 12 to 30 mm. In a deliberately filled ditch in the kitchen area, some wattles were preserved by the water-logged conditions. The larger examples were identified as wood hazel (*Corylus avellana*), the smaller as willow (*Salix alba*). Wattles are the product of pollarding or coppicing, and there is thus direct evidence from the excavation for woodland management in the locality.

The ubiquitous boulder clay is a suitable material for making daub, and will have been obtained somewhere nearby – possibly from the large irregular pits found about 50 m further south in the 1984 and 1985 seasons of excavation. The roof may have been shingled.

Medieval buildings usually consist of small oaks felled when between twenty-five and seventy years of age. Old Court, Corpus Christi College, Cambridge incorporates 1,400 oaks, mainly under 0.25 m diameter. The fifteenth-

Fig. 35. Junction of the south transept and the east range. The west and south walls of the transept are of one build with deeper and broader foundations. The west wall of the east range makes a butt join with the short spur projecting from the transept.

century roofs of Norwich Cathedral comprise 680 oaks of about 0.4 m basal diameter (Rackham 1976, 76). In contrast the best preserved timber from the largest aisled building at Norton (fig. 26) was from a tree aged about 200 years when felled (information from Dr Alan Hibbert, Liverpool Polytechnic) which had a diameter of at least 0.5 m (0.30 m by 0.40 m scantling). Even the wall timbers of this building were of 0.22 m by 0.18 m scantling (*c.* 0.3 m diameter).

Construction of the church

As soon as temporary accommodation for the canons had been provided, a start would have been made on the masonry structures. The excavation provided clear evidence that at Norton the church was the primary masonry building. The south transept was built with a pair of buttresses projecting southwards where the walls of the east range were intended to join later (fig. 35). The junction of the west range walls with the church was complicated by the late twelfth-century demolition of the early west range and the presence of a later drain. However it seems that small walls were built, bonded in with the south wall of the nave, in the position of the intended west range. Thus the positions of both east and west ranges

were determined from the outset, but their construction awaited completion of the church (fig. 36).

The church walls were provided with surprisingly shallow foundations, only 0.15 m deep. They consisted of trenches dug into the boulder clay about 0.25 m broader than the wall they were designed to carry. They were filled with sandstone rubble and rounded pebbles from the clay. Although the foundations were so slight, there was no

evidence that any of the walls suffered subsidence, despite the many later modifications that were made to the church. The south wall of the nave even became the foundation of the pedimented three storey north front of the Brookes' Georgian mansion, but the medieval foundations still proved adequate on the boulder clay.

The local red sandstone is an ideal stone for ashlar construction, being easy to dress but reasonably robust (in contrast to the Chester sandstone for example). Thus it is not surprising that the masons constructed the walls of the church with ashlar faces and with a rubble and mortar core (fig. 35). The blocks of sandstone were cut to provide a rectangular outer face dressed obliquely with a chisel.

Fig. 36. Twelfth-century masonry buildings and drainage ditches. Destruction of a substantial part of the east (dormitory) range in the eighteenth century makes it difficult to judge whether it reached this considerable length in the original plan.

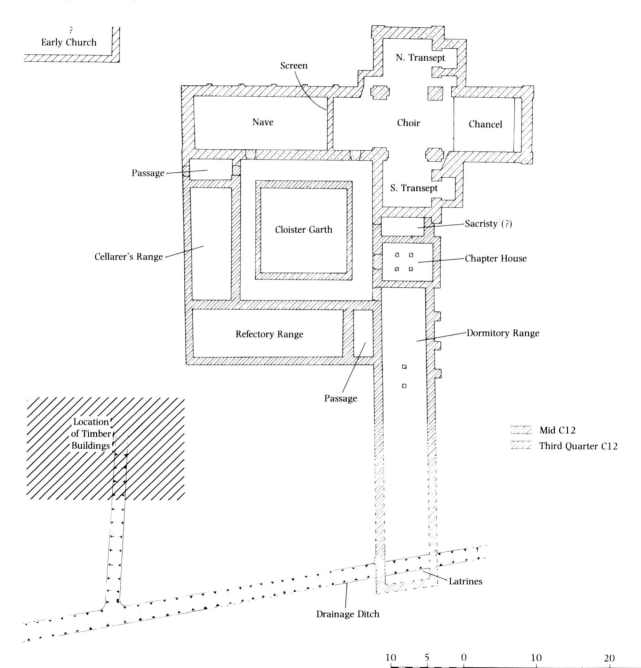

They varied from 240 mm to 460 mm long. Each course consisted of stones of uniform height, the courses within a narrow range from 220 mm to 240 mm. The four sides of the blocks were chisel-dressed to a depth of about 0.15 m to permit a close joint to be made with neighbouring blocks. The remainder of the depth of the blocks was roughly tapered (adze- or axe-dressed) to provide good bonding with the core. This consisted of lime and sand mortar with broken sandstone rubble. The north and west walls of the surviving west range revealed further information about constructional methods. A large area on both walls had been stripped of its late twelfth-century ashlar to accommodate the deeper ashlar of the façade of the Georgian house. When the remnants of the eighteenth-century façade were removed a large area of corework was exposed. It was possible to distinguish a series of horizontal layers by observing the positions of the fragments of sandstone rubble and by detecting subtle differences in the composition of the mortar. Each layer was equivalent in thickness to a course of ashlar. It can therefore be deduced that the walls were constructed by laying one course of ashlar at a time and filling the space between with rubble and mortar. As the group of masons worked round the walls of the building, completing no doubt a length of one course each working day when conditions allowed, the core would have a chance to set before the next course was added. The chemical processes involved in the setting of mortar take place over a considerable period of time but the crucial changes from a semi-fluid to a near solid state occur relatively quickly. After a few days therefore the next course of ashlar could be bedded (using mortar) and the new layer of core added. This avoided the danger of the existing wall being distorted by weight produced by several courses of ashlar and core being added in one stage.

Variations in the composition of the layers of core material are easily understood. By the time one course of masonry had been completed round the circuit of the building, new supplies of some of the materials would have been obtained. Rubble with a different size range, or sand of a different hue, or lime with a different proportion of adventitious charcoal, could all produce the slight variations that were observed.

It was a frequent practice to construct a monastic church in two separate campaigns. First the eastern end (choir, transepts and presbytery) would be built, enabling services to take place as soon as possible. Construction of the nave could then follow. An example is Lilleshall in Shropshire, where there is a butt join in the south wall of the nave to the west of the eastern processional door. Everything to the east of this point was completed in late Romanesque style, whereas the nave must date from the early thirteenth century (Rigold 1969, 9–10). There is no reason to believe that the primary church at Norton was built in two campaigns. There is no evidence of a junction

in the nave wall, and there is no difference in the character of the masonry between the eastern and western parts of the church, nor was there any sign of a stratigraphical break in the layers within the church.

The building operations must have required the use of wooden scaffolding, which is shown in many medieval manuscript illustrations. However, nowhere in the site has any trace of post holes for scaffolding been found. It must therefore be assumed that instead of the scaffolding having vertical poles set in the soil, it was erected with poles resting either on planks or on stones. A mid-thirteenth century drawing of masons and carpenters (Cambridge University Library Ee.3.59) shows scaffold poles and a windlass set on what must be stones or wooden blocks. Scaffold post holes have been identified at Bordesley Abbey (Hirst, Walsh and Wright 1983, 29) and Fountains Abbey (Gilyard-Beer and Coppack 1986, 158).

The plan of the original church (fig. 36)

Norton Priory was founded in 1134 not as a new establishment, but by the transfer of an existing group of canons from Runcorn where construction was presumably still taking place. It is therefore likely that a master mason and a workforce were available to start work immediately. The church that the masons laid out and began to erect had a simple cruciform plan. It comprised a presbytery, a crossing which would have accommodated the choir and above which a tower was placed, two transepts with tiny transept chapels, and a nave. A screen (the pulpitum) separated the choir from the nave (figs. 95, 96); the choir occupied not only the crossing but the easternmost part of the western arm of the building (fig. 84).

Measurements and proportions

During the archaeological work at Norton all measurements were carried out using metric units. In the case of structures such as the church an accuracy to 0.01 m (i.e. 1 cm) was achieved. In the following table a series of measurements of the church and the period one cloister is given in metric units with Imperial equivalents. The third column requires explanation. Measurements taken at Bordesley Abbey suggest that a foot of 0.295 m was used as the basic unit in laying out the original church – a unit which has also been found at a number of other English and Continental Cistercian abbeys (Hirst, Walsh and Wright 1983, 224). To test the possibility that this unit was used at Norton the metric measurements have been converted into 'medieval feet' using the 0.295 factor, with the result expressed in feet and inches. In all cases below measurements were taken to the faces of walls, which with the high quality of ashlar masonry vary only slightly from place to place (± 0.01 m).

An examination of the two columns of feet and inches measurements does not immediately reveal which variety was used by the medieval masons. However, in trying to work out how the church was laid out, the writer has found the use of medieval feet to be the more likely unit. Furthermore it has proved possible to postulate a scheme whereby the church was laid out using medieval feet, as follows.

A striking and significant relationship exists between the overall length of the church, 152'11" and the total length across the transept, 76'6". The precise ratio of 2:1 can only be deliberate on the part of the masons.

A second significant relationship exists in the breakdown of the length of the church. The nave is 59'9", the choir 59'8", and the chancel 33'7". The demarcation between the nave and the choir is the pulpitum screen base, and between the choir and the chancel it is a row of sandstone blocks which must have supported a threshold step or a screen. It is not improbable that the internal space was divided up as follows: nave 60', choir 60', chancel 30', a ratio of 2:2:1. It is perhaps significant that there is a gap of 1.08 m (3'8" medieval feet) between the back of the altar pace and the east wall which would bring the size of the presbytery within one inch of 30'.

In view of such a neat division of the length of the church, it is worth examining the length across the transepts. This is listed in the table as 26'0" south transept, 24'8" choir, and 25'10" north transept, the measurements being taken from the inner faces of the south and north transept walls to the projected line of the inner faces of the nave and chancel walls. If however the measurement is taken from the transept wall to the projecting bases which supported the arches into the transepts, using the top of the chamfer of the base as re-

presenting the face of the arch, it is found that three lengths of 7.53 m are the result. The total length across the transepts therefore resolves itself into three sections of 25'6", a simple ratio of 1:1:1, each section being precisely one sixth of the total length of the church.

In examining the dimensions of the church a fourth relationship has become apparent. The combination of two of the above sections is 51'0" (i.e. the choir plus either transept). The distance from the pulpitum screen to the west side of the transepts is 8.27 m (28'0"). The sum of this and the width of the transepts is 51'2". The co-incidence of the two figures is significant, as will be explained.

Laying out the church

On the basis of the four relationships described above it is possible to suggest how the masons set about laying out the church. They are likely to have followed these steps.

1. Establish a base line along the intended line of either the north or the south wall of the nave and chancel. Both of these are very precisely built with their inner faces following near-perfect straight lines.
2. Lay out the nave by measuring 60' from the western end of the line, 25' as the second side of a right-angled triangle, and 65' as the third side. 25, 60 and 65 constitute a Pythagorean set. 25' is the required width of the nave, 60' its length. Having established two sides of a rectangle the other two sides can simply be measured in using two strings, one of 60' and one of 25'.
3. The eastern end of the rectangle forms the line of the pulpitum. The choir can be laid out by measuring a

	Metric	Statute feet	'Medieval' feet
Total length of church	45.13 m	148'1"	152'11"
Length of nave (to pulpitum)	17.61 m	57'9"	59'9"
Length of choir (pulpitum to chancel)	17.60 m	57'9"	59'8"
Length of chancel	9.92 m	32'7"	33'7"
Width of nave	7.31 m	24'0"	24'9"
Width of chancel	7.30 m	23'11"	24'9"
Length of north transept	7.62 m	25'0"	25'10"
Length of south transept	7.67 m	25'2"	26'0"
Total length across transepts	22.57 m	74'0"	76'6"
Width of north transept	6.83 m	22'5"	23'2"
Width of south transept	6.84 m	22'5"	23'2"
Depth of north transept chapel	2.19 m	7'2"	7'5"
Width of north transept chapel	2.73 m	8'11"	9'3"
Depth of south transept chapel	2.10 m	6'10"	7'2"
Width of south transept chapel	3.10 m	10'2"	10'6"
Width of cloister walk	2.65 m	8'9"	9'0"
Length from east range to west range	8.26 m	59'11"	61'11"
Cloister garth – overall width with arcade wall	13.00 m	42'8"	44'0"
Cloister garth – internal width	10.60 m	34'9"	35'11"
Internal width – west range	5.91 m	19'5"	20'0"
Internal width – east range	6.12 m	20'1"	20'8"

further 60' along the base line and constructing a rectangle again, or by simply extending the long sides of the first rectangle for a further 60' and checking the width. The 65' diagonal can also be checked.

4. The 30' chancel can be laid out in a similar manner; the 39' diagonal can be checked (25, 30 and 39 being another Pythagorean set). The extra 3'7" extension presents no problems, simply being a continuation of the rectangle of the chancel. It would have been possible of course to lay out both nave and chancel on the simpler 3:4:5 set, but the fact that dimensions lend themselves to the sets described here does raise the possibility of their use.

5. The next step is to lay out the transepts. Having decided that the length across the transepts is to be half of the length of the church, the division of 153' into six units of 25'6" provides the module for the transepts and choir. Again, the pulpitum line is used in laying out. Two overlapping squares are constructed with sides of 51' using the pulpitum and north side of the nave for the right angled corner of one of the squares and the pulpitum and south side of the nave for the other. The eastern internal sides of the transepts are provided by the eastern edge of the squares. The line of the inner face of the north transept is provided by the north side of the northern square; likewise the southern one.

6. The reason for the choice of 23'2" as the width of both transepts is not clear, but it may result from a desire to provide spaces that were square in plan as the distance from the inner face of the transept arch is close to this measurement. Having decided on that width, the laying out of the western sides presents no problems, simply requiring a measurement of 28' back from the line of the pulpitum to provide the inner face.

7. The church having been laid out, the outline of the cloister had to be established. As has already been explained, provision was made in the south transept south wall and the nave south wall for the construction of the east and west ranges. A right angle was already provided by the south side of the nave and the west side of the south transept. The east side of the cloister could therefore be provided by projecting the latter southwards. The other dimensions of the cloister coincide closely with the postulated 0.295 m foot – cloister walks 9'0" broad, the length across the cloister to the edges of the cloister arcade walls of 44'0", and the length of the cloister garth to the inner side of the arcade walls of 35'11". The distance from the west wall of the south transept to the east wall of the west range was 61'11", and the internal width of the west range 20'0". Once all these dimensions had been established, the detailed

laying out of the cloister would wait until the construction of the church was approaching completion.

The above scheme, based upon the proposed foot of 0.295 m, works so well that it seems very likely that this was indeed the unit employed by the medieval masons; the perch of 5.03 m (Fernie 1985) does not appear to have been used here. Once the laying out had been completed, the digging of foundations would have commenced. At this stage, and also with the laying of the first ashlar course, minor discrepancies will have crept in. The transept chapels, which in contrast to all other features of the church lack symmetry and precise measurement, may have been planned after the initial layout of the church had been completed.

Details of the plan of the church

The walls of the church were 1.40 m broad at the base, narrowing on the second course by 0.10 m where a simple chamfer was present. This chamfered plinth seems to have been used on the complete external circuit of the church with the exception of the south wall of the nave. Here the cloister roof protected the foundations; elsewhere the chamfer would have deflected falling drops of water away from the wall.

The north wall of the church had a series of shallow pilaster buttresses which must have been present more for the sake of appearance than to enhance the stability of the building. The exposed corners of the building (north west corner of the nave and the corners of the north transept and the chancel) had shallow clasping buttresses.

The crossing tower was supported on four masonry piers. The south west pier was integral with the south wall of the nave and the west wall of the south transept. The other three piers were built separate from the junctions of the other walls. A narrow passage around the north west pier was created by constructing a right-angled projection into the angle between the nave and transept. A small passage around the north east pier was made possible by enclosing the space between the north transept chapel and the north wall of the chancel. The south east pier was separated by cutting back both the pier and the junction of the chancel and transept.

The arrangement of the piers supporting the transept arches, the chancel arch and the nave arch appear to relate to the 0.295 m foot. The faces of the two transept arches facing the choir have already been identified as significant, coinciding with the unit of 25'6" into which the length across the transepts and the choir is divided. The width of the transept arches (again measured to the top of the chamfer which represents the inner vertical face of the arch piers) is 5.33 m (18'1" medieval feet). The distance between the inner sides of the nave and chancel arches, which lack a chamfer, is 6.50 m (22'0"). It is not surprising that these two pairs of dimensions were accurately measured, for the round arches which in turn supported the central tower were determined by their precision.

Within the chancel was an altar pace which occupied its whole width and which was faced with an ashlar step on the east and west. The pulpitum screen base survived in fragments. It had a simple vertical rounded moulding and a horizontal rebate, presumably for a wooden screen (Figs 95, 96).

Churches with a similar ground plan to that at Norton

Two other Augustinian churches have a ground plan and other architectural features in common with the original church at Norton, Portchester in Hampshire and Leonard Stanley in Gloucestershire. Portchester was founded in 1133 by William Pont d'Arch with the help of Henry I; it was abandoned by its canons sometime between 1145 and 1153 in favour of Southwick (Knowles and Hadcock 1971, 174). As a result its church (fig. 37) has survived little altered, apart from the loss of the south transept. It has a cruciform plan with a squat tower over the crossing. Its total internal length is 35.5 m and the internal width of the nave and chancel is 7 m. These dimensions are taken

Fig. 37. The church of the short-lived Portchester Priory in Hampshire, now a parish church. Beneath the tower can be seen the roof lines of the chancel and south transept. The (blocked) transept arch is clear. The windows and pilaster buttresses stop at the point of junction with the lean-to cloister roof. The scar in the masonry at the left end is where the west range joined the church.

from Cunliffe 1977, fig. 67, in which Baker suggests that the chancel may in fact have been of two bays (41.5 m). It has four pilaster buttresses on the north wall of the nave, and clasping corner buttresses as at Norton. It once had transept chapels – the roof line of the north transept chapel is visible, showing that it projected in the same way as at Norton. It has an impressively carved west door and two processional doorways to the cloister.

Leonard Stanley was founded some time after 1121 as a house of Augustinian canons by Roger de Berkeley who died in 1130. His son, in a grant confirmed in 1146, alienated the house to Gloucester Abbey and it became a cell of Benedictine monks (Swynnerton 1921). This reduction to a comparatively humble status must explain why much of the original church has survived little altered. It has a simple cruciform plan with a tower over the crossing. There were transept chapels (now demolished); they were not apsed, although it has been suggested that they were (Middleton 1880 – who in fact shows just one chapel, on the south transept). The church is 128' (39.0 m) long and the chancel, which is narrower than the nave, has a width of 16' (4.8 m) according to Middleton's plan; the nave is 25'7" (7.8 m) wide according to his text. An excavation by the church architect revealed that the transept chapels were of an unusual design, rectangular in plan, 7'3" wide and 10'6" deep (2.2 m by 3.2 m) but with a shallow apse projecting a maximum of 2'6" (0.8 m) in the centre of the back wall (Swynnerton 1929, 21). The apse chapels shown in Cunliffe 1977, 116, fig. 70 are therefore incorrect.

Leonard Stanley also has a feature, absent at Port-

chester, that brings it even closer to Norton's plan. A short angled passage, now blocked at its north eastern end, runs diagonally round the back of the south east pier base from the south transept to the chancel, just as at Norton. There is evidence for a passage around the north east pier, again similar to Norton. The Leonard Stanley passages were discovered on the removal of plaster, when the south east one was unblocked (Swynnerton 1929, 13). The explanation of these openings must be that they permitted communication between the transepts and the chancel which the presence of choir stalls on the north and south sides of the choir would otherwise have prevented. In a fully aisled church such a device would be unnecessary.

The close kinship between the three churches, built within a few years of each other, is not surprising. They are a simple and straightforward response to the requirements of a priory of modest resources, and probably intended for a complement of canons not exceeding thirteen in total. The plan was by no means the simplest that was available. Excavations at Haughmond (plan, Webster and Cherry 1980, 240–1 fig. 6) have demonstrated that the earliest church was a small cruciform structure just 17.0 m (56'8") in length; when the community was regularised in the second quarter of the twelfth century the nave was extended, bringing the total length to 31.5 m (105'0"). The nave and chancel were 6.3 m (21'0") wide; the tiny transepts had no chapels. It was completely demolished to make way for a much larger church at the end of the twelfth century.

At Norton and Haughmond, excavation has revealed the plans of the early churches; at Portchester and Leonard Stanley the early church has been 'fossilised' as a result of the peculiarities in their histories. It would be interesting to know more about the original plans of other Augustinian churches founded in the first half of the twelfth century. The Augustinians still found this plan appropriate at the end of the twelfth century. At Mottisfont (Hants.) the remains of the priory church founded in 1201 that are incorporated in an existing mid-eighteenth-century country house indicate that in plan and size it was similar to Norton (National Trust guide book 1973, 2).

The unaisled cruciform church was by no means restricted to the Augustinian canons. The first Cistercian abbey in England was founded at Waverley in Surrey on 24 November, 1128. Thirteen monks were brought from L'Aumône in Normandy. The remains of the church that was built for them were investigated between 1899 and 1902 (Brakspear 1905, plan of early buildings, 9). It consisted of a square chancel, transepts with one eastern chapel to each, and a long nave without aisles. The total internal length (taken from the plan) was about 54 m (177'); the width of nave and chancel was stated by the excavator (*ibid.*, 18) to be 24' (7.3 m). It was therefore of a very similar scale to the first church at Norton, where the equivalent dimensions were: length 45.13 m (148'1") and width 7.31 m (24').

In 1131 another band of pioneer Cistercian monks was sent from L'Aumône, this time to Tintern (Craster 1956, 3; the plan of the site is the source of the dimensions below). Their first church was very similar to that at Waverley – a simple unaisled cruciform structure, but with two chapels to each instead of one. The overall internal length was 48.5 m (159'0") and the width of the nave was about 8.4 m (27'6") – again, of a similar order to Norton. A plan which is almost a twin of Tintern's is Torre Abbey (Devon), a house of Premonstratensian canons (e.g. Gilyard-Beer 1959, fig. 6, viii). Again the dimensions are similar: total internal length 168' (51.2 m), width of nave 25'8" (7.8 m). Ewenny Priory (Glamorgan) is an example of a Benedictine use of this simple plan (Radford 1952). The most recent discovery of a church of this type is that started in 1135 at Fountains Abbey. It had pairs of chapels on each transept, arranged *en échelon*. It was about 36 m long with a nave width of about 5.2 m (plan in Gilyard-Beer and Coppack, 1986, 179).

It can therefore be concluded that square-ended aisle-less cruciform churches were not the sole prerogative of the Augustinians – they were also built by Cistercians, Premonstratensians, and Benedictines. The basic reason for the similarities in plan and scale between the churches at Norton, Portchester, Leonard Stanley, Haughmond, Waverley, Tintern, Torre, Ewenny and Fountains is that the objective in each case was the same: to provide a simple church to serve about thirteen brethren with modest resources and expectations (although in several of these cases such modesty was short-lived and expansion soon followed).

The unusual feature of the plan of the first church at Norton is the projecting passage around the back of the north west tower pier. Although unusual, it is not unique. A similar feature is present in the Augustinian priory of Kirkham in Yorkshire, founded sometime between 1122 and 1130 (Peers n.d., b). Kirkham was subject to a campaign of rebuilding which started at the east end in the first quarter of the thirteenth century. This obliterated details of the east end of the original church, but it is clear that it must have been similar in plan to the aisle-less churches discussed above. Peers gives its overall length as 180' (55 m) with the internal width of nave being 33' (10 m). The passage is contrived within the west wall of the north transept and the north wall of the nave. It provided access to the north transept from the nave immediately west of the pulpitum. Although the pulpitum at Norton was situated further west, it seems likely that the passage was present to enable access from the nave to the transept without intruding upon the choir. What reason could there be for such an arrangement? One group of lay people who might have been permitted access to the east of the pulpitum were benefactors. Perhaps the altar that was set up in the north transept chapel had a particular significance for such a group. What is certain is that during the twelfth and thirteenth centuries the north transept chapel at Norton underwent a series of rebuilding and enlargements, necessitated primarily by the burial of members of the Dutton family within the chapel which was dedicated to the Blessed Virgin.

An almost identical arrangement was present at Lilleshall (Rigold 1969). The abbey, an Augustinian house of Arrouaisian affiliation, was founded in 1148. The original plan was very similar to those of Norton, Portchester and Leonard Stanley, an unaisled cruciform church with a tower over the crossing. Just as at Norton, the north west, north east and south east tower piers were built partially free standing, with passages around the 'back' of each of them. In the case of the north west pier, this required the construction of a passage which had to project from the angle between the north transept and the north wall of the nave, as at Norton. The south west pier was built as one with the nave and transept walls, an arrangement identical with that at Norton. To contrive a freestanding south west pier would have been virtually impossible; a projecting passage would have disrupted the corner of the cloister and would have displaced the eastern processional door.

A difference between Lilleshall and the three examples previously described is in the design of the transept chapels. Instead of Norton's short chapels opening from the transept east walls but unconnected with the chancel, the builder of Lilleshall constructed longer chapels with lean-to roofs against the chancel walls. As a result the chapels are larger, their construction simpler, and access around the back of the piers simplified. This improvement in design can be seen in the context of the later date of the foundation of Lilleshall (1148 compared to 1134 Norton, 1133 Portchester, and before 1130 in the case of Leonard Stanley). The arrangement is, in effect, a partially aisled chancel, the introduction of which facilitated circulation at the east end in a much more dignified manner than previously. Similarly, the construction of Augustinian churches with a north aisle

allowed easy access from the nave to the north transept without crossing the choir. Many originally aisle-less churches, such as Lilleshall and Norton, eventually had a north aisle added to the nave. By the later part of the twelfth century, however, aisle-less churches were being built infrequently. Most new Augustinian churches had a north aisle. An example is Brinkburn Priory (Northumberland) founded in 1135, but with a church built at the end of the twelfth century. In most aspects it is little different to the aisle-less cruciform churches. The internal length of the church is 131' (40 m); the chancel and nave are of equal width, 23' (7 m) and a pair of square ended chapels opens off each transept (dimensions taken from plan by W. H. Knowles 1903, in *VCH Northumberland*, facing p. 484). Only the presence of the aisle distinguishes it from the simple aisle-less cruciform churches.

Other examples of newly built or largely reconstructed Augustinian churches with a north aisle are Burscough (Lancashire) and Lanercost (Cumbria). It is often stated (e.g. Gilyard-Beer 1959, 19) that the reason for this is the avoidance of reconstructing existing claustral buildings. In the case of the simple addition of an aisle as at Norton this is clearly true, but where the church is part of a new foundation (Burscough) or where rebuilding is on the major scale of Lanercost it cannot be the reason. The popularity of the single aisle must have a functional explanation. Its effect was to unite the nave with the north transept and the north transept chapels. As these seem frequently to have been the place where benefactors might be buried, it might have been regarded as a good investment to provide a 'corridor' between the nave and the transept chapel.

Comparative dimensions of aisle-less cruciform churches

The dimensions of the churches mentioned in the foregoing text are brought together here for the purposes of comparison. They are listed in the order in which they

Religious house	Length of church	Width of nave	Length across transepts	Source
Norton	45.13	7.31	22.57	Excavation
Portchester	35.5 (poss. 41.5)	7	21	Plan, Cunliffe 1977
Leonard Stanley	39	7.8	20.5	Plan, Middleton 1880
Haughmond	17 (later 31.5)	6.3	16	Plan, Webster and Cherry 1980
Mottisfont	65 (conjectural)	7.6	25	Plan, N.T. Guidebook
Waverley	54	7.3	18.3	Plan, Brakspear 1905
Tintern	48.5	8.4	22.7	Plan, Craster 1956
Torre	51.2	7.8	27.7	Text, Watkin 1914
Ewenny	44	7	26.5	Plan, Radford 1952
Fountains	36	5.2	21	Plan/text, Gilyard-Beer and Coppack 1986
Kirkham	55	10	34	Text, Peers n.d.b
Lilleshall	66	9.4	31	Plan, Rigold 1969
Brinkburn	40	7 (plus) (aisle)	21.3	Plan, VCH

occur in the text. The measurements are all given in metric units, with differing precision in the various sources reflected in the extent to which subdivisions of metres are expressed here. All lengths are internal.

The early cloister and its buildings (figs. 36, 38)

Just as the church was built to a simple straightforward plan, so were the claustral buildings. To the south of the south transept, where the east range abutted the church, was a rectangular room 6.12 m long by 2.53 m wide. On analogy with other sites, this might have been either a sacristy or a passage leading from the cloister to the canons' graveyard east of the church. The latter interpretation is less likely in view of the fact that when the chapter house was extended its northern wall would have blocked the eastern door of the passage.

The building further south was the chapter house. This was rectangular, measuring 7.30 m long by 5.16 m wide. Its eastern side projected 1.1 m beyond the general line of the east range east wall, suggesting a roof line at right angles to the axis of the range. The vault was supported by four piers. A band of clay, 0.5 m wide and 0.3 m deep, was present along the north and south walls, and either side of the door on the west (on the east, later modifications obscured the evidence). It can be interpreted either as the base upon which benches had been set, or possibly as a clay packing in a robbed foundation for the benches. Benches in these positions for the canons to sit on during Chapter are to be expected on analogy with other monastic sites, e.g. Finchale, which has stone benches

Fig. 38. Model of Norton Priory in the twelfth century based on the evidence of the excavation and comparison with Augustinian buildings such as Portchester (fig. 37).

lining the walls of the chapter house, including an elevated seat in the centre of the east wall for the prior (Peers n.d.a).

Evidence for the doorway to the cloister was present as faint traces of mortar on the ashlar of the west wall, two courses of which were present below the threshold. The course of ashlar blocks which included the base of the door jambs had been set on the mortar. The return for the south jamb was clearly visible, and on the assumption that the door was placed symmetrically a width of 2 m can be computed (though this may be a later modification of a narrower original door – see below).

South of the chapter house was another entrance from the cloister: one rebated stone which had formed part of a doorway survives. It is possible that this represents the entrance to the day stairs which are to be expected in the vicinity, giving access to the first floor dormitory. No trace of night stairs was found in the south transept: throughout the history of the priory either they must have been of wood, leaving no trace, or the cloister walk was used as access to the choir. The east wall of the east range had a series of buttresses, projecting 0.84 m and 1.08 m wide.

Unfortunately, the southern part of the east range was badly damaged when the southern (servants') wing was added to the Brookes' Georgian mansion in the late eighteenth century. A fireplace was set into the west wall later in the priory's history, so it seems likely that from the beginning the warming room was situated to the south of the chapter house. The eighteenth-century foundations, and a nineteenth-century brick-built water cistern and culverts between them removed all further information. As a result it cannot be certain how far south the east

range extended in its first plan. However, it must have had a rere-dorter at its southern end served by a drain. The earliest drain in this part of the site consisted of lengths of hollowed elm tree-trunk, 0.65 m diameter, laid end to end in a trench cut into the natural clay. The tree trunk drain emptied into a ditch which ran on the same alignment to the west (fig. 31); this has been examined at a number of points further west. The ditch which served the second phase of timber buildings fed into it (fig. 70). A contemporary wall immediately south of the tree trunk drain consisted of layers of flat unworked sandstone set into a construction trench dug from the same ground surface as the ditch containing the wooden drain. It is possible that this foundation, very different in character to the early ashlar faced walls of the other buildings, supported the south wall of a wooden temporary rere-dorter building, connected somehow to the dormitory range. The dormitory would therefore have been some 48 m in length.

The south and west ranges (fig. 36)

Excavation to the south of the nave revealed the foundations of an early cloister wall, and the northern part of the early west range. Some of the foundations of the eastern wall were present, and an east–west cross wall. The latter had created a rectangular room alongside the nave. It was in the equivalent position to the passage in the standing west range, and presumably had the same function. The walls were built in the same way as the other early masonry buildings, with ashlar facing (only one course of which, intermittently, survived) and rubble-mortar core, set on rubble packed trench foundations. The foundations of the east–west wall were continuous with those of the standing east wall of the later west range. This proved that the latter wall had been rebuilt on earlier foundations, no doubt reusing much of the same stone. No more of the west range could be found as a result of its removal during later remodelling of the cloister.

Traces of the eastern and western ends of the north

wall of the early south range were found, the central portion also having been removed by cloister remodelling. The south range was 6.62 m wide and 25.25 m long internally. The west range, which extended from the church to the south range, was therefore shorter, 18.65 m long and 5.91 m wide. It is probable that both ranges were completed before they were demolished, for the foundations of the cloister arcade wall were present. It is unlikely that construction of the arcade wall would have been started before completion of the ranges, as the roof of the cloister would have been built lean-to against the ranges. Additionally, if the cloister walk was built when the ranges had reached only the height of the lower storey, its roof would have made the erection of scaffolding to build the upper storeys very difficult.

The complete lengths of the north and east arcade foundations were found, and the start of the western foundation at its northern end, and the southern on the east. The remainder had been removed in later remodelling of the cloister. The foundations were trenches filled with sandstone rubble and smoothed pebbles from the boulder clay. There were no buttresses. The cloister garth measured 11.60 m north–south by 10.60 m east–west. The overall size of the cloister, including the cloister walks, was 18.86 m by 18.20 m respectively.

In the angle beyond the west and south ranges may have been the kitchens, but little can be said about them as preservation of later walls over some of the area prevented further excavation, and the devastating effects of the Georgian house and its drains rendered other areas sterile. Some of the timber buildings were probably the early kitchens, positioned to serve the canons' temporary accommodation, which retained their function after the new quarters had been completed.

Comparison of the early cloister buildings with others elsewhere

It might be thought that provision of sleeping accommodation for a convent of thirteen individuals, and a room

Monastery	Foundation date	Chapter house			Dormitory		Cloister			Source
		Length E–W	Width N–S	Area	Length	Width	E–W	N–S	Area	
Norton	1134	7.30	5.16	37.67	48 (approx)	6.12	18.26	18.86	344.38	Excavation
Portchester	1133	–	–	–	24	6	19	19	361	Cunliffe 1977
Waverley	1128	9.3	6	55.8	24	8.1	28.8	28.8	829	Brakspear 1905
Buildwas	1135	12.9	9.6	123.8	–	–	27	24.3	656	HMSO Guide 1946
Basingwerk	1131	7.3	6.6	48.2	31.5	7.3	24.5	28.5	698	HMSO Guide
Lanercost	1166	8.1	4.5	36.5	30	6.3	22.5	23.4	527	Moorman 1945
Monk Bretton	1154	8	5.5	44	29	8.1	26	24	624	Rigold, in *Archaeological Journal* 125, 1968, 323
Lilleshall	1148	11.5	7.1	81.7	–	–	31	34	1054	Rigold 1969

in which they might meet, would result in dormitories and chapter houses of a uniform size. The standard arrangement of the church, dormitory, refectory and cellarer's range around an approximately square cloister might, in the case of monasteries designed for thirteen brethren, also result in a uniformity of size for the cloister. In fact, such uniformity does not exist, as the data set out on p. 88 demonstrate. Only houses founded around the middle of the twelfth century, and thought to be for thirteen brethren, have been included. Unfortunately the size of the original building of most monasteries is unknown due to later rebuilding or the limitations of excavated evidence. Thus it is not possible to include Leonard Stanley, Haughmond and Tintern.

In the case of the chapter house and dormitory, the dimensions (metres) are internal. The cloister measurements include the cloister walks. Norton had a very small cloister and chapter house in its original form, but a very long dormitory.

Masonry building in twelfth-century Cheshire

The building operations at Norton, and previously at Runcorn, were a notable instance of the way in which the establishment of a religious house could introduce new ideas, skills and techniques to a locality which can have had few masonry buildings previously. There is no evidence for pre-Conquest masonry buildings anywhere in Cheshire. No churches have Saxon masonry surviving – indeed, very few have Romanesque masonry. If the church of St Bertelin at Runcorn was constructed of stone, it must have been the only masonry building in a large area. It is not known when the baron of Halton built masonry structures into his castle, but certainly none of the existing stonework can be earlier than the thirteenth century. In Chester, St Werburgh's Abbey and St John's church (the cathedral from 1075 to 1095) probably had masonry Saxon buildings, and rebuilding had been started in stone by the time Runcorn Priory was founded in 1115, but had not been completed. Thus when Norton was founded in 1134, it is probable that the only substantial masonry buildings to be seen in the earldom were the two major churches in Chester. The start of construction of masonry Romanesque buildings at Runcorn required the introduction of men with experience and skills that could only have been found in Chester, or outside the earldom.

The twelfth-century master mason

The name of the master mason who contracted to build the original church at Norton is known – an unusual circumstance in respect of twelfth-century buildings. Hugh de Cathewik was granted pasturage for 100 sheep by Eustace fitz John on condition that he made a final end to building the church of Norton (Tait 1939, 16). It has been suggested (Beamont 1873, 159; *VCH Chester*, 3, 165 footnote 38) that Hugh de Cathewik is likely to be Hugh de

Keckwick, the township bordering Norton on its eastern side. VCH Chester suggests also the alternative Hugh de Dutton – presumably Hugh, son of Odard, one of the priory's original benefactors – and discounts Tait's suggestion that Cathewik is the village of Catwick near Beverley in Yorkshire. In fact there is strong evidence that Tait is correct. He put forward no supporting argument but the various spellings in early grants and confirmations certainly lend weight to his assertion – for example Catthevic, Cattingewic, Cattewic, Catewic and Cathwic (Farrer, 1916, 46–9). There are no other possible candidates for identification with Cathewik in Ekwall 1960. In contrast, the name Keckwick has the following variants: Kekwic 1154, Kecwyk 1287, Kequik 1288, Kekwike 1295, Kekwyke 1295, Kekewyc end of the thirteenth century, Kekwyk *c.* 1320, Kekweke 1454, Kekwik 1479, Keekwicke 1534, Kekwick 1580, Keckewick 1594 (Dodgson 1970, 151). It can therefore be assumed that the master mason working at Norton came from the village near Beverley. Yorkshire in general and Beverley in particular were the scene of considerable building activity in the eleventh and twelfth centuries – just the sort of area to produce a mason capable of taking on the construction of the buildings at Norton. Other affinities with Yorkshire will be discussed later.

Another interesting aspect of Eustace fitz John's grant is the statement that the church was to be finished 'in every part according to the first foundation of William fitz Nigel'. It was he who founded the priory in Runcorn in 1115, so the implication is that a specification for the church was established then, which at the refoundation was transferred to Norton. It is even possible that Hugh de Cathewik had been involved in the construction of the Runcorn church, and was committed to a brief established in 1115.

The charter must date between *c.* 1144–5, when Eustace fitz John succeeded William fitz William as fourth baron of Halton, and 1157 when he was killed (Barraclough 1957, 4). It is a pity that closer dating is not possible. It can be stated only that the church had not been completed at a date which is at a minimum ten years after the foundation, and a maximum of twenty-three years after the foundation. The grant seems to imply some impatience with Hugh de Cathewik's rate of progress. However, if the construction of the church and claustral buildings took forty or fifty years to complete it would not have been exceptional. Lilleshall Abbey (Rigold 1969), founded in 1148, has Romanesque details in the eastern part of the church which are likely to date from well into the second half of the century. The east and south ranges were completed before the construction of the nave in the early thirteenth century. The Lilleshall buildings therefore took in excess of fifty years to complete.

The second church at Waverley, admittedly a much larger structure than at Norton, had its foundations laid in

1203 but it was not until 1278 that it was dedicated (Brakspear 1905, 10). The church at Beaulieu took forty-three years to complete (*ibid.*, 24). At Croxden (Staffs.) building began in 1179, but not until 1254 was the church dedicated (Reynolds 1946). At Cleeve in Somerset, the east end of the church was begun in 1198 but it was not until 1232 that the choir stalls were made (with oak given by Henry III). Then the dormitory and refectory ranges were tackled before the nave and west range were completed by the end of the thirteenth century (Gilyard-Beer 1960, 9). Long building campaigns must have been particularly uncomfortable for brethren housed in temporary quarters. During Vale Royal Abbey's troubled history of building, Abbot Peter moved his convent in 1330 from the 'unsightly and ruinous' buildings which they had occupied since 1281; despite this the claustral buildings were still far from completion (*VCH Chester*, 3, 160). Ultimately, it was the resources at a monastery's disposal that determined the speed with which it could be completed. Hailes Abbey (Gloucestershire) is an example of an astonishingly rapid building programme which started in 1246. Five and a half years later work was sufficiently far advanced for a dedication ceremony in the church; the cloister, dormitory and refectory were also complete. Ten thousand marks had been expended by Richard, earl of Cornwall, to achieve this end (Coad 1969). Hugh de Cathewik did not achieve this rate of progress, but it is unlikely that he was any slower than most of his fellow master masons.

Masonry mouldings associated with the early priory buildings

The number of moulded stones from the site as a whole is small, as a result of the thorough demolition of the buildings in the centuries following the Dissolution. Often, where such stones have been found, it is impossible to relate them to their original context as they have been utilised in foundations of later buildings. Fortunately, a number of interesting moulded stones survive from the original priory buildings for which an architectural context can be suggested.

In the foundations of a chapel built alongside the south wall of the chancel were found nine blocks that probably formed part of the corbel table of the early church (fig. 39). On the outer face they measure 0.46 m by 0.23 m deep. To a depth of 0.16 m on the underside of each is cut a half-cylindrical hollow, emphasised by a small quirk and roll-mould, and containing a triangular projection. The face of the projection, which is flush or slightly recessed from the rest of the outer surface of the stone, is decorated either with small bosses, or foliage-like carving. The presence of dressing marks on the underside of the block each side of the hollow indicates that these parts were not intended to be seen: they were presumably hidden by projecting corbels.

The corbel table must have been removed when the south-east chapel was about to be built, to allow the chancel roof to be extended over the chapel or for a double-pitched chapel roof to be attached to the chancel.

Unfortunately, the practice of lowering twelfth-century roofs has removed evidence of many possible corbel tables – at Leonard Stanley and Portchester for example. However, there are widespread parallels for the Norton corbel table. At the church of St Peter's in the East, Oxford (*c.* 1150) the corbel table consists of rectangular

Fig. 39. Corbel table blocks found incorporated in later foundations.

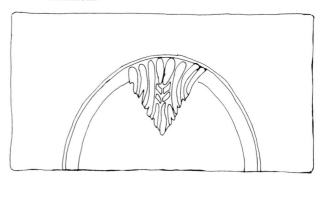

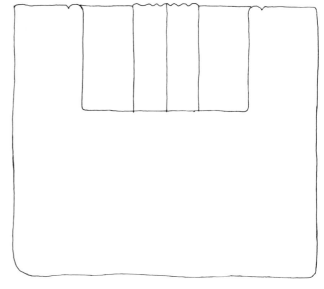

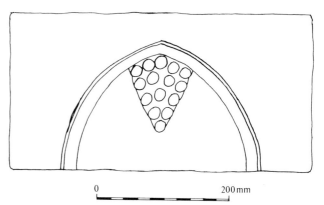

0   200 mm

blocks with half-cylindrical hollows, but undecorated; the blocks rest on carved corbels (Parker 1874, 79, fig. 60). At Iffley, Oxfordshire (*c.* 1160) part of the corbel table has similar blocks, with quirks cut to emphasise the hollows (Rickman 1862, 128). The corbels of the south transept of Winchester Cathedral support a corbel table consisting of blocks with a half-cylindrical hollow spanning between neighbouring corbels. It has been dated soon after 1107 (Zarnecki 1951, 30 and pl. 33). Romsey Abbey, Hampshire, has a corbel table comprising blocks with pairs of half-cylindrical hollows (Parker 1845, 2, pl. 37; Gardner 1951, 68). Ketton church (Northants.) has half-cylindrical hollows emphasised by a quirk; Adel church (Yorkshire) has blocks with a triangular hollow from the two faces of which is a carved projection (Parker 1846, pl. 23). The corbel table with half-cylindrical hollows is

Fig. 40. Beak-head voussoir from the original chapter house doorway.

0   100mm

therefore found widely in England. It also occurs in France, for example at Silvanes Abbey in the Rouergue. The church of 1157 has a series of such blocks (Dimier 1962, pl 44). However, the Norton corbel table appears to be unique in having triangular projections within the half-cylindrical hollow.

Information is also available about another feature of the early masonry buildings, the decoration of important doorways. In the chapter house, the vaulting was altered when a new chapter house was built to the east. An entrance to the new chapter house was made in the east wall of the original building, and to strengthen the wall masonry was added to its west face. In this added masonry, used as rubble, was found a carved beak-head voussoir (fig. 40). It is very likely that the voussoir formed part of the original doorway to the chapter house from the cloister. A doorway to the chapter house is known from mortar traces to have been 2 m wide. This may be the new entrance which replaced that incorporating beak-heads, which the existing voussoir indicates was 1.54 m wide.

Another beak-head voussoir was found in a layer of rubble within the later west range. It seems likely that it had formed part of one of the original doorways of the church. The beak-head was deposited amongst rubble make-up for the earliest floor of the west range reconstructed at the end of the twelfth century. At this time a new door was inserted into the south wall of the nave to communicate with the new west cloister walk. Its predecessor was blocked up, and it is possible that the voussoir came from its arch. Certainly the measurements are consistent – the width of the door to the inner face of rebated frame was 1.25 m, the computed size of the arch of which the voussoir was part was 1.30 m (small for the west door of the church which is another possible location for decorated voussoirs).

On the basis of this evidence, it seems probable that two doors at Norton had beak-head voussoirs. The processional door from the choir into the east cloister walk, of which only the plan is known, might also have been embellished with beak-heads.

Beak-heads are a characteristic of English Romanesque, apparently originating in the use of Anglo-Saxon animal head terminations such as that at Deerhurst, combined with the common Romanesque chevron ornament on arches (Zarnecki 1953). The earliest beak-heads that have been recognised are those which decorated the cloister arches of Reading Abbey; they must date from 1130. Two regions where the beak-head became particularly popular were Oxfordshire and Yorkshire (*ibid.*, 7); Norton had links with both. The ownership of Pirton church may have brought some members of Norton's community into contact with an area in which beak-heads could be seen. Both St Ebbe's in Oxford, and St Michael's at Barford had elaborate doorways embellished with beak-heads in about 1150 (*ibid.*, 54). It is the Yorkshire link however that is the stronger. The probability is that the original canons came from Bridlington Priory. Bridlington had beak-heads in the second half of the twelfth century (*ibid.*, 7). This in itself would be a rather tenuous connection with Yorkshire

Fig. 41. Door with beak heads at Malton Priory, Yorkshire. The chapter house entrance and west door of the church at Norton may have been of similar appearance.

were it not for the evidence, provided by Eustace fitz John's grant, that the master mason was a Yorkshireman. Eustace fitz John had extensive Yorkshire possessions, and was heavily committed to the support of religious houses in that country. It is therefore in Yorkshire that one might expect to find affinities with masonry of Norton.

The doorway of St Wilfrid's church, Brayton, is likely to be one of the earliest works of the Yorkshire school of masons, dating from about 1150 (Zarnecki 1953, 59).

The outer of the four orders of the arches of the doorway consists of beak-heads, smaller than those at Norton; the bird beak-head corbels however are closer in size. More like the Norton beak-heads are the voussoirs of the west door into the north transept at Malton Priory – which was founded by fitz John in 1150 (fig. 41). On the evidence of Eustace fitz John's grant, it is unlikely that the Norton church was finished much before 1155 or perhaps 1160. The chapter house would have had the highest priority when work started on the claustral buildings. Both doors may therefore date to within a decade of 1155, and the evidence from Yorkshire would appear to support such a chronology.

Beak-heads are rare in the north west. The only other church in Cheshire to have them is Bruera, where the chancel arch has four single beak-heads. They are crudely carved, and not comparable with the Norton beak-heads. Lancashire has only one example, at Overton. The near-absence of this motif to the west of the Pennines, in contrast to the heavy concentration in the east, is illustrated by Henry and Zarnecki 1958, 21, fig. 8.

Bell casting

Masons were not the only craftsmen to be brought to Norton. A bell maker was commissioned to make a bell that was probably intended for the tower of the priory church. Portchester has a pair of bell louvres, one each side of the abutting gable, on each face of its squat tower; in view of the affinity of the plan of Portchester to that of Norton it is likely that a similar arrangement existed at the latter church also. In 1979 excavation took place about 50 m to the north of the priory church. Various phases of semi-industrial use were discovered, including iron working and tile making. The earliest activity however was bell casting. A rectangular pit was found cut into the boulder clay from the original ground surface. Along the centre of the base of the pit a shallow channel had been cut. Overlying it were the remains of the core of a bell mould. Lying where they had been discarded after casting were numerous fragments of the cope (the outer part of the mould). A discussion of the techniques used to cast large bells in the medieval period will be left until the other casting pit found at Norton is described (pp. 118–22).

The absence of dateable artifacts from the bell pit, or any useful stratigraphical relationship that might have provided an indication of date, necessitated the use of radiocarbon dating. Charcoal from within the pit was identified as the residue of brushwood that had been used as fuel in metal melting furnace. It provided a date span of 1080 ± 60 (Harwell HAR 3885) which is consistent with a casting for the original church. Judging by the remains of the core and the fragments of cope, the bell was a large one, about 0.8 m wide at its rim.

There is no evidence that more than one bell was cast for the twelfth-century church. The Observances of Barnwell Abbey (Clark 1897) make frequent reference to the ringing of bells for signalling the start of services and for summoning the canons to attend other events in the monastic day. A bell was also tolled during funerals. Contemporary practice at Cistercian Waverley relied upon just one bell from its foundation in 1128 until 1218 when the abbot obtained a 'great bell'. Another great bell was obtained in 1239, though possibly this was a recasting of the 1218 bell (Brakspear 1095, 35). However, general Cistercian practice seems to have been for two bells (*ibid.*, 34). The chaos which might result from one monastery's bells being audible to a neighbouring monastery is exemplified by Rievaulx, and the brethren who were forced to move to Byland as a result of the nuisance their bells caused (Peers 1952, 3).

6
The priory expands

A dramatic expansion of the priory's buildings occurred soon after the first plan was complete. In summary, the changes included the demolition and rebuilding on a larger scale of the south and west ranges, the extension of the church to the east and west, the enlargement of the transept chapels, the construction of a new chapter house to the east of the original one, and the construction of a new rere-dorter (fig. 42).

The west range undercroft

Of the new buildings, it is the undercroft of the west range (figs. 43, 44) that has survived virtually intact, and which can therefore provide most information about the expanded plan. It has been noted above that the east wall of the new west range was rebuilt on the foundations of the west wall of its predecessor. This re-use of part of the original building also applied to material from the demolished range. It is probable that the walls and vaulting of the new building contain re-used stone. The southern four bays of the undercroft have ribbed vaults, semi-circular in profile along its length, but pointed across it. The three northern bays are square in plan, with groined vaults and transverse ribs only. It is in these three bays that the greatest re-use of material probably occurred. The original undercroft would have had groined vaults and much of the material from these, including transverse rib voussoirs and piers, would have been suitable. At the northern end of the range is a passage, communicating between the outer courtyard on the west and the cloister on the east. The cloister doorway is an example of re-use. It is round-headed, and has a continuous half-round roll moulding (fig. 43). Evidence that it has been re-set in this position is presented by an examination of the courses of the wall. The heights of the courses vary, but within every course the blocks are of uniform height. However, in the vicinity of the door there is a ragged break in the coursing, and adjacent stones are of the same height as the doorway blocks. It is clear that the doorway has been inserted in this position, probably by simply 'turning round' what had been the west door of the original range.

The west doorway of the new passage was more elaborate. It is very fragmentary, but sufficient of the lower part survives to give an idea of its form. It was recessed to accommodate a detached shaft each side, the bases of which are still present. They both have a water-holding torus moulding, indicating a date towards the end of the twelfth century. The moulding of the head of the doorway has gone but for one stone of the inner order. It has a half-round roll moulding which does not follow the semi-circular arch of the door, but curves more markedly, indicating a more elaborate arrangement – possibly a multi-cusped head (cf. the refectory door and the warming room door at St Werburgh's Abbey, Chester – both Early English features of the claustral buildings, Pevsner and Hubbard 1971, 146–7).

The interior of the west range passage

It is within the passage that the most impressive decoration is situated (figs. 45–50). Along both walls are benches, the upper stones of which project and have a chamfered lower angle. There was originally an additional layer of material on top about 0.08 m thick – a masonry or possibly timber surface to the seat. Until the recent work of conservation took place an eighteenth-century barrel vault set on the two benches lined the complete passage (fig. 45). Its removal revealed an elaborately carved blank arcade on each side (figs. 46, 47). The arcade consists on each wall of two groups of four round-headed arches, with capitals, free-standing columns, and bases set on the benches. Each group of four arches corresponds to the two bays of passage vault. The vault was pointed, with diagonal and transverse ribs. The ribs spring from double columns in the corners of the passage, and triple columns in the centre of both sides. The crown of the vault is missing (fig. 48), possibly destroyed during alterations to the Brookes' house or even as early as the fifteenth century when the Abbot's Tower was built. The south east part of the arcade was damaged by the insertion of a circular staircase.

In spite of the vicissitudes suffered by the passage, it remains a very fine structure. The quality of the carving is high: accomplished but also experimental in some details. In its overall design, the passage is a product of the transition from Romanesque to Gothic architecture. The (re-used) east doorway is purely Romanesque; the west doorway with its water-holding bases and multi-cusped head shows the influence of Gothic design. The passage vaults are pointed, but the arcades are round-headed. The mouldings of the passage show a similar duality. The majority (fifteen) of the capitals are based on the late Romanesque acanthus leaf derived pattern with volutes at the upper corners. There are also three water leaf capitals, one incurved cone capital, and five others in the cushion capital tradition, much devolved. A closer examination shows that almost every capital is different. The capitals with volutes have a variety of embellishments, such as

Fig. 42. Norton Priory in the thirteenth century. The scale of the expansion which occurred at the end of the twelfth century and the beginning of the thirteenth is apparent by comparing this plan with fig. 36.

pellets. Some are transmuted into arum lily shapes, with the leaves grouped round the fruit. The bases have an interesting variety of forms. Some have water-holding torus moulding, while others are convex in shape with decorations such as raised medallions and bosses. The central group of bases on the south side is decorated with the torus of the central base replaced by a 'twisted rope' and with a band of chevrons on the convex surface of the base.

At first sight, it might be supposed that the variety of capitals and bases results from the incorporation of

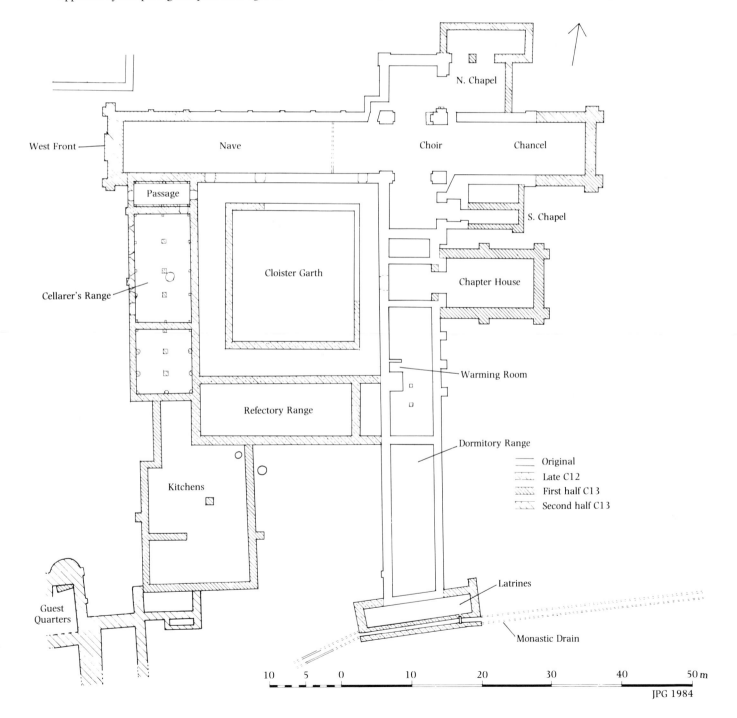

JPG 1984

Fig. 43. The late twelfth-century west range undercroft, before restoration. A cupboard (for books?) with a rebate for doors, is on the left. On the right is the door to the passage, reused from the earlier west range.

Fig. 44. Interior of the undercroft, after restoration and in use as part of the museum for a temporary exhibition (compare its condition with fig. 2).

Fig. 45. The passage arcade, being revealed by the removal of the eighteenth-century brick barrel vault in 1974.

material from an earlier building, but this is not so. All the capitals are carved as one with their abaci, and all the latter have an identical profile: square upper angle, quirk and rounded lower angle.

The capitals are in character predominantly late Romanesque, but the moulding of the arches reveals strongly Gothic forms. The north west and south east arcades have deeply undercut mouldings with fillets, and the north east arcade has a keeled moulding. The south west arcade has a chamfered moulding, and on the surface of the chamfer is dog-tooth embellishment. The dog-tooth has details that seem to be experimental. Whereas most of the bosses are simple flat-faced pyramids, drilled at the apex and carved at the base, a few have lines cut on the faces to emphasise the outline. One of the latter had been left rough within the lined areas to heighten the contrast. The impression given is of a mason trying out a new decorative technique (fig. 49).

The vault ribs are also Gothic in style: the diagonals all consist of three rolls, whereas the transverse rib is simply chamfered. The wall ribs consist of one roll.

The date of the west range passage

The question of the date of the construction of the west range must be decided on the basis of the passage decoration. It has sometimes been suggested that Cheshire suffered a 'cultural lag' in the medieval period, and that architectural styles may be later in date here as a result (F. H. Crossley, in Richards 1973, and Crossley 1938, 75–6). This possibility can be ruled out in the case of the Norton passage. Although some aspects of the work can be regarded as experimental, there can be no doubt about the technical skill of the mason responsible for the carving. Both the free carving of capitals and bases and the template cutting of arcade and rib mouldings are of a high order of execution and finish (fig. 50). It has been shown that Norton received considerable benefactions in the

Fig. 46. The arcade, bench and vault ribs on the north side of the passage.

Fig. 47. The arcade (partly missing at its eastern end) on the south side of the passage.

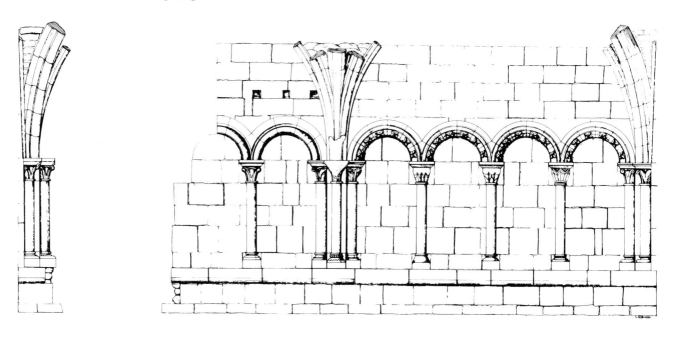

Fig. 48. The passage looking towards the cloister walk during restoration and before the erection of the protective roof over the undercroft, 1974

second half of the twelfth century. There can be little doubt that these resources were used to pay for good quality, up to date work.

Cartmel Priory is important for dating architectural details of this period. It was founded in 1188 by William Marshall, earl of Pembroke, for Augustinian canons. The

Fig. 49. Detail of the dog-tooth embellishment of the arcade, including 'experimental' treatment of two of the bosses with added lines.

eastern arcades of the church have pointed and round arches, some with dog-tooth ornament, and must be later than about 1190. But unlike the products of the first building campaign at Cartmel which ran from about 1190 to 1220 (Pevsner 1969, 87) the foliage at Norton has not developed into true stiff-leaf, although capital four strongly hints at it, and the arum lily capitals also have 'proto-stiff leaf' foliage. The arum lily element is itself a Transitional feature, part of the general popularity of

Fig. 50. Carved capitals of great variety and excellence of carving, north arcade.

semi-naturalistic foliage in the late twelfth century. There are parallels in the carving of the west door of Ledbury church, Herefordshire (Bond 1906, 418), where the arum berries are enclosed in a spathe as at Norton.

The incurved cone type of capital is also a product of the last quarter of the twelfth century. It is specially characteristic of the late Transitional or early Gothic school of west country masons, with examples at Worcester (west nave), Hereford (east transept), Lichfield (arch to north aisle of choir), Cheltenham (tower) (Bond 1906, 414). It also occurs at Abbey Dore, Herefordshire; a number of variations of the incurved cone are used on the capitals of the belfry arcade at Christ Church (St Frideswide's) Oxford, where it has been dated to about 1180 (Parker 1845, 2, pl. 5).

The presence of 'Early English' features such as the keeled moulding profiles, the heavy undercutting and use of fillets and dogtooth, the water-holding bases and the 'proto-stiff leaf', all used in conjunction with water leaf and other late Romanesque capitals supporting both round and pointed arches, suggest to the writer a date at the end of the twelfth century. In all probability the passage was erected as an integral part of the west range in the last two decades of the century (i.e. 1190 ± 10).

Apart from Cistercian houses, where the use of the west range by lay brothers was a complicating factor, most monasteries have a passage through the west range adjacent to the church. Where a passage survives, or where the wall of the church retains traces of a demolished passage in the equivalent position to that at Norton, it is usually functional and plain. Indeed, the writer has yet to see a west range passage that in any way approaches the elaboration of that at Norton. It can be regarded as a measure of the pretension and ambition of the priory at the close of the twelfth century – a self-esteem which the generosity of benefactors would seem to have justified.

The upper floor

The arrangement of the undercroft of the west range provides some clues about the layout of the upper storey. The substantial wall which forms the join between the groined and ribbed vault parts of the storage range plays no part in the ground floor arrangements. Its function must have been to carry a dividing wall across the first floor of the building. The upper storey can consequently be interpreted as comprising a chamber at the southern end, separated by the cross wall from a hall over the groined vault area. A small chapel may have occupied the space over the passage; it would have been orientated correctly in this position. This arrangement was first suggested by Gilyard-Beer, who drew a parallel with Bradenstoke (Gilyard-Beer 1959, 31). As such, it would have provided suitable accommodation for the prior of Norton.

Construction of the west range

There is good reason to think that the whole of the west range undercroft was built as part of one campaign, in spite of differences in style between parts of it. A building

Fig. 51. Timber centering supporting one of the vault ribs during the dismantling and re-erection of the groined vaults of the undercroft, 1974.

sequence can be postulated. The first operation would have been the construction of the walls to the height from which the vaults would spring. Construction of the northern-most groined vault would then have commenced. For each pair of bays, the central pier would be placed in position, and the side walls would have been continued upwards until the inner ashlar, cut to shape, had the semicircular profile of the intended vault. Wooden centering for each of the transverse ribs, between piers and from the piers to the walls, would then be assembled and the ribs would be built (fig. 51). The main vault centering could then be made, in the form of two intersecting barrel vaults (fig. 52). Each vault would then be built, starting at the corners. Blocks of sandstone would be mortared together, and the masons would carry the vault up until the last wedge-shaped blocks were placed in position, and the centering removed. Construction could then start on the next pair. When the wall dividing the two parts of the undercroft was reached, it appears that a different form of vaulting was adopted, using similar piers but with diagonal ribs in addition to the transverse ribs. Centering would be required for the erection of the ribs, but not for the rest of the vault: the smaller area of the vault and the greater number of ribs made it unnecessary. The reason for the change in design can only be guessed at. If the northern bays were incorporating material from the

Fig. 52. The upper surface of the centering (two intersecting barrel vaults) ready for re-erection of one of the groined vaults. They would have been built in precisely the same way in the twelfth century.

demolished early west range, then a repeat of the groined vault would have been the obvious choice. By the time the masons started work on the southern part of the range, they may have realised that although the groined vault spanned a large area, it had inherent weaknesses: the centre would tend to sag, and the lateral pressure on the side walls would tend to push them out of vertical. The ribbed vault could not sag, and although the chosen area was less, lateral pressure was spread over a large number of points on the side walls, reducing the danger of their collapse. Whether or not the masons were aware of these points and were influenced by them cannot be known for certain. However, the groined vaults certainly turned out the weaker. The southern-most pair were completely rebuilt and refaced in 1868. The remainder required total reconstruction due to sagging and spread of the side walls in the consolidation programme in 1974 (figs 51, 52). In contrast the ribbed vaults merely required repointing. Alternatively, the explanation may simply be the adoption of a new technique as the building progressed; medieval masons were not constrained by a dominating desire for uniformity but were prepared to innovate as they built.

The differences between the passage and the rest of the building are a reflection of their different functions. The main body of the undercroft was the storage range, in which the bulk of the priory's more important commodities and goods were kept. The architecture is therefore basic and functional, the only concession to decoration being the scalloped capitals of the piers. In contrast, the passage was the main link between the

cloister and the outside world. On the seats would sit those who waited to speak to the canons: tenants, merchants, etc. Through the passage would be ushered benefactors such as Sir Geoffrey de Dutton and his wife, on their way to sign an agreement in the chapter house in 1262 (Beamont 1873, 166). Such an important room required decorative, modern masonry. The contrast can be underlined by comparing the two western doors of the west range. The door to the passage has already been described; it had shafts and apparently a multi-cusped head. In contrast, the door to the body of the undercroft is simple: it has only a half-round roll moulding and a narrow hood mould with small lozenges as decoration.

The whole undercroft is thus a fascinating piece of building, transitional not only in the decoration of the passage, but also in the methods of construction.

Fig. 53. The late twelfth-century Norman doorway.

The Norman doorway (figs. 53, 54)

The importance of the Norton passage for the architecture of the north west has been recognised since its discovery in 1974 (Crossley 1976a, 74 and 79). The outstanding feature to have been given attention by earlier writers is the Romanesque doorway set into a Victorian porch entrance added in 1868 to the west front of the Georgian house. Photographs and drawings of the doorway have appeared in numerous publications. However the doorway has not been fully described or considered, though its importance in the context of the paucity of Romanesque survivals in Cheshire has been recognised: 'With the exception of Norton, the doorways remaining in Cheshire give but a dim reflection of the glories to be found elsewhere' (Crossley 1938, 78); 'the most elaborate Norman portal in the North West' (Crossley 1976b, 7).

Where was the original situation of the doorway? It

The priority expands 103

might be thought that the most fitting position would be either the west front of the church, or the chapter house entrance. However, neither of these can be possible. The original west front of the church was demolished following the extension of the nave westwards, which was probably complete by about 1155; the later one is unlikely to be much earlier than 1200. The surviving doorway however falls between these two dates. In any case, the Buck engraving suggests that no vestige of the west front was standing in 1727 (fig. 18). Similarly, the Randle Holme manuscript drawing shows that no claustral buildings such as the chapter house were standing in the seventeenth century (fig. 17).

Two other possible contexts for a door of this quality are the east and west processional entrances from the cloister into the church. The eastern doorway must have

Fig. 54. The medieval doorway in the setting created for it when the porch was added to the country house in 1868.

been provided fairly early in the building sequence, so the surviving doorway is stylistically unacceptable there. The refectory was demolished to make way for the Tudor house, so the door cannot be an entrance similar to that at Kirkham.

The remaining possibility is the entrance to the nave from the western cloister walk. This hypothesis can be supported on two grounds: the date of the doorway, and a chain of reasoning to explain its survival when so much else has vanished. It will be seen later that it must have been constructed in the late twelfth century. This fits in well with the construction date of the newer west range; when it was built the original entrance from the cloister to the nave was blocked, and a new one created further west. The size of the opening of the latter doorway matches that of the Romanesque door. The southern face of the nave wall (as far as it survives) could have accommodated the carved stonework. Thus it appears that the opportunity was taken to provide a splendid new portal.

There are many parallels for the provision of elaborate doorways from the cloister to the church in other monastic houses. Usually it is the eastern processional doorway that attracts embellishment. Examples include the Augustinian Cartmel Priory and Lilleshall Abbey. St Werburgh's Abbey, Chester, also has a good late twelfth-century eastern cloister doorway. In all these cases the western doorway is comparatively plain. Elaborate western processional doors are less common, but they do exist. An impressive example is at the Augustinian Haughmond Abbey, where the richly carved late twelfth-century western doorway was further embellished with the carving of Saints Peter and Paul in the thirteenth century. The supreme example is at Ely, where the so-called Prior's Doorway is in this position (Gardner 1951, 71, pl. 121).

How did the doorway survive? The details of the carving are still crisp, and this is not a result of Victorian restoration as comparison with the replica doorway, itself much more mechanical and precise in its finish, makes clear. The conclusion to be drawn is that the doorway has always been protected from the weather. During the medieval period the roof of the cloister walk would have sheltered it. In the post-Dissolution period, it must be assumed that the doorway was protected by the Tudor house. Examination of the Randle Holme sketch plan shows a building projecting eastwards from the main range at this point. The Georgian country house made use of the nave wall, as part of the north front of the house. The north front may have been rebuilt in the late eighteenth century by James Wyatt, the tradition for which is strong although there is no direct documentary evidence for it (Wyatt is cited in Pevsner and Hubbard 1971, 297). By the late eighteenth century all the remaining medieval buildings had been demolished, so perhaps then, with the rise of interest in medieval architecture, the value of the doorway was at last recognised and it was extricated from its original position to be re-erected in a place of safety.

The safe location that was chosen was beneath the double staircase on the west front of the house (fig. 99). The evidence for this is a series of passing references such as: 'Norton Priory, the present mansion, now the seat of Sir Richard Brooke, Bart, is a modern building, but part of the substructure of the monastery, in which is a door of Saxon architecture, still remains, being fitted up as a cellar' (Lysons 1810). The 'Saxon' door, so worthy of note, must have been the Romanesque door.

In 1868 (the date is recorded on a keystone) the double staircase was demolished, and a porch was built in its place. The southern part of the undercroft was turned into the entrance hall, which opened onto the internal staircase which gave access to the first floor. A theatrical touch was the incorporation of the Romanesque arch and the replica into the east wall of the porch (fig. 54). Beamont recorded the event as follows 'Since he came to the estate, Sir Richard (the seventh baronet) has cleared and re-opened, after it had been hidden since the building of the present mansion, the original doorway of the old priory, a beautiful piece of work, and almost as perfect as when the Norman masons left, which is once more devoted to its original purpose and made the entrance to the house' (Beamont 1873, xxv).

The doorway is elaborate, with three orders of shafts in an unusual arrangement – the outer two on each side are paired to stand parallel to the line of the wall in which the door was set. This arrangement would have permitted the door to be set into the comparatively narrow south wall of the nave while still retaining the impressive appearance given by three orders. All six capitals have late Romanesque volutes. The bases all have a water-holding double torus moulding on a square base. Both the inner order shafts are circular in section; their freshness and dressing suggest that they are modern replacements but the bases indicate that the originals were also circular. The two outer pairs are most unusual in that they are slightly keeled, and the bases are consequently ovoid in plan.

The inner frame of the portal is decorated with a chevron pattern that runs in a continuous band around the outer face of the frame. An identical chevron decorates the sides and soffit of the frame. The frame consists of individual blocks and voussoirs, each bearing a pair of chevron units with the points facing the angle between face and soffit. They are separated by a keeled moulding around the complete frame on the angle. Most units of the chevron are enriched with a group of three leaves, rendered in typical late Romanesque formalised manner. The remainder have a single many lobed leaf.

The inner order has a vault consisting of thirteen voussoirs with a roll moulding on all three visible angles, and a diagonal rounded moulding on the face and the soffit. Thus a lozenge-shaped recess is created on each pair of voussoirs.

The outer order consists of seventeen voussoirs. The pattern is similar to that of the frame, in that a continuous band runs round both the face and the soffit of the door arch. However, it differs in the treatment of the angle between the face and the soffit. In the case of the frame the angle is emphasised with a continuous keeled moulding, but on the outer order the points of the chevrons meet across a recessed angle three-quarter round moulding. As in the case of the frame, the chevron units (a pair of which occupy the face and soffit of each voussoir) have a trefoil within the triangular spaces. The door is completed with a hood mould consisting in section of a half-round roll, a semi-circular hollow, and a triangular quirk on the outermost edge. Apart from the innermost shafts there appears to have been little restoration.

There are no features in the decoration of the door that make it possible to distinguish any particular regional influence in its design. All were current in the late twelfth century, and the presence of a keeled profile to the outer shafts and the frame angle mould, together with water holding shaft bases, emphasises its late date. The use of the chevron on two faces, with joining apex and with identical fillings of the triangular spaces (trefoil and multi-lobed leaves), is found on the great five-order west door of Selby Abbey, which dates from the late twelfth century. The chapter house entrance at St Mary's Abbey, York, has affinities with the Selby door. It too had chevrons enriched with foliage of a very similar type. It 'dates from the late twelfth century, but probably before 1190' (Wilson, in Thompson 1983, 100–21, pl. XLII). It is tempting to see a Yorkshire influence, as earlier in the century. However, the foliage enriched chevron voussoir occurs very widely, making specific influences difficult to trace. One example at a considerable distance is the church at New Shoreham, Sussex, where the enrichment of the chevrons includes foliage trefoils very similar to the northern examples (illustrated for example in Rickman 1862, 131). Indeed, such enrichment was probably much more common than is now apparent. Chevron vault ribs excavated at St Augustine's Abbey, Canterbury, in 1974–5 still had vividly coloured painted enrichment. The flat surfaces of the 'V's were painted with black, red and white trefoils (Geddes, in Thompson 1983, 95 and pl. XXXIVb). The use of polychromy in Romanesque architectural sculpture has been recognised for many years (e.g. Parker's additions to Rickman 1862, 138) but recent studies emphasise just how common it was. Fragments found during the excavation of the chapter house at St Albans (Kahn, in Thompson 1983, 74); the Canterbury material described above; and the chapter house doorway at St Mary's, York (Wilson, in Thompson, 1983, 103) were all enhanced with colourful surface treatment to architectural elements that were also covered with carved decoration. The Norton door was therefore probably painted when first erected – it must have been a dazzling embellishment to the church. So too must have been the west doorway of

Ledbury church (Herefordshire) which has much in common with the Norton door – keeled shafts, chevrons separated by a keeled roll moulding, and chevrons joining at each apex. It lacks foliage enrichment of the chevrons, but is this an instance where paint once provided the detail? The door dates from a building phase that was completed *c.* 1210; the detail of the carving of the door is 'very late Norman' (Pevsner 1963). There seems a strong probability, in view of the detail of the Norton door, and by analogy with portals such as Selby and Ledbury, that it was carved and erected within the period covered by the 1180s and 1190s. Chevrons with enrichment meeting across a roll-mould could occur as late as 1210, as the doorway in the north porch at Wells proves; there it is associated with early stiff-leaf foliage (Webb 1956, pl. 83).

To summarise, the most likely location for the portal is the entrance from the west cloister walk into the nave of the church. This entrance was inserted into the nave wall as part of the building campaign which included the reconstruction of the west range *c.* 1190. The probable date of the doorway, sometime during the last two decades of the twelfth century, is consistent with that theory.

Construction of the new cloister

The building of a new cloister was an integral part of the expansion scheme of the late twelfth century. The size of the cloister garth increased from 10.60 m (E–W) by 11.05 m (N–S) to 15.72 m (E–W) by approximately 17 m (N–S). The foundations of the original cloister wall were retained on the unchanged north and east sides, though extended to the new length. New south and west walls were built. The new cloister wall, like the old, was without buttresses. The ashlar face on the garth was built lower than the ashlar on the cloister walk. It must have formed the side of a drain surrounding the cloister garth, which would have received large quantities of rainwater from the roofs of the surrounding buildings.

The requirements of ritual, in particular the Sunday morning procession, required the speedy construction of the cloister walk as soon as the south and west ranges were complete. A construction date of about 1200 is therefore probable. No information on its form has survived but it is likely that a low wall supported paired shafts which in turn carried an arched wall upon which rested a roof built lean-to against the surrounding buildings. This type of cloister wall arrangement still exists at many continental religious houses.

Extensions to the church (fig. 42)

Reconstruction of the west and south ranges was followed by expansion of the church. Extensions were built onto the chancel and the nave. In the latter case there is no doubt that the new west end was erected after the completion of the west range, as an examination of the junction at the south west corner of the nave proves. The erection of the

east end cannot be related by direct archaeological means to the sequence at the west end. However, the expansion of the priory buildings probably resulted from an increase in the complement of canons. An increase in the size of the choir would be necessary, and this could be achieved by building a new chancel further east, allowing the choir stalls to encroach on the existing sanctuary. A similar situation may have occurred at Easby Abbey, where an extension to the chancel was built in the fourteenth century and the choir may have been moved east (Thompson 1948, 7). If priority were given to ritual arrangements rather than domestic accommodation, the building of the new chancel would take place before the reconstruction of the south and west ranges, and the expansion of the nave. However, the small amount of evidence – the style of the ashlar, and masons' marks – suggests otherwise.

The ashlar of the west front has much in common with the ashlar of the west wall of the undercroft. It is characterised by neat oblique chiselling of the corner blocks of buttresses and the chamfered plinths, and adze or axe dressing of the remainder. The plinth course is identical in treatment, and in thickness of the course of sandstone blocks (0.20 m), but this is not to achieve a uniformity between the west range and the west front, as the plinths do not meet at the junction. Rather, it seems to be a continuity in the treatment of a particular architectural element, which suggests that although the construction of the west end commenced after the completion of the undercroft, they were not long separated. In contrast, all the east end blocks are finely chisel dressed.

In the original priory buildings there are no masons' marks. In the rebuilt west range they occur only in the ribbed vault portion, where simple squares, crosses and strokes are the three types of mark found, all on the vault ribs. The west front has one mason's mark, a triangle. In contrast the ashlar of the single surviving course of the east end has masons' marks on most of the blocks, including a star and an 'N'. The work must have been carried out either by a different team, or by a team that adopted marks after completing the western buildings.

Thus the evidence suggests that the rebuilding of the west end occurred at an earlier date than the rebuilding of the east end. A sequence can be proposed: the rebuilding of the south and west ranges and extension of the east range to form a larger rere-dorter; the construction of a new cloister walk; the extension of the nave; the extension of the chancel; the building of a new chapter house; the enlargement of the transept chapels.

The new chancel was built to the same width as the existing eastern arm and measured 8.83 m long internally, including the breached earlier eastern wall. No details of internal arrangements were found – only one course of ashlar survived except for a single block of the chamfered plinth, and no floor surfaces. Georgian gardening activities had removed all stratification down to mortar and rubble floor make-up.

The extension to the nave fared little better than the chancel. Robbing of stonework removed much of the north wall of the extension and most of the west wall down to the foundations. Eighteenth-century construction and landscaping destroyed all floor levels down to foundation level, and a huge sewer trench cut through the middle of the nave and its west wall. Luckily, the south west corner buttresses survived, albeit cut about by other drains, to give important information about the west front. Two buttresses, of identical size, project on the corner to the south and west. The second ashlar course is narrowed by a 0.10 m chamfered plinth on the second course. The rubble and mortar footings of the north west corner indicate that similar buttresses must have been present there. The ashlar of the west wall projected by 0.25 m in the middle part of the west front: only one ashlar block of this survives, but is important in trying to reconstruct the appearance of the west front. The extension was built to project beyond the western face of the west range by 2.75 m.

The fact that the front projects suggests that this arrangement was adopted to enhance the visual impact of the church. By projecting, the south west pair of buttresses could stand unencumbered, and symmetry with the north west pair could be achieved. In addition, projection would have allowed the west front to dominate the western assemblage of buildings by perspective as well as height. If the west range was built in about 1190, then the west front of the church was probably finished in the early years of the thirteenth century. The suggested emphasis on symmetry, and architectural dominance of the west front, is in complete accord with what one would expect by comparison with other religious houses of similar stature at this date. Three examples can be cited, all Augustinian houses. The west front of Lilleshall (Shropshire) built in the early thirteenth century (Rigold 1969, 10) lacks complete symmetry due to the massive north west tower, but undoubtedly possessed a great architectural presence. Above the large round-headed west doorway were shafted lancets, probably three in number. On the flanking buttresses were decorative arcades. At Brinkburn (Northumberland) there are buttresses at both angles, framing a composition that consists of blank shafted arcades at the bottom, surmounted by three tall shafted lancets, and three small lancets in the gable. The church was built during the period 1195 to 1220 (Knowles and St Joseph 1952, 190), the west front presumably towards the end of that period. Lanercost priory church was completed at its west end in the period 1200–20 (Moorman 1945, 17). The church has a very impressive west front. Above the door is a decorative blank arcade, and above that three tall shafted lancets. In the gable is a niche for a statue of St Mary Magdalene.

Other Augustinian houses built magnificent west fronts to their churches later in the thirteenth century. Bolton Priory and Canons Ashby Priory completed theirs in the middle years of the century, and Newstead Abbey in the late thirteenth century (priors and abbots arriving for the general chapter would have been impressed by the west front, which in fact gave a greatly exaggerated impression of what lay to the east). Norton probably had the elements which can be found in the west fronts completed in the early decades of the thirteenth century, i.e. a central door, a blank arcade and triple lancets, framed by the pairs of buttresses (fig. 29). We have seen how the generosity of benefactors was matched by the quality of architectural decoration in the passage and the

Fig. 55. The late twelfth-century monastic drain, with sandstone flagged base and a single course of ashlar blocks surviving. Here the drain was incorporated in the end wall of the latrine block; the row of seats was probably situated above the drain at first floor level, convenient for the dormitory.

western processional doorway, and so there is every reason to think that the composition of the west front would have been of a similarly high order. Fragments of shaft and shaft-rings found in demolition rubble immediately west of the west front support the suggestion that it had a blank arcade.

The projecting ashlar in the central part of the west front was probably a device to increase the impact of the door. By projecting the ashlar, an extra order of shafts could be accommodated and the doorway could be given extra depth. Parallels can be drawn with Fountains Abbey, where a similar projection has a horizontal sloping

head above the door to establish a uniform wall line above, and Kirkstall Abbey, where the head is gabled.

Enlargement of the east range

Unlike the west and south ranges, no rebuilding of the east range took place – it was not necessary as demolition of the other two sides was sufficient to allow the cloister to be enlarged. Since it was the canons' dormitory, its demolition would also have caused greater disturbance to the life of the household. In the thirteenth century (on pottery evidence) a new rere-dorter (latrine) block was built, twice the length of the previous one, with a similar rubble and clay foundation wall. The new block was provided with a sandstone drain which had a slab base and ashlar sides (figs. 20, 55). The timber termination of the east range was rebuilt in masonry up to the enlarged rere-dorter, which thus formed a T-shape set on the slant. This doubling of the size of the rere-dorter is another of the measures necessitated by the increase in the number of canons. The internal east–west width of the new rere-

Fig. 56. A group of burials in the original chapter house, placed here after it had become the vestibule to the new chapter house. The adult skeleton is that of a man – presumably the father of the three children, all of whom died and were buried at the same time. He must clearly have been important to have been interred in this location.

dorter was 15.82 m, compared to 6.30 m of the original. The extended east range was very long – 52 m in total from the south transept to the southern wall of the rere-dorter.

The new chapter house

An increase in the number of canons would have made the original chapter house rather cramped for the daily meeting of the brethren. A new chapter house was constructed, probably early in the thirteenth century. The ashlar is different from the other buildings of the expanded plan. The blocks, which are finely dressed, are larger, especially in the surviving buttress, which measures 1.51 m wide and projects 0.80 m from the face of the south wall. The differences in the size of the ashlar, and the larger buttresses, suggest that the construction of the new chapter house was the final project undertaken during this building phase.

The chapter house was built to the east of the original chapter house, which henceforth must have become a vestibule in which a group of burials took place (fig. 56). The vaulting was modified and the four pier bases were removed. The discovery of the beak-head voussoir built into masonry associated with these structural modifications suggests that the door to the cloister was widened to the 2 m indicated by mortar traces on the upper surviving course of ashlar. Much of the east wall of the existing chapter house was demolished to give access to the new building.

The new building was longer and wider than its predecessor. Its internal length was 12.29 m, its width 7.21 m, compared to the length of 7.30 m and width of 5.16 m of the earlier building. The comparative areas are 88.61 and 37.67 square metres. It was no doubt also taller. Buttresses were provided in the centre of both long sides, and the rubble foundations showed that a further pair projected from each of the eastern corners. The main body of the chapter house was not excavated due to the desirability of preserving some good yew trees at this spot. Some of the internal levels were observed at the western end. A simple stratigraphical sequence consisted of a layer of sandstone rubble and mortar, which was the make-up for the original floor. Cut through this was a grave containing a slab-sided wooden-based coffin – presumably that of a prior. Later, a thick layer of clay was spread across the chapter house interior. It was probably this floor surface that was replaced by the mosaic tile floor, much of which was found dumped alongside the chapter house. Nineteenth-century gardening had removed all layers above the clay.

Expansion or rebuilding of chapter houses is something which occurred at a number of monasteries in the thirteenth century. At Chester, the magnificent chapter house was constructed in the second quarter of the thirteenth century and a vestibule was provided to the west (Crossley 1976a, 78–9). At Lanercost, a new chapter house of similar dimensions to that at Norton was built to the east of the existing chapter house. Its internal dimensions were 12.3 m long by 6 m wide (Thompson 1939, fig. 9). The construction of a chapter house to the east of the earlier building would have allowed it to be a lofty building in keeping with its status. The vestibule, where the chapter house had been, could then be of a height to allow the dormitory to run across it. It has been suggested, in discussion of the original buildings of Norton's east range, that the original chapter house had a roof that had its ridge at right angles to the axis of the east range. This would have inhibited access from the dormitory to the south transept. The construction of the new chapter house was coupled with a removal of the piers that supported the vaults of its predecessor. This modification may have been to permit the dormitory to run across what was now a vestibule, permitting the canons to process directly from the dormitory to the church for their midnight and dawn services in the more normal manner (though no evidence for night stairs in the south transept was found).

The expansion of the buildings – summary and discussion

The radical rebuilding programme took place at Norton over a period that probably encompasses the last two decades of the twelfth century and the first two or three decades of the thirteenth. The conclusion reached by Knowles and Hadcock (1971, 168), before evidence from the excavation was available, that Norton became one of the larger houses of the order for probably about 26 canons must be correct. The expansion of the buildings can be explained only by an increase in the establishment of the priory. The study of the growth of Norton's possessions also supports that view. By 1195 the canons' property had increased substantially compared to their foundation endowment, which was itself a generous allowance. It was the income from temporal and spiritual possessions that enabled a larger number of canons to be housed and fed at Norton. The income also paid the masons and others who carried out the reconstruction programme. The quality of work shows that highly skilled masons could be attracted to Norton. The canons were not only concerned to expand their accommodation. The degree of embellishment of the west range passage and the cloister door demonstrate a commitment to rebuild the priory in an impressive manner. The construction of a new west front was not necessary as a means of increasing the accommodation of the nave – probably the least used part of all the monastic complex. It was instead a device to bring forward the west front of the church beyond the new west range to dominate the outer courtyard (fig. 29). Visitors could thus be impressed by a west front incorporating an elaborate doorway, and tall lancet windows, more in tune with the pride and ambition of the expanding house than the more homely Romanesque west front.

A major rebuilding programme to provide accommodation on a larger scale has been revealed by excavation at a number of sites. In some cases it involved not only the claustral buildings, but also the church, as has already been described in the cases of Waverley, Tintern and Haughmond. Evidence has been revealed of a total rebuilding of the church at Fountains – for which the catalyst was the fire of 1147 (Gilyard-Beer and Coppack, 1986). Excavation of the Benedictine nunnery at Elstow showed that the early to mid-twelfth-century claustral buildings were rebuilt in the mid-fourteenth century (Baker 1970). Furness underwent major rebuilding following the amalgamation of the Order of Savigny with that of Citeaux (Dickinson 1965 and 1967).

Excavation would doubtless reveal more examples of rebuilding and enlargement on the scale that occurred at Norton. It is a dramatic example of the scale of change that was possible when adequate resources were available.

7
From priory to abbey –
and dissolution

The fire of 1236 and its effects

A terse statement in the Whalley Abbey annals reads '1236: Combusta est ecclesia de Northon et claustrum' (Taylor 1912, 184). This entry records a major disaster in a religious house that shared with Whalley the barons of Halton as founders and patrons. The annals would have had no interest in exaggerating the incident, so it can probably be taken at face value. There is ample evidence

from the excavation for a widespread fire. An extensive layer of burnt material was found in the area occupied by the choir and the transepts, comprising charcoal, ash, lead droplets, nails, and sandstone roof slab fragments. An ash layer was found in the north east part of the cloister walk. The most spectacular evidence was found during the excavation of the kitchens. A thick layer of charcoal covered all of the area. It was not ash from ovens – it was not fully oxidised, and did not contain refuse. The decisive evidence was the presence of six burnt planks lying on the clay floor and a burnt wooden bowl (fig. 57). The place of the burnt deposit in the stratigraphical sequence, and pottery associated with the clay floor it covered, make a thirteenth-century date for the fire a probability. The most likely context therefore is the fire of 1236. It is possible that the fire started in the timber kitchens, and spread from there to the claustral buildings and the church, fanned by the south westerly winds that predominate on the west side of Cheshire. Roof timbers would be the most combustible parts of the buildings, as well as the furnishings. The choir of the church, which no doubt had wooden choir stalls and screens, would have burnt fiercely, the tower acting as a chimney. The major walls of the buildings, and particularly those parts of the complex that had masonry vaults, probably escaped permanent damage. However, following the fire a major repair operation must have been undertaken. The annal entry implies that the church and all the buildings around the cloister were burnt. Re-roofing the buildings would have been a priority, as well as the repair of floors and other wooden structures. Re-furnishing the buildings to make them habitable would have followed. Construction of new choir stalls to enable

Fig. 57. Burnt remains of planks and a wooden bowl, found lying on the clay floor of the kitchens under a widespread layer of burnt material, probably resulting from the destruction of the building by fire.

religious life to return to normal would have been an urgent consideration. In the case of the kitchens total reconstruction was required, but rather surprisingly the evidence indicates that they were timber-framed once more, and remained so until the Dissolution.

There is circumstantial evidence to suggest that the cloister arcade suffered severely in the fire. Evidence will be presented to show that a new arcade was constructed in the middle years of the thirteenth century. The only reasonable context for rebuilding at that time is the requirement to repair damage caused by the fire of 1236. The destructive effects of a fire on the cloister walk need cause no surprise. The cloister arcade is likely to have consisted of arches supported by pairs of slender shafts, as at Rievaulx. There would have been a lean-to timber roof, supported by the arcade and resting against the walls of the buildings on the four sides of the cloister. The roof would have burnt in the fire, and its collapse as well as the impact of debris falling from the surrounding buildings would have made short work of such a fragile structure. Total reconstruction would have been the only course open to the canons.

Fig. 58. Four bays of the mid-thirteenth-century cloister arcade, reassembled from fragments recovered in the excavation.

The mid-thirteenth-century cloister arcade (figs. 58–63)

The structure and decoration of the new arcade can be described in detail. This is due, ironically, to its demolition in the early sixteenth century. At that date yet another rebuilding of the cloister took place, probably to provide a wall with glazed windows instead of the draughty open arcade. Amongst the foundations of the last cloister wall were many fragments of its predecessor, used as rubble (fig. 98). It consisted of those parts of the arcade that had no value for re-use – arches, shafts and other decorative details.

It has proved possible to reconstruct four bays of the cloister arcade (fig. 58). The arcade was a remarkably fine structure. A dwarf wall must have existed as the lowermost part. On this the arcade would have been set. It consisted of slender, cylindrical shafts in groups of three set on a triple base of simple profile. Each group of three shafts, which were probably about a metre in length (only fragments were found) supported a capital. Only one capital survived intact, but fragments of others were found. Each capital had three shaft-rings which provided a setting for the three shafts. Above the shaft rings were short lengths of expanding shaft, which merged to form the underside of the capital. In the surviving complete example six bunches of stiff-leaf foliage originate as stems

on the expanding section of shaft, and overhang the edges of the capital (fig. 63). It is clear from fragments that other capitals had human heads alternating with the stiff-leaf foliage, and probably also animals. The upper surface of the capital was in the form of a large flat trefoil with a shallow beaded edge. From the trefoil the arches sprang.

The arches were of trefoil design. Spanning from one capital to the next was a pair of arch elements, each having as its soffit two quarter circles meeting at a cusp. Together they created the trefoil form of the arch. The flat upper side of the two arch elements provided the seating for a total of six moulded voussoirs that formed the outer part of the arch. The moulding projected forward, and rested on a springing block that was seated on the central lobe of the capital trefoil top and formed the junction between each pair of arches. The voussoirs formed a slightly pointed apex to frame the rounded trefoil below.

Fig. 59. The finely carved head of a woman from the cloister arcade (210 mm in height).

The upper side of the arch voussoirs supported blocks of stone that formed the spandrels, which at the top of the wall provided the horizontal surface that carried the wall plate of the lean-to cloister roof. The blocks were shaped to fit neatly against the curving surface of the voussoirs, and to form horizontal courses. The spandrels were the most remarkable of all the features of the arcade. Three fragments were discovered. The most complete one had a scar where a semi-relief figure had broken away. Still surviving was the left hand of the figure, holding an open book. One of the fragments had carved in semi-relief a hand, palm outward, apparently with a nail set in the palm. The other piece had the lower part of the torso of a semi-relief figure. The subjects of the spandrels thus seem to have included events of the Passion, and figures of the Evangelists or other sacred writers.

The embellishment of the spandrels with figures completed a highly decorative cloister. The embellishment of the capitals with stiff-leaf foliage, human heads and animals has been described. The arches themselves were

also enriched with high quality carving, with subjects of the same three categories. The two positions on the arches that provided an opportunity for the mason to exercise his creative skills were the blocks from which the outer voussoirs sprang, and the narrow spandrels which occupied the space between the two semi-circles and cusp of the inner order, and the moulding of the voussoirs of the outer order. The carvings used for the former situation in most cases projected from the plane of the outer order beyond the edge of the arcade capitals. As a series they would have caught the eye of anyone looking down the cloister walk. The subjects included a head of a woman with uncovered straight hair combed back, a frown on the forehead and finely executed features set in a serious expression (fig. 59). Another woman's head was shown wearing a wimple. A stern-looking man's head with beetling eyebrows, a frowning forehead and wavy hair projected from one block (fig. 60). A group of exquisitely carved stiff-leaf foliage covered another. It is not only the composition of this particular foliage that demonstrates the skill of the mason – it is also the manner of its execution. The leaves are carved in such a way that they grow up both sides of the block to form a pair of sheaths from which the moulding of both voussoirs emerges. The foliage meets across the centre of the block forming a bridge that is carved in full relief – a testimony to the ability of a mason fully confident of his mastery of the red sandstone.

The subject of another block is an otter-like creature, with a rounded friendly looking face, pointed ears laid flat

against the neck, and a coat in tightly curled waves. The animal emerges from a bunch of stiff-leaf foliage, with its front legs and feet resting on the upper part of the foliage. Another subject is a creature with a monkey-like face, small even teeth, whiskers, and a body which looks like that of a serpent and which terminates in stiff-leaf foliage that wraps around the body. In contrast to the fantastical nature of that creature is the head of a canon (fig. 61). It is realistically, even ideally, carved. The canon has a tonsure and the cowl of his habit is drawn halfway across the crown of his head. The face is rather expressionless compared to the women's faces and the stern man – an idealised canon provided less scope for the mason. Interestingly he is shown with a closely cropped beard, which presumably indicates that beards were not uncommon for Augustinian canons in the thirteenth century.

The narrow spandrels within the arches provided less scope for relief carving, but the mason nonetheless made the most of his opportunity. Stiff-leaf foliage was ideal for filling the space and this accounts for most of the decoration that has survived. One block however has an animal carved in semi-relief stretched full length along the long spandrel. It is similar in appearance to the 'otter' described above, but with a smooth coat (fig. 63).

The form of the cloister arcade can be described in summary as follows. Trefoil bases were set on a dwarf wall. Cylindrical shafts in groups of three supported large capitals enriched with stiff-leaf foliage, human heads and animals. These in turn supported trefoil arches with deeply cut mouldings and embellished with human heads, animals and foliage. The spandrels of the arcade had relief figures carved on them.

The width of each bay of the arcade was about 1 m, with a variation of about 30 mm from the average. Each

Fig. 60. The head of a young man with a pronounced brow and long hair, staring intently at passers-by in the cloister walk (160 mm in height).

side of the cloister was about 16 m in length, so the complete arcade must have consisted of sixty-four bays, though the central pair on one or more of the sides may have incorporated doors giving access to the cloister garth.

The relief figure (fig. 62)

A seated figure, which unfortunately lacks the feet and upper part of the torso, was found packed into the foundations with the other arcade elements. The figure was carved in the round but with the back left plain where it must have been set against a wall (e.g. the back of a niche). The seated figure has its left arm folded across the waist, holding a closed book which has a fastened cover. Some drapery is gathered and falls over the arm and down between the knees towards the ground. The right arm is raised from the elbow; the loose sleeve hangs below the arm. The shaft of what may be a cross, a crozier or a staff is placed to the inside of the right arm; the right hand

Fig. 61. An Augustinian canon, with the hood of the habit drawn half way across the tonsured head. He is represented idealistically, and is shown wearing a neat close-cropped beard and moustache (170 mm in height).

(which is missing) may have grasped it or have been raised in a gesture of benediction. The drapery of the robe hangs in folds, and is stretched smoothly over the knees. A tiny arm and hand are carved on the figure's right side, with the hand touching the garment on the lower part of the leg.

In the absence of the upper part it is not possible to identify the subject with certainty. A figure holding a book could be one of the Evangelists or the Fathers of the Church (such as St Augustine). The shaft could be part of either an episcopal staff, crozier, a pilgrim's staff or a cross. However, a strong case can be made for identifying the figure as Christ in Majesty. The presence of the hand touching the garment is one indicator. It is probably derived from Biblical references to miracles performed by the act of touching the hem of Christ's robe. The mid-thirteenth-century figure of Christ in Majesty which is placed in a niche over the chapter house door at Lichfield Cathedral retains a fragmentary arm and hand touching the hem of Christ's robe – probably the remains of one of the supporting angels. The size of the figure and the fact that it was carved to stand against a flat background support its identification as Christ in Majesty. The figure is

much larger than the figures that occupied the arcade spandrels. One of these, as has been described, holds a book in his left hand, open to the observer. There is a probability that it was one of the Evangelists, or the Fathers of the Church. With up to sixty-four spandrels available, a series of such personages would have made a suitable subject for the cloister walk. The other fragment with a hand bearing a stigma may be one of a series about the Passion and Resurrection of Christ. For either of these

series an appropriate culmination would be a figure of Christ in Majesty. The usual setting for such a statue would be above a door or entrance. It can be speculated that if there was a pair of doors giving access to the cloister garth, a niche could be set between them in the intervening spandrel, or a bracket could project to carry the figure. Its larger size and dominant position would then provide the correct iconographic relationship with the subjects of the neighbouring spandrel series.

Christ in Majesty is a common subject in medieval iconographic masonry. The relationship to doors and entrances has been mentioned – in the twelfth century this was often through location in the tympana of doorways.

Fig. 62. The seated figure – possibly Christ in Majesty. The upper torso is missing; note the book with its clasp, the rod of the staff or cross, and the tiny hand touching the hem. The scale is in 10 mm divisions.

The Prior's Door at Ely, the west door at Rochester, the south door at Barfreston (Kent) and the south porch at Malmesbury are all outstanding examples. More modest examples of twelfth-century Majesties are to be found in the typanum of Rowlstone (Herefordshire) and in niches over doors at Rouse Linch (Worcestershire) and Lullington (Somerset). In the thirteenth century Christ in Majesty continues to be a popular subject for this location. At Lincoln the statue which forms the centrepiece for the Judgement Porch dates from about 1280 (Gardner 1951, 145). In all the examples mentioned above Christ is shown with his right hand in a gesture of benediction. In his left hand he holds a book in all except the Lincoln example. A figure of Christ in Majesty placed over an internal passage rather than the doors listed above is at Lichfield, where it is placed above the entrance to the chapter house passage – a work of 1249. A very mutilated but magnificent example of the subject is the over-lifesize Christ in Majesty which dominates the refectory of Worcester from its east wall; it dates from 1220–30 (Pevsner 1968, 15).

A staff or cross does not seem to be a usual feature of Christ in Majesty. However examples can be found outside the limitations of twelfth- and thirteenth-century masonry. A relief panel at Breedon-on-the-Hill (Leicestershire) has a Christ with a right hand raised to bless and holding in the left hand a long rod with a cross head. Christ holding a rod with a cross head can be found in some manuscript depictions. In an Ascension scene (D'Ancona and Aeschlimann 1969, pl. 39) Christ holds a cross in his right hand. An Ascension in an Italian volume of Gospels produced in 1170 shows the enthroned Christ with right hand raised in blessing, and holding a cross headed rod in his left hand (*ibid.*, pl. 66). The tympanum of the Prior's Door at Ely has the figure of Christ in Majesty with an open book in his left hand above which is a small cross (illustrated in Gardner 1951, 71). A figure of Christ in a niche at Leigh, Worcestershire (date *c.* 1100), holds a long shafted cross in the left hand (Parker 1874, 74). Thus the presence of the shaft, although unusual, does not prevent the identification of the Norton figure with Christ in Majesty; that remains the most likely of the several possible alternatives.

Affinities of the cloister arcade

The number of English cloister arcades of twelfth- or thirteenth-century date about which there is information is very small indeed. The construction of early cloister arcades in timber is a possibility that has yet to be proved (Butler 1982, 93). The twin-shafted arcade built at Rievaulx in the late twelfth century has already been mentioned as one of the few for which details are known at that date. A recently discovered arcade, dated to *c.* 1200, is that at Haughmond, Shropshire (Blair, Lankaster and West 1980). Like that at Norton, it was demolished in the late fifteenth or early sixteenth century and fragments

were incorporated in the foundations of its successor. It was a cusped round-headed arcade which had paired capitals, shafts and bases. A fine sculpture of the Virgin and Child was probably situated at a corner of the walk. Fragments of contemporary foliage carving may have come from panels in the wall surface above the arcade.

The highly decorated arcades of the thirteenth century at Haughmond and Norton are unlikely to have been unusual in their elaboration. In the twelfth century the opportunity to embellish cloister walks was certainly taken at a number of places. The fragments of the cloister built in about 1130 at Reading Abbey show that it had considerable sculptural decoration, both on its capitals and in the form of carved panels (e.g. Zarnecki 1951, pls. 59 and 67). Fragments of the highly enriched twelfth-century arcade from Bridlington Priory have been re-assembled and are displayed in the nave of the church. These two cloister arcades, from Cluniac and Augustinian houses respectively, contrast with the plainer arcade from Cistercian Rievaulx. The narthex arcade at Fountains provides another example of a simple Cistercian arcade – the cloister was doubtless similar. There are other fragments of twelfth-century arcades at Winchester, Westminster, Norwich and Canterbury (Webb 1956, 56). The date of the twin-shaft Norwich arcade has been assigned to the second decade of the twelfth century (Franklin, in Thompson 1983, 56–70). Thirteenth-century arcades are similarly few in number – examples are Newminster (Northumberland) (re-erected), Southwark (fragments), Butley (Suffolk) (fragments of a cloister with twin shafts); Forde Abbey (Dorset) has a wall arcade on the north wall of the north cloister walk. The best surviving example of an early thirteenth-century arcade is that at Mont Saint-Michel, which has English affinities (Webb 1956, 58). It is unusual in form – instead of paired shafts, there is a double arcade with single shafts that are staggered. The simple pointed arches are supported by Purbeck marble shafts; the spandrels facing the cloister walk are decorated with naturalistic foliage and also figures including Christ upon the Cross and Christ in Majesty (Brooke 1974, pls. 347, 348 and 350).

From the above it is clear that twelfth- and thirteenth-century cloister arcades have left little evidence of their form of construction in Britain, despite the fact that many hundreds must have existed. The task of assessing the Norton arcade is therefore a difficult one, though the richness of its decoration was part of a tradition which is exemplified by non-Cistercian houses such as Reading, Bridlington and Haughmond. The feature for which the writer can find no parallel in any cloister arcade in Britain (or elsewhere in Europe) is the use of groups of three shafts. Single shafts were by no means uncommon, but the most popular form by far was the use of paired shafts, in practically every country in Western Europe from the fourth century to the fourteenth.

To find the origin of the Norton arcade, architectural schemes other than cloister arcades must be examined. In particular, it is wall arcades (both external and internal) on major ecclesiastical buildings that are likely to be of a similar scale to Norton's cloister arcade. The west front of Wells Cathedral, built in the 1220s, has several tiers with round trefoil arches and capitals with bunches of stiff-leaf foliage; however the trefoils have no separate hood mould, the shafts are single and the capitals have a prominent abacus (illustrated e.g. Gardner 1951, 129, pl. 237). The additions to the Norman west front of Lincoln Cathedral, built in the 1240s, consist of various tiers of arcading. The southern extension has one tier of blank arcade that is very similar in appearance to the Norton arcade – trefoils within a slightly pointed hood mould with projecting heads at the springing, and triple independent shafts with stiff-leaf enriched capitals. The Angel Choir (finished *c.* 1280) has on its interior walls a profusion of shafts, many in groups of three on the clerestory with bases and capitals very similar to those at Norton.

Thirteenth-century spandrel sculpture

The spandrel decoration of the Norton arcade has no parallels among thirteenth-century English cloisters with

Fig. 63. The highly enriched arcade with human heads, animals and superbly carved stiff-leaf foliage.

the possible exception of Haughmond, where the evidence is very fragmentary. However, there are a number of important internal wall arcades where spandrel sculpture is a feature. The eastern end of Worcester Cathedral is an outstanding example. Wall arcades line the eastern transepts, the eastern chapel and the eastern part of the choir, with St John's Chapel on the south. There is uncertainty about the date of the eastern work, but it must have been undertaken after 1218 (Singleton 1978). The wall arcades consist of pointed trefoils with single shafts. The springing is decorated with foliage, not heads. The spandrel decoration is heavily restored, but the original work has figures, stiff leaf, beasts and grotesques. There are some excellent groups of relief figure sculpture including subjects such as masons at work, the Damned, The Expulsion and Visitation (Gardner 1951, 106–8, pls. 198–202).

Westminster Abbey is widely acknowledged as the most influential English building of the thirteenth century; in the middle years of the century wall arcades were built as part of the ambulatory and transept chapels. The installation of later monuments has badly damaged the wall arcades, but it is clear that the spandrels contained both foliage and figure sculpture (Webb 1956, 106; Gardner 1951, 108, pl. 203). Despite restoration and the presence of monuments, the continuation of the wall arcade into

the nave is easily seen on both north and south walls. Its form is very similar to that at Norton – rounded trefoil arches within a broad hood mould which is slightly pointed at the apex. There is carving in the same situations as the Norton arcade, that is in the spandrels between the arches and also between the cusp of the trefoil and the hood mould. The former location has angels and painted heraldry as its main subjects; the latter beasts and grotesques and semi-naturalistic foliage. The hood stops on the springing blocks are very battered, but consist of human heads and beasts. The arcade has single shafts.

Spandrel sculpture reached its peak in the Angel Choir at Lincoln, constructed between 1256 and 1280. The large spandrels of the main structural arcade of the choir house subjects ranging from angels playing instruments to Christ showing his wounded side, all with mature stiff-leaf foliage in association (Gardner 1951, 110–23, pls. 217–30).

Mention must also be made of two other churches with spandrel sculpture in wall arcades. At Ely the trefoil arcades are within the east end that was begun in 1235 (Webb 1956, 106). At Salisbury the chapter house was begun in 1259; it has a wall arcade with a series of skilfully executed spandrel sculptures which have been dated to *c.* 1270 (Gardner 1951, figs. 204, 5 and 6). A figure of Christ in Majesty dominates the entrance – it is a product of the restoration by Burges but justified by the original symbols of the Evangelists which support the aureole.

A cloister mason

The cloister arcade, unique as it is in many respects, is nonetheless part of an architectural movement that embellished some of the greatest churches in England with figure sculpture in the spandrels of arcades for the greater part of the thirteenth century. It is particularly impressive that Norton was able to attract a mason who was fully conversant with the type of work being carried out in the greater churches, and was able to adapt the approach to create a cloister for a medium sized priory that was both original in its conception and highly skilled in its execution. The quality of work is outstanding in the region. It might be expected that the mason might have worked at Chester before moving to Norton, but there is no similar work to be seen at St Werburgh's Abbey. The refectory pulpit, fine though it is as a composition, is greatly inferior in its detail. It dates from *c.* 1290 (Pevsner and Hubbard 1971, 147). The lady chapel was built *c.* 1260–80 (*ibid.*, 139) but it too has no details which are similar to the Norton arcade. Another major church which might have had a school of masons that could have produced the Norton mason was Lichfield Cathedral. The chapter house and the passage leading to it, built in about 1249, have wall arcades consisting of trefoil arches with hood moulds and mould steps, mainly heads and foliage. However, there is no spandrel sculpture, and the

treatment of foliage is quite different to that at Norton.

If the Norton sculptor did not come from Chester or Lichfield, where did he come from? It is assumed that just one mason was responsible for the embellishment of the cloister arcade because the carving appears to the writer to be in one, highly accomplished hand. It would be possible to look across the Pennines to Yorkshire, but it is difficult to find mid-thirteenth-century carving there with the same mix of elements that the Norton arcade possesses.

It is to the west country that one has to turn to find a widespread use of the three elements exhibited at Norton – foliage, heads and animals (fig. 63). Interestingly, a similar source has been suggested for architectural decoration found in several Irish churches of the same period (Stalley 1971). A mason who worked at Droitwich and Overbury in Worcester has been shown to be the man who designed the nave of Christ Church, Dublin, between 1213 and 1234. The decoration of the Worcestershire churches and Christ Church is characterised by the use of heads and foliage in combination. This combination occurs in several churches in the west of England, with the ultimate source of the formula apparently the sculpture of Wells Cathedral (*ibid.*, 68). It is unlikely that the same man was responsible for the Norton work, but a similar process of recruitment may well have taken place.

Cheshire, with its relatively low level of activity in church building in the thirteenth century, was unable to sustain an architectural tradition of its own. Like church builders in Ireland who wished to see their churches built and decorated in an expert contemporary manner, the prior of Norton appears to have turned to a west country mason for his expertise.

The bell foundry

In 1976 excavation in the outer courtyard of the priory revealed a large pit in which a bell had been cast (fig. 64). Fragments of the mould were subsequently re-assembled. The mould had been used to cast a large tenor bell, which most probably hung in the tower of the church. It was of an identical size to the bell which was cast in the twelfth century, the casting pit for which was found in 1978.

The need to cast a new tenor bell may have been another of the consequences of the fire of 1236. The burning of the church tower would have brought the bells crashing down; they would have shattered on impact with the floor. It is always tempting to ascribe archaeologically observed events to historical occasions. Nonetheless the fire of 1236 is a credible explanation for the casting of a new bell. A radiocarbon date obtained from charcoal found in the pit is 730 ± 80 bp, i.e. *c.* 1220 ad ± 80 (HAR 2279) which would be consistent with this hypothesis, though of course the recasting may have been necessitated by a fracture on a different occasion. The acquisition of a bell was an activity for which the canons of Norton required specialist craftsmen from outside the

Fig. 64. The bell casting pit with the peripheral drainage channel, T-shaped channels with wooden wedges, and the mark of the rim of the bell.

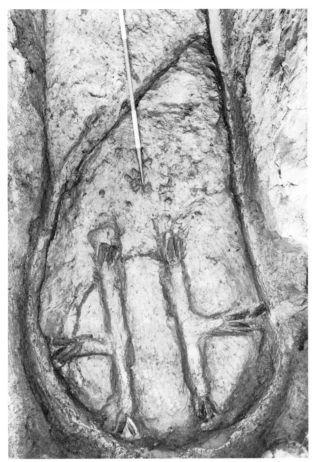

locality. It is not possible to say from where the bell makers travelled, but presumably it was a town sufficiently large to support a foundry producing difficult castings. It was easier to travel to the customer, set up a foundry and cast a bell on site (fig. 65) rather than transport a bell weighing about 750 kilos (an estimate based on the size of the bell mould and the density of bell metal) with the danger of cast bell metal being damaged in transit.

The pit (fig. 66) was cut 1 m into the natural clay. It was more than 9 m long (the limit was not reached) and almost 2 m wide. It had parallel sides and a rounded end. The sides were near vertical, and the base was almost flat, though channels had been cut into it. One channel followed the rounded end of the pit, and then continued along its northern side with a gradual fall to the north west. It became clear during the excavation that its function was to act as a drain. Sand filled fissures in the boulder clay acted as natural drains and water continuously trickled into the pit from them. The peripheral

Fig. 65. Casting a bell. The five stages are 1: the core of the mould is built up (using a revolving arm called a strickle); 2: a 'false bell' of clay is made, again using the strickle, to the precise form of the intended bell; 3: the outer mould (the cope) is built up over the false bell, and is then heated to harden it. It can then be lifted off, the false bell removed, and then the cope replaced in its exact position for casting; 4: the mould for the canons is placed on top of the cope, and then molten bell metal is poured through channels in rammed sand in a box in a single continuous casting operation. The displaced gases and excess metal can escape through the central vent at the top. 5: the bell is rigidly attached, using the canons, to a pivoting beam.

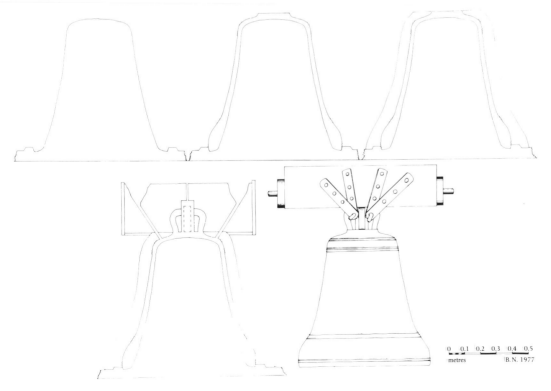

0 0.1 0.2 0.3 0.4 0.5
metres   B. N. 1977

channel removed the water. The other two channels were shaped like equal armed Ts, with the tops adjacent and parallel. Small wooden wedges were found at the ends of these channels. It seems likely that they accommodated a wooden framework, which would have held the two halves of the bell mould together during casting, and which would have facilitated hoisting the completed bell out of the pit.

On the bottom of the pit was a groove, only a few millimetres deep, in the form of part of a circle. It must have been produced by the rim of the bell pressing slightly into the clay (fig. 64). A mound of pale yellow clay containing fragments of straw was found above the charcoal filled channels and groove. Scattered around the base of the pit were pieces of bell mould (fig. 67), a black material which on analysis was found to comprise clay, manure and sand. About two hundred fragments were found, some of them quite large and readily identifiable, for example as pieces of the cope (the outer portion of the two part mould) shaped to form the shoulder of the bell and the sound bow – the thickened part struck by the clapper. Other fragments were parts of the mould for the canons, the loops by which the bell would have been

attached to a beam. It seems likely that the yellow clay with straw was the decomposed remains of the mould core. The organic content of the mould was essential – as the molten metal was poured the air could escape through thousands of tiny apertures where straw and grass had burnt out. The presence of air bubbles, which would have weakened the casting, would therefore be avoided.

It proved possible to re-assemble the fragments to form the complete cope of the bell mould (fig. 68). It had been used to cast a bell about 1 m high and 0.8 m in diameter at the lip. The bell was 'long-waisted' – the shorter bell was introduced during the thirteenth century as change ringing became popular. A replica of the bell was cast at Thomas Platt and Company's Foundry in Widnes, following medieval practices. The exercise emphasised the high degree of skill required for an operation of this kind (fig. 69).

The pit contained a layer of sandstone rubble above the mould fragments. The rubble turned out to be fragments of the furnace that had been used to melt the metal; it was fortunate that they survived as no trace of the furnace base was present. From the fragments it was possible to establish that the furnace had a bowl, made of roughly rectangular shaped blocks of sandstone about 0.2 m long set in clay, and with a clay lining. Much of the stone and clay showed the effects of considerable heat. Some fragments of baked clay were apparently part of a runner, a channel through which the molten metal was tapped during the casting operation.

Blobs of metal that had escaped during casting were analysed by BICC Metals Limited. The bell metal comprised the expected metallic elements, copper and tin, with small quantities of others, notably gold and silver. These occurred as a tiny proportion of the total, but nonetheless more than would have been expected to derive from the ores of copper and tin. Their presence lends support to the tradition that patrons would give articles or coins of gold and silver to be thrown into the molten bell metal in the (mistaken) belief that their act of piety would improve the tone of the bell.

Bell casting pits have been found in a number of excavations of churches. Examples found since 1970 and mentioned in summaries in *Medieval Archaeology* include the following at parish churches: St Michael's Church, Thetford (volume 15, 1971, 130); Thurleigh, Beds. (16, 1972, 177); Castle Rising, Norfolk – the church in the castle (16, 1972, 181); Hadstock, Essex (19, 1975, 221); St George's Church, Norwich (19, 1975, 247); Thornton, Leics. (20, 1976, 182); Barton upon Humber, Lincs. (23, 1979, 239). Monastic sites with bell foundries are Pontefract Priory (16, 1972, 176 and 17, 1973, 157) and Taunton Augustinian Priory (22, 1978, 161) as well as Norton.

Unless a monastic house or parish church was situated in a town where a bell foundry existed a specialist

Fig. 66. Plan of the bell pit.

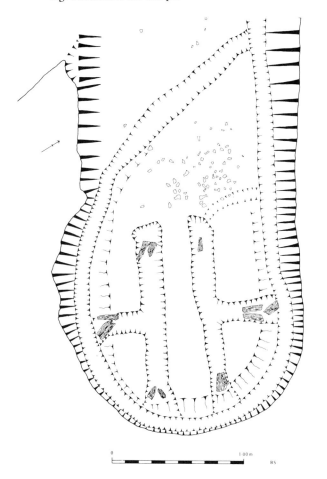

0   1.00 m

Fig. 67. Fragments of the bell mould on the bottom of
the pit: the shiny surface is the inner face of the cope
(500 mm scale).

Fig. 68. The reassembled mould fragments forming the
cope, supported by dental plaster in a wooden frame.

Fig. 69. The replica bell hanging in the museum gardens on the occasion of a ceremony performed by Professor Sir Bernard Lovell, 23 May 1977.

bell founder had to be engaged to travel to the place where the bell was required. It could be a protracted business. At Croxden in 1303 the monks engaged Master Henry Michael of Lichfield to cast a bell to replace one that had cracked. He laboured throughout the summer but at the first attempt his casting failed. It was not until All Saints Day that he was successful (Hibbert 1910, 95). It is possible that when the canons of Norton engaged a bell founder a half-century earlier they too had looked to Lichfield, the administrative centre of the diocese.

The guest quarters

Buildings found on the south side of the outer courtyard stretched westwards from the kitchens and approximately followed the line of the monastic drain. The situation of the buildings, close to the kitchens and facing on to the outer courtyard, would be appropriate for guest quarters and this is their most likely function.

The buildings were erected in an area which had previously been crossed by ditches which provided the early drainage system of the priory. They became defunct when the masonry drain was installed as part of the

expansion of the priory around 1200 (the drain is an integral part of the enlarged rere-dorter). Clay and rubble were tipped into the ditches to consolidate them in readiness for the erection of two of the masonry buildings (fig. 70). A date in the first half of the thirteenth century would be consistent with the date of a short cross penny of John from a context immediately predating their construction. It is a type which was minted until 1218 and remained current until 1247, giving an effective currency for the coin of *c.* 1210 to 1250 (information from Marion Archibald, BM Department of Coins and Medals). The more westerly of the two buildings terminated in a rounded front on the north – an architectural feature of some pretension overlooking the outer courtyard (an oriel window?).

Further west another large building was discovered which proved to be contemporary with the round based masonry drain with corbelled capping which replaced the early thirteenth-century drain in the fourteenth century (fig. 71). The foundations of its west wall were no less than 2.5 m broad, consisting of large blocks of sandstone bonded with clay. As with the thirteenth-century buildings the depth and breadth of the foundations was needed to avoid subsidence into earlier ditches. This building had been of some importance, for alongside its western wall, amid the discarded fragments of roofing slabs, were numerous pieces of painted glass. There can be little doubt that the glass was smashed to remove lead during demolition. Clay pipe evidence indicates a demolition date in the early eighteenth century; the previously described pair of buildings were demolished in the sixteenth century. There is a strong possibility that the building was the guests' hall – it could not have been a chapel, and few other buildings on the outer courtyard would have merited windows of painted glass.

Elsewhere at Norton only small fragments of highly devitrified glass has been recovered. All the guest house glass had become opaque as a result of devitrification but nonetheless a great deal of its detail could be discovered. Many of the quarries survived intact with the original shape identifiable from the grosed edges; traces of painted decoration including geometric motifs, foliage such as oak leaves and acorns, and a lion's face.

The provision of hospitality for travellers was an obligation of most religious orders. Norton must have been well used by travellers journeying north or south who crossed the Mersey at the Runcorn Gap. The adoption of St Christopher (fig. 72) as a subsidiary patron saint was an apposite choice in view of the proximity of the river. The giant late fourteenth-century statue of St Christopher probably stood in the outer courtyard where it is shown in

the 1727 Buck engraving (fig. 18). It would have provided comfort to those who stayed in the guest quarters and who shared the common medieval conviction that to look upon his image ensured safety from death for that day.

The growth of the north transept chapel

The original transept chapels were small rectangular projections from the east wall of each transept, measuring internally only 2.73 m (N) and 3.10 m (S) wide and 2.79 m (N) and 2.10 m (S) deep. As such, they would have been sufficient in size to accommodate an altar and one celebrant. They were soon given an additional function as burial places.

The north transept chapel was lengthened by demolishing its east wall and extending the side walls eastwards. This made the chapel 5.90 m long. The

Fig. 71. The fourteenth-century drain with a round base and, here, corbelling to support the additional weight of one of the guest house buildings. It replaced the flat based drain (fig. 55) west of the latrine block. Its steeper fall and rounded base would have considerably increased its effectiveness.

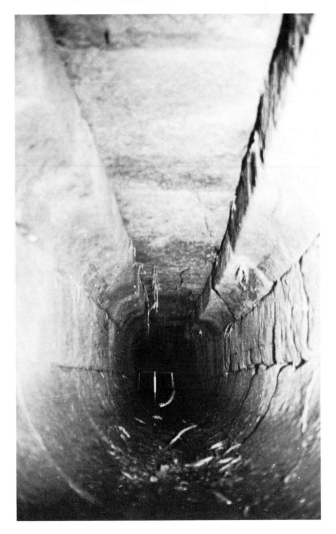

Fig. 70. Foundations of the probable guest quarters overlying twelfth-century ditches, and cut by an eighteenth-century drain and brick wall.

opening in the east wall of the transept between the chapel and the chancel was retained, and the extension of the chapel thus created a passage alongside the north wall of the chancel. The date of the extension is not known, though it must have taken place after the building of the church in the mid-twelfth century and before the mid-thirteenth century, when the chapel was further extended.

Unfortunately knowledge of the north east chapels is

Fig. 72. Statue of St Christopher carrying the infant Christ, which probably stood on the outer courtyard (it can be seen on fig. 18). The right forearm and staff are missing.

limited by the amount of disturbance which occurred in this area. Extensive landscaping and gardening work was undertaken to remove stonework and to level the ground to create the gardens of the Georgian country house. All floor surfaces were removed, and nearly all wall ashlar.

The second extension to the north transept chapel involved a complete replanning of the north east part of the church. The extended chapel was demolished along with much of the east wall of the transept to create a much larger opening into a new chapel (fig. 74). This new building extended 3.37 m further north internally (4.37 m externally) than the north transept. Eventually the chapel was extended 14.06 m eastward again to a new east wall in line with the extended chancel (fig. 73).

The internal floor area of the chapel in its final form was 182 square metres. This is a very considerable size, and there are few parallels in other monastic houses. Thetford Priory (Cluniac) had a large lady chapel of *c*. 190 square metres which was built in the north east part of the church in the early thirteenth century, as a result of a series of visions, which included the insistence by Our Lady that it should be of stone rather than timber. It became frequented by pilgrims, and the proceeds allowed the monks to rebuild the east end of the church on a larger scale (Raby and Reynolds 1970, 2–4). At Castle Acre (Cluniac) a lady chapel of 80 square metres was built in the fifteenth century to replace an apsidal chapel on the north side of the chancel (plan in Raby and Reynolds 1952). At Lilleshall (Augustinian) a free-standing lady chapel was built in the north east angle between the chancel and north transept. Its internal dimensions were 21 m long by 7.5 m wide – a floor area of 157 square metres (plan in Rigold 1969). This situation is similar to that at Ely where the early fourteenth-century lady chapel is a separate building to the north east.

The considerable size of the chapel is notable, but the provision of chapel-cum-aisles alongside the chancel is a feature that Norton shares with several Augustinian churches, including Lanercost, Kenilworth, Lilleshall and Llanthony (Gwent).

The date and function of the north east chapel

When and why did the series of expansions to the north east chapel occur? The answer to both questions is provided by the large number of burials that have been excavated in this area. Many of the burials were in sandstone coffins, some with elaborately carved lids surviving. The conclusions to be drawn are that benefactors were being buried in the chapel and that its size reflects not only the financial support the priory managed to attract and the ambitious tastes of the donors, but also the pressure on space resulting from many burials. The sandstone coffins are placed in many cases side by side (fig. 10). What now appear to be gaps were in fact filled with burials in wooden coffins.

Fig. 73. Model of the church from the north east. From the Romanesque north transept and tower (which has been heightened in the thirteenth century with crenellation and pinnacles added in the fifteenth century) the north east chapels, the chancel and impressive east chapel all project (see fig. 4).

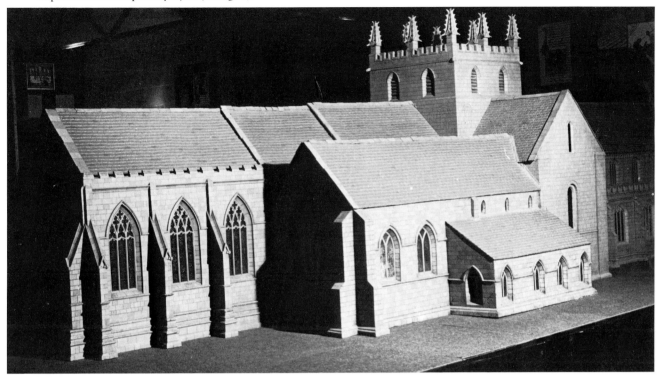

Fig. 74. Entrance to the north east chapels. The band of mosaic tiles forms the threshold; they have subsided into a grave, and on the right partially cover the masonry of the entrance to the original, tiny chapel.

Fig. 75. Photograph taken in about 1870 during the display of coffin lids in the gardens. Note the pile of rubble beyond the fence – doubtless the result of deep trenching by the gardeners on the site of the church.

Fig. 76. Coffin lids displayed in the garden (see fig. 75), surrounded by a wall to support a glazed cover, reburied in the 1920s and rediscovered in 1971. The two elaborate thirteenth-century coffins were found to be *in situ*; the twelfth-century coffin on the right had been moved to this position.

A threshold of mosaic tiles (fig. 74) clearly related to the large chapel as it spanned the complete width of the entrance, sealing the demolished remains of the entrance to the earlier chapels. The enlargement must therefore pre-date the production of mosaic tiles at Norton, which it will be argued later took place in the first quarter of the fourteenth century.

In the nineteenth century a number of coffins were discovered, and put on view in the garden. Beamont records the event: '. . . a series of handsome sepulchral slabs . . . each lying *in situ*, were disclosed for the admiration of the reflecting spectator' (Beamont 1873). A

Fig. 77. A highly carved lid which had partially collapsed into its coffin. Vines flank a central cross. One arm is carved above the cross, and nearby some locks of hair are visible; the rest of the bust, and the part of the inscription naming the person buried in the coffin were unfortunately missing.

photograph in the Norton Priory Museum collection (fig. 75) shows the coffins soon after their discovery. Seven are placed, side by side, in a rectangular pit with a gravelled base. The sides have just been turfed, the surrounds await turfing. Beyond the fence is a sombre sight – two large heaps of stones. It is clear that the area has just been 'dug over' and all the stone encountered has been cleared. This explains the lack of surviving archaeological deposits. The coffin lids were rediscovered in 1971 in the positions shown on the photograph. A stone wall was found surrounding three of the lids (fig. 76). Sir Richard Brooke, the last occupant of the Georgian house at Norton, described to the writer the purpose of the wall – it supported a wood and glass top 'rather like a cold frame'. He had the coffin lids covered with soil when he moved from Norton in 1922. Of the seven coffins, only two complete ones and fragments of a third can with confidence be described as being *in situ*, whilst the others may well have been moved for the purposes of display. The third *in situ* complete lid was not found by the Victorian gardeners. It survived undisturbed, albeit shattered, until its discovery in 1972 (figs. 77, 78).

The two lids that were in their original positions in the nineteenth-century frame both have cross designs which use stiff-leaf foliage (fig. 76). The decoration is carved in relief within a frame which is chamfered along the outer edges of the lid. On one lid the terminals of the cross head expand in stiff-leaves which overlap and form a circular wreath, surrounded by a circular frame which unites with the stem of the cross. The stem terminates in a further group of stiff-leaves. The other lid has a design which is also based on a cross, but with more imagination. The cross head consists of an annular band around eight radiating stiff-leaves and a central rosette. The shaft sprouts stiff-leaves in pairs down its length, terminating in a triple leaf. These two lids have much in common. The coffins beneath them have similar characteristics as well, in particular stone cushions in the head recess, a feature not found in any other coffin on the site.

The complex stiff-leaf designs indicate a date in the later thirteenth century. The third phase of the chapel must have been erected by the time the coffins were placed in it, so construction in the mid-thirteenth century seems likely. A date for the fourth, final phase of the chapel is provided by the mosaic tile floor. A threshold of tiles was present at the entrance from the transept. There can be no doubt from the tiles found in many of the graves dug into the final eastern extension that a mosaic floor existed there as well. The final extension of the chapel had to be standing in order for the tile floor to be installed, and it is possible that the extension of the chapel and the creation of the floor were part of one building operation in the early part of the fourteenth century.

The layout of the final extension, damaged though it was by eighteenth- and nineteenth-century gardening, could nonetheless be determined. The eastern portion was completely lacking in burials; presumably it had an altar and a sanctuary upon it. The western part was heavily occupied by burials (fig. 9). None of these were in stone coffins. Presumably the fashion for marking the position of graves with sandstone coffin lids had passed, to be replaced by tile panels and effigies (one fragment of a mailed arm from the stone effigy of a knight was found in the vicinity).

The four phases of the north east chapel can be summarised as follows:

	Size (sq m)	Date
Phase 1	9	Part of the original church, started 1134
Phase 2	19	Probably second half of twelfth century
Phase 3	98	Erected by mid-thirteenth century
Phase 4	182	Erected by early fourteenth century

The Dutton family and the north east chapel

The relationship between the two branches of the Dutton family and Norton Priory has been described. As the barons of Halton, founders of Norton Priory, grew more remote from the early thirteenth century onwards, the Dutton family became the dominant benefactors. In return for their material support, members of the family would have expected to be buried at Norton with the advantage of prayers regularly offered for their souls by the canons. There are three wills of Duttons who were buried at Norton – Lawrence de Dutton in 1392, Sir Geoffrey Warburton in 1448 (in which he mentions the

Fig. 78. A fantastic beast from the foot of the coffin (fig. 77). The shaft of the cross pierces this representation of evil; from the dead beast comes life in the form of the vines growing from the dragon's head and the dog's head on the tail.

chapel of the Blessed Mary) and Sir Lawrence de Dutton in 1527 ('and I will that my body shall be buried and interred amongst my ancestors in the chapel of our Blessed Lady within the monastery of Norton'). The lady chapel is likely to be the north east chapel. This identification is confirmed by the special tiles which include panels representing the effigies of knights designed as grave covers and tiles which form the Dutton coat of arms (fig. 11). Those tiles form part of the early fourteenth-century mosaic floor.

The south transept chapel

A small chapel projected from the east side of the south transept of identical size to the original north transept chapel. It too underwent expansion, but not in the same way. As with the series of northern chapels, damage as a result of landscaping and gardening was severe. Not a single block of ashlar of the walls remained to be found, and no floor surfaces were present. Knowledge of the south transept chapels is derived purely from the rubble-filled foundation trenches. The first expansion consisted of the building of a wall from the east side of the transept, returning opposite the end of the original chancel. The south wall of the chancel was strengthened by the addition of an extra row of ashlar blocks alongside its southern face. It is probable that the wall was pierced by arches to make the chapel into an aisle. It probably had a lean-to roof resting against the chancel wall. There is no evidence by which to date the extension.

The extension was then rebuilt on a slightly narrower plan, and its eastern wall was thickened. The reason for the rebuilding is unknown. The carved stonework incorporated in the new south wall foundations indicates that the rebuilding occurred at a time when demolition was also taking place. The corbel blocks of the twelfth-century church were found here: perhaps they were removed during the re-roofing of the

chancel. Another carved fragment must be part of an Early English arch of considerable size, with a filleted roll flanked by rounded hollows, and a relief carved group of leaves on the flat surface. The chapel may therefore have been rebuilt in the second half of the thirteenth century.

Subsequently, the chapel was extended further east, to a line continuous with the end of the extended chancel. The foundations at the east end are constructed from the same level as those of the second chancel extension, and are of the same character. The latter, as we will see, must date from the end of the thirteenth century or the beginning of the fourteenth, so the enlarged chapel-cum-aisle can be assigned a similar date. An interesting feature of the south wall of the extended chapel is the presence of a stone coffin built into the wall. Its sides are built up with blocks of ashlar neatly assembled. It is possible that the burial is that of the person who provided the finance for building the extension. Other burials were found in the chapel, including several in sandstone coffins. In addition a rectangular base is present in the eastern part. It consists of one course of ashlar with a moulded chamfer on the corner angles. It is 2.03 m long and 0.82 m broad. It seems

Fig. 79. The east chapel in the foreground, and the church beyond. The north wall had been thoroughly robbed. Foundations of the east range and the west range undercroft beyond can also be seen.

likely that it is the base upon which a tomb with an effigy was set.

In the case of the southern transept chapels, as well as the northern, the emphasis is on the provision of places of burial, probably for the local gentry. The desire for family altars and chantry chapels was clearly met by expansion from both transepts to the maximum extent. However, the southern chapel could not grow to the size of that on the north because of the presence of the chapter house immediately to the south.

The eastern chapel

By the early thirteenth century, the church had been lengthened by the construction of a new chancel and an extension westwards of the nave. These modifications increased the internal length of the church from 45.13 m to 65.10 m. This was not to be the final length however. The excavation revealed the presence of a second extension of particularly impressive design at the eastern end (fig. 79). The building continued the internal width that had been established in the twelfth century. The foundations were broader, and considerably deeper than the earlier structures. The robber trench of the northern foundations was over a metre deep. In plan it was markedly different, possessing large buttresses, paired at the corners and projecting from the sides at two points; the

structure was therefore three bays in length. The size of the foundations in both width and depth, and the presence of the buttresses, suggest that this building possessed masonry vaulting, unlike the rest of the church, where the roof structure would have been of timber.

The lack of surviving stratification in the eastern part of the church has already been referred to. Only one block of ashlar remained, and no floor surfaces were found due to ploughing of the area beyond the garden fence. The southern and eastern foundations were intact but the northern foundation had been dug out in the eighteenth century; only the northern ends of the buttresses had escaped. In the robber trench dating evidence for the structure was found. Several pieces of tracery were recovered, which are likely to have been part of a very large window, almost certainly the east window of the chapel. The tracery has cusps springing from the soffit of the moulding, an early characteristic, and gables bearing crockets within the tracery. This unusual feature is to be found in two dateable windows, Merton College chapel, Oxford (east window) and St Albans Abbey lady chapel (east window). The former was built in 1290–6 (Sherwood and Pevsner 1974, 160) and the latter 'as early as 1308' (Pevsner and Cherry 1977, 305). Thus a date for the construction of the Norton east chapel is likely to fall somewhere in the two decades 1290 to 1310. This date range is confirmed by John Maddison (correspondence). An attempt to reconstruct the appearance of the window has been made on the model in the museum (fig. 80).

At first sight it is very surprising to be drawing parallels between Norton Priory, an Augustinian house in the comparatively poor county of Cheshire, and the likes of Merton College and St Albans Abbey. However, Norton was valued by the local gentry as a place of burial and its endowments were substantial. Revenue may have been obtained from pilgrims, as will be explained below. We have seen how from its foundation Norton had been able to engage masons of considerable quality; thus the canons might employ a master mason familiar with architectural developments in southern England. In addition, the castle and town building activities of Edward I in North Wales and the construction of his abbey at Vale Royal had brought to the north west large numbers of masons from ecclesiastical building projects all over England. In consequence this was a period of rapid transmission of architectural ideas.

Only one stone coffin was found in the east chapel, in marked contrast to the other chapels. There is reason to think that it was there before the chapel was built. It was filled with skulls and seems to have served as a charnel container for graves disturbed in building the chapel. Other burials were present in the area, but these probably pre-date the chapel, for the canons' graveyard would already have existed to the east of the chancel. The graves

were not excavated, as a small scale investigation found that the bones were in a very decayed state due to the low pH of the soil here. In the absence of floor levels, it would in any case be impossible to establish the relationship of most of the burials to the east chapel.

The function of the east chapel

The most obvious identification of the east chapel at Norton is that it was a lady chapel, dedicated to the cult of the Blessed Virgin. Many churches terminated at the east in lady chapels – for example the cathedrals of Chichester, Exeter, Gloucester, Hereford, Lichfield, St Albans, Salisbury, Southwark, Wells, Winchester and York. Other monastic houses, particularly the more wealthy urban ones, also built lady chapels at the east. Chester, Sherborne, Tewkesbury, Pershore, Romsey and Great Malvern are examples.

The dedication of a church to the Virgin was no obstacle to the establishment of a lady chapel in part of it. Norton's church at Great Budworth is one example. The church was dedicated to St Mary and the north transept was known as the lady chapel. In it was kept a gilded wooden image of the Virgin (Leycester, quoted in Ormerod 1882, 1). Nantwich church was also dedicated to St Mary, but still had the north transept north bay as a lady chapel (Richards 1973, 250).

Two wills, both of which refer to a lady chapel, indicate that in fact it was *not* the east chapel. Sir Geoffrey Warburton, in 1448, desired to be buried 'between the high chancel and the chapel of the Blessed Mary' – clearly referring to a specific part of the church next to the chancel. Lawrence de Dutton in 1527 willed that his body should 'be buried and interred amongst my ancestors in the chapel of our blessed lady'. There can therefore be no doubt that the Norton lady chapel was the Dutton burial place – the north east chapel. This is an acceptable position for a lady chapel, as the examples of Thetford, Castle Acre, Lilleshall, Ely and Great Budworth prove.

If the east chapel was not a lady chapel, what was it? Ecclesiastical buildings might be erected as a result of benefactors' generosity or of the ambition of the principal of the establishment. A third circumstance however could often lead to a major building operation – the discovery or acquisition of a relic with miraculous powers. The military advantages to the English in their operations against the Scots resulting from the possession of the Banner of St John of Beverley was exploited from 1292 by the chapter of the Minster. The chapter embarked upon a massive building campaign to provide a suitable setting for the miraculous relics of the saint (Stone 1955, 171). At Hailes, the community was presented in 1270 with a phial of the Holy Blood. As a result the whole of the east end of the church was rebuilt and extended as a chevet. It accommodated an ambulatory around the shrine containing the precious relic that became the focus of considerable pilgrimage (Coad 1969, 4). Walsingham was the foremost Augustinian shrine (Dickinson 1956). Vale Royal Abbey in Cheshire was given a relic – a portion of the Holy Cross brought back by Edward I from the Holy Land – at its foundation (Brownbill 1914, 9).

Fig. 80. The model of the east chapel. The position of the buttresses, and the window in the broad span of the east wall, can be compared to the foundations on fig. 79.

Norton also had a miraculous relic in the late thirteenth century. In an entry for 1287, the Whalley Abbey annals state that 'speech lost for five years by one person, and sight by another, have been restored by virtue of the holy cross of Norton' (Taylor 1912, 187). The fact that the miracles were known at Whalley, and that apart from the fire of 1236 this is the only reference in the annals to Norton, indicates their sensational nature. The

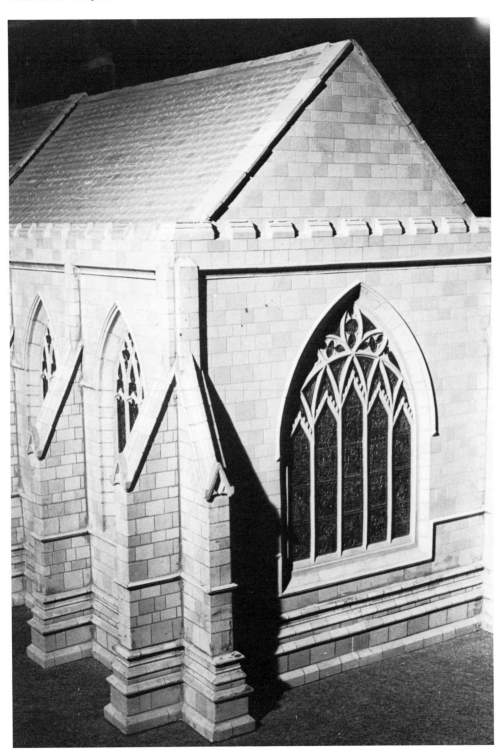

value of the cross as a pilgrim attraction may well have permitted expenditure on an east chapel worthy of the relic. No other record of the cross has been found; it may have been the victim of changing fashions in pilgrimage which resulted in fluctuations in the popularity of many shrines (Robinson 1980, 259).

Fig. 81. Excavation of the mosaic tile floor in the centre of the nave – which had to await the felling of the large elm visible on fig. 79. The presence of tree roots and rootlets infiltrating the tiles made excavation difficult.

The mosaic tile floor (figs. 81–92)

Just as the late twelfth–early thirteenth century was a time of major building work at Norton, so too was the late thirteenth–early fourteenth century. In the latter period, as we have seen, a large chapel was added to the east end of the church and the two transept chapels reached their fullest extent. The other significant development was the manufacture and laying of a mosaic tile floor in the church and chapter house.

Previously the church floor had consisted of clay or

mortar surfaces. At Bordesley a sequence of clay and mortar floors was found, and a flagged phase, before the first tiles were laid at the early date of *c.* 1200 (Hirst, Walsh and Wright 1983). No evidence of any flagged flooring was found at Norton. By the early fourteenth century a floor more in keeping with the standing and wealth of the priory was required. The tile floor which was installed was of a quality that matched the standards of the stone-masonry at Norton. By very good fortune a substantial area survived the vicissitudes of refloorings, burials, the demolition of the church, gardening, drain trenches, etc., to be revealed in the excavation. About 80 square metres remained – the largest area of a floor of this type to be found in any modern excavation (figs. 81–4).

The floor was installed in all of the choir of the church (i.e. east of the nave screen), in the transepts and no doubt in the chancel as well although with the higher floor level gardening had removed all traces. As the tile floor was almost certainly laid after the erection of the eastern chapel it is very likely that this too was provided with a mosaic floor. The presence of the tile floor in the north transept chapel has been established but there is no evidence for a tile floor in the southern chapel. No floor survived in the chapter house but a dump of tiles immediately to the south probably came from it. Other mosaic tiles were found in two patches to the west of the nave

screen where they appear to have embellished a pair of nave chapels.

Thus the floor originally covered some 500 square metres. The number of tiles needed for a particular pattern averages 80 tiles per square metre. The complete floor therefore required the manufacture of about 40,000 tiles.

The tiles were laid within the body of the church in the form of bands of decoration aligned with the central axis (fig. 84). The bands were separated from each other by borders which consisted of long rectangular tiles at the most simple, to a border of stars and hexagons at the most elaborate. The bands of patterns mainly consisted of geometric motifs. The central band along the axis of the choir comprised eight-pointed stars and squares with quatrefoil centres. On each side, continuing into the transepts, other patterns were placed so that there was a symmetry about the central axis. Thus alongside the central band to the north and to the south was a band of 'lemon' shaped tiles – in reality circles extended to points by ogival curves, each one set within bands of curving tiles. Beyond that on each side were tiles which formed a pattern of large six-petalled flowers. A total of twelve patterns occurred in the bands of decoration, three of which were also used in the borders. Four other patterns were used only as borders. In addition, two patterns were not found *in situ* but can be inferred from tiles found loose in other layers; there were thus eighteen different patterns in total (fig. 85).

All tiles were glazed. The main colours were black, produced by adding substantial quantities of copper to a lead glaze, green (using less copper) and yellow – an effect achieved by having a surface skim of light coloured clay which when fired with a lead glaze coating gave a yellow

Fig. 82. Band of flower pattern mosaic tiles on the south side of the choir, where the presence of the wooden stalls had protected the glaze. The deep depressions had been caused by impact from blocks of masonry – presumably during demolition of the tower after the Dissolution. 500 mm scale.

Fig. 83. Bands of mosaic tiles in the chapel next to the pulpitum screen on the south side of the nave. Part of the base of the altar is visible top left.

Fig. 84. The tile floor in the choir, cut by land drains, pipe trenches and a sewer with its inspection chamber. Part of the later floor is visible on the right projecting through the doorway to the east cloister walk.

Fig. 85. Mosaic tile patterns found at Norton Priory.

colour. Some tiles were orange, where the glaze was applied direct to the orange boulder clay that is the basic material from which they were made. On a number of tiles where differential glazing was attempted a dark brown or black was created by the addition of iron (analysis by ICI Mond Division revealed the colour producing constituents of the glazes). The colours were arranged in the patterns to alternate dark and light coloured elements.

Many of the tiles were embellished by stamped decoration (fig. 92). Experiments at Norton proved that wooden stamps were used to impress the moist clay. Motifs such as rosettes, leaves and a beautifully drawn lion's face occur frequently. There is evidence that templates were used to produce shaped tiles. A template would be placed on a sheet of moist clay and a knife would be used to cut around its edge. The knife was held at an angle to undercut the edges so that a tight join between the upper surfaces would result. Small holes on some of the more complex designs showed where the template had incorporated a number of spikes which, pressed into the clay sheet, would prevent the template slipping while the tile was being cut out. The templates were probably made of wood. It has been suggested that metal stamps and templates were used because wood would not have a sufficiently long life without suffering loss of detail (Eames 1980, 40–3). Experiments at Norton suggest otherwise, and later wooden stamps do exist (Keen 1969).

A notable aspect of the floor was the presence of 'special' tiles. The greatest concentration of these was

found in the north east chapel – the lady chapel in which the Duttons were buried. An account of the finds made there has been given (fig. 11). Here it is sufficient to say that the tiles included individually produced examples, some with clay inlay, some differentially glazed, some with the decoration incised with a knife, some finely drawn on the surface. Subjects included a life-size knight, large mosaic lions and probably a large pictorial panel.

The good fortune of finding such a large area of tile floor in position was compounded by the discovery of the kiln in which the tiles were fired (fig. 86). The presence of a large quantity of wasters, both in the fill of the kiln and also built into its structure, extended knowledge of both the range of products and the techniques of the tile makers.

The kiln was the usual double flued type, but of rather a small size, measuring 1.9 m long by 1.4 m wide to the outside of the walls. It was set within a large flat based pit cut 0.5 m into the natural boulder clay. The internal dimensions of each stoking chamber were 1.1 m by 0.35 m, separated by a spine wall 0.18 m thick at its base. The walls were constructed primarily of clay, but they also incorporated waster tiles. Two short arched tunnels communicated between the stoking pit and the stoking chambers. The arches were constructed of clay voussoirs. The internal dimensions of the Norton kiln were 1.1 m long by 0.9 m wide, which can be compared with kiln 1 at Danbury, Essex, which measured 2.2 m by 2 m internally (Drury and Pratt 1975, 105), and the second kiln at Naish Hill, Lacock, which was 3 m by 1.85 m (McCarthy 1971, 180). Indeed, all other excavated kilns of which the dimensions are known are larger than that at Norton.

Experiments were carried out at Norton Priory to investigate the methods used by the medieval tile makers.

Fig. 86. The kiln in which the mosaic tiles were fired. The stoking pit is in the foreground, and fill remains in the arches to the pair of firing chambers. Many waster tiles have been incorporated in the structure.

A replica kiln was constructed on the basis of information derived from the excavated kiln (fig. 87). This exercise established the probable form of the original. The replica was fired on a number of occasions, and it was used to fire replica line impressed tiles made from the local boulder clay (fig. 88). Clay pits had been found in the excavation adjacent to the kiln. A considerable amount of information about the methods of making line impressed mosaic tiles was obtained (the full results are presented in Greene and Johnson 1978; two other articles describing the experiments are Greene 1980 and Greene 1981).

On the basis of the experimental data it was calculated that to produce 40,000 tiles the kiln had to be fired fifty-four times, assuming an optimum load of 750 tiles. With good organisation one firing a week would have been possible, so the floor could have been completed in two years. In late autumn, winter and early spring firing would not have been practicable because of the difficulties of drying both tiles and fuel – crucial factors, as our experiments showed. Presumably during the winter

months the floor could be laid, clay could be dug for weathering and brushwood for fuel could be gathered.

The date of the tile floor – evidence from the excavation

The most closely dated artifact to be found in a context that can be related to the mosaic floor is a silver penny of Edward I that was minted in 1302 (report supplied by Marion Archibald of the Department of Coins and Medals, British Museum, in which she emphasises the potentially long period of circulation). The coin was found in a deposit of mortar which had been used to fill a depression in the strip of tiles which formed the threshold up to the lady chapel within the opening from the north transept (fig. 74). The depression had been caused by the subsidence of the floor into the softer fill of a grave, which had been cut from the floor surface which preceded the tile floor. It is likely that the floor was laid soon after the grave had been filled and before the fill had compacted. If this is correct, the subsidence of the tile floor must have occurred soon after it was laid. No attempt was made to dismantle the floor and relay it – the depression was simply filled with

Fig. 87. Experimental kiln, made of clay dug on the site, and fired to test the effectiveness of the excavated tile kiln, the dimensions of which it replicated. Brush wood was the most effective fuel. A drying shed can be seen in the background: having thoroughly dried tiles proved essential for successful firing.

Fig. 88. Replica tiles – products of the experimental kiln, and all exact copies of tiles found in the church at Norton.

mortar. If it took say ten years for this to take place, and if the coin had been in circulation for, say, two decades, it would put the construction of the floor at about 1312. It would be safer to say that the probable date, on the basis of the coin evidence, is 1312 ± 10. When the affinities of the floor are discussed it will be suggested that a date towards the end of that span is in fact correct. It must also be noted that the coin could have been in circulation for much longer before its deposition. Coin evidence alone could not therefore be relied upon to provide a date for the floor.

Characteristics of the Norton Priory mosaic floor tiles

Two main classes of mosaic tile floors are found in Britain. Plain tile mosaic was used in the east end of the Corona of St Thomas in Canterbury Cathedral before 1220; there is a possibility that it was being made at Byland Abbey as early as 1197 (Eames 1980, 34). This type of floor consists of small shaped tiles which when assembled form geometric arrangements. It is thought to have originated as a less expensive substitute for stone and marble mosaic (*ibid.*, 72). The thirteenth century is the period during which plain tile mosaic was used. It proved particularly popular in the Yorkshire Cistercian abbeys, but it is also found at many sites elsewhere in Britain and on the Continent.

Although occasional tiles which formed part of otherwise plain mosaic floors have inlaid decoration or line impressed decoration these are rare characteristics. The class of mosaic tile floor to which the Norton pavement belongs has line impressed decoration as a common feature (fig. 92). It is therefore known as line impressed mosaic. Other characteristics are the relatively large size of the tiles compared to plain mosaic, and their lesser thickness.

The Norton tile makers employed a variety of techniques to achieve a range of effects. An examination of their considerable versatility presents the best chance of identifying affinities between the Norton floor and others elsewhere. The full repertoire of techniques is listed here; some are illustrated in figs. 85 and 92.

1. Plain tiles bearing no surface decoration other than the glaze

These are mainly large tiles which when assembled form the recurring centrepiece of a design such as the six-petalled flowers, or very small elements such as the hexagons in the stars and hexagons border. The variety of the floor is such that whereas in one panel the centrepiece tiles might be plain, elsewhere they might have line impressed decoration or even individually drawn embellishment – see 7 and 8 below.

2. Tiles with impressed lines which emphasise their shape

This particularly applies to the background tiles of the patterns which include large centrepiece tiles such as the lemons, the six-petalled flowers, and the elongated pointed quatrefoils. One interesting aspect of this technique is that it reveals the intention of the tile makers to create cusps on some designs. In most cases the cusp is represented purely by the shape of the tile and the emphasis of the lines, but the tile makers experimented with ways of further emphasising the cusp. Two methods were used. One was to excise the slip in the triangular area demarcated by the cusp. All the background tiles are yellow, so removal of part of the spread of light coloured clay revealed the darker body beneath it. The second method was to add iron to the glaze covering the triangular area. This fired to a dark brown or black colour, but had a tendency to spread. Whether by simply using the impressed lines, or by excision or by differential glazing there can be no doubt that the intention of the tile makers was to create the effect of a reticulated cusped tracery. A band of cusps emphasised by differential glazing was found *in situ* in the southern nave chapel.

3. Pseudo-mosaic geometric tiles

Elizabeth Eames distinguished a technique which she classified as pseudo-mosaic whereby medieval tile makers used surface lines to give the impression that an individual tile was made up of a number of constituents. The practice can be observed on several types of mosaic tile from Norton, most commonly on geometric shapes. Both six- and eight-pointed star shaped tiles invariably have straight lines radiating from the centre to each indented angle, to give the impression that the tile is made up of six or eight small lozenge shaped tiles. The large lozenge (as well as being left plain or with stamped decoration) exhibits a variety of lines – in some cases dividing it into four, sometimes into nine, and sometimes nine with the centre unit removed and replaced by a small lozenge tile glazed a contrasting colour. This technique is sometimes used with square tiles which likewise can have a contrasting centre with a surround of eight units. They too are found divided into nine and four, left plain or bearing stamped decoration. A few inlaid tiles with lines to demarcate the inlaid part have also been found.

4. Line impressed tiles

The wooden tile stamps used to impress a decorative motif on the Norton mosaic floor include rosettes of a number of kinds, a 'smiling lion' face and a three-lobed leaf. The impressions are found on a wide variety of the tiles, including those described in their plain state in 1, the background tiles described in 2, the pseudo-mosaic tiles (3) and also rectangular border tiles. They do not appear on every tile, but their use within a particular pattern is consistent.

5. Inlaid two colour tiles

One method of producing an inlaid two colour tile was to stamp the moist clay and fill the cavity with clay of a contrasting (light) colour. This technique was used to produce a number of square tiles that formed a border between two bands of pattern. The design has a vine leaf growing from a stem from which a berry also grows; a bird on the stem pecks at the berry. The tiles alternated to produce a continuous, sinuous vine stem. The inlay is deep and a feature of its surface is the enhancement of the design with inscribed lines on the leaf and the bird – the eye and feathers for example. Individually produced inlaid tiles were also made.

6. Differentially glazed tiles

The use of iron as an additive to the glaze to emphasise the cusps has been noted above (2). A type of tile which is closely allied to those described in 5 also exhibits differential glazing. These square tiles were also used as a border, and have as their subject birds sitting on a plant. The overall glaze was slightly green, but iron was added to give parts of the background of the design a dark brown appearance which thins to an orange colour at the margins. The technique is also found on some of the special tiles described below.

Special tiles

The six categories of tile described above all formed part of the main floor. They were all manufactured by repeating the various techniques to produce series of tiles of the same type. 'Special' tiles, however, were either produced as single, individual tiles, or were standard tiles to which individual non-repeating embellishment was added.

7. Background tiles with writing

A number of tiles which formed the background to one of the patterns were found with individually inscribed cursive script, written on the curve to follow the shape of the tile and using the emphasising line (see 2) as a guideline. A few were found *in situ* in the south transept. Unfortunately the script has proved intractable, but that it is a genuine script there can be little doubt. Some of the tiles seem to have Roman numbers in addition to the script. Their significance may be in association with 8.

8. Mosaic tiles with individually drawn designs

A number of the larger mosaic tiles described in the plain condition above (1) have been found with designs inscribed upon them individually. They formed part of the floor in both transepts. Subjects include figures on horseback (hunting?) and birds in a tree. There is a possibility that the tiles with cursive inscriptions (7) were laid in association with these pictorial tiles, providing a text or captions.

9. Rectangular 'calendar' tiles

Two rectangular pictorial tiles were found as wasters in the kiln. One shows the lower half of the figure of a man treading grapes in a barrel (fig. 89). The other has the upper half of a man (apparently a religious man because he has a tonsure) with a plant, possibly pruning it. It is probable that the tiles are two from a set of twelve representing the labours of the months. Their size (*c.* 200 mm by 400 mm) and the fine surface detail suggest that they may have been designed as wall panels, but they

could also have been intended for risers of steps in a liturgically important location such as the entrance to the presbytery or the edge of an altar base. Their use in the floor cannot be eliminated on the basis of the easily worn detail of the design, for the undoubted floor tiles described above (8) are equally fine in their detail. The style of 8 and 9 is very similar. The calendar tiles were intended to have

Fig. 89. Tile with drawing of man (wearing minimal clothing) trading grapes in a barrel while holding onto a bar. This waster tile was found on the kiln site – it is underfired and the glaze has not formed properly. Scale in 10 mm divisions.

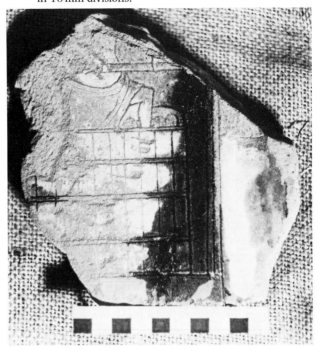

Fig. 90. Tile with parrot-like bird, open beak, crest and hollowed eye. Note the skilful drawing and use of inlaid pale clay to produce two colours. It was found incorporated in the back wall of the kiln (fig. 86). Scale in 10 mm divisions.

a polychrome appearance through a combination of different surface clays (red slip is used in addition to white on the grape-treader) and differential glazing. The evidence of small dots on the second calendar tile for pricking the design is an interesting aspect of the tile makers' technique. Presumably the design was drawn on parchment first. A third waster tile, built into the structure of the kiln, can be associated with the calendar tiles on the basis of a broad border strip common to all three. It features a bird, drawn in fine detail, including feathers, eye and large beak, and employs inlay and differential glazing to achieve its effect (fig. 90).

10. Large mosaic lions

Elements of large mosaic lions were found as wasters in the kiln, and loose within the area of the north east chapel. They were intended to constitute several different designs when they were assembled. One tile featuring an eye and part of a mouth was part of a large (c. 0.25 m) lion's face which stared directly out of the pavement (fig. 91). Other lions were shown in profile – a tile with jaws and nose must be part of a lion passant sinister. A large foot with claws found in the dump of tiles near the chapter house must be part of a large lion passant.

The tiles must have been assembled in panels which Elizabeth Eames has classified as mosaic *opus sectile* (Eames 1980, 36–9). Other tiles from Norton are shapes which were clearly intended to form the background.

The detail of the mosaic lions – mane, jaws, teeth, eyes, etc. – was executed freehand with a sharp blade. The mane and other hair is represented by characteristic flame-like details, cut deeply through the fairly thick (*c*. 2

to 3 mm) layer of light clay which forms the surface of the tile). The lions were glazed to appear yellow against a dark green background. They must have been a very impressive element of the floor of the north east chapel (and possibly elsewhere).

11. Other opus sectile *tiles*

Several tiles were recovered in the excavation from which the presence of other subjects can be inferred. One is a green glazed wing (once part of a gryphon or an angel?) which on the underside has a symbol cut out, in appearance similar to the numeral 6. One background tile bears the same symbol – an aid to the tile makers in locating elements of the same pattern after the tiles had been fired in the kiln? Other tiles are shaped to represent tree leaves (the veins are inscribed on the surface) and one tile is apparently the back of a head with hair drawn as grooves which follow the curve of the edge of the head. There is a strong possibility that these tiles once formed part of a picture mosaic panel.

12. Tiles associated with burials (fig. 11)

Tiles discovered in the north east chapels can be associated with the burial of members of the Dutton family. There are several types, all of which appear to have formed elements of one or more tomb covers. Long, narrow rectangular tiles have finely drawn Lombardic lettering inscribed into the surface of the light slip clay which covers the tiles. They must have been assembled to form a marginal inscription. Tiles with decoration intended to represent chain mail, again in the light clay surface, formed a life size *opus sectile* knight. A large shield, about 0.5 m high, bearing the Dutton fret, was found as wasters in the kiln; the successful product is likely to have formed part of the knight panel. Another waster tile can be associated with the grave cover. It has a design of inlaid clay emphasised by inscribed lines which is unmistakably a triangular crocketted canopy. The north east chapel had therefore at least one grave cover made of tiles in the manner of a memorial brass: a figure of a mailed knight with a full shield bearing his coat of arms, under a canopy and surrounded by a marginal inscription.

Analogies with memorial brasses

The features found in tiles at Norton can all be paralleled in brasses of the late thirteenth and early fourteenth century. For example, four brasses illustrated in Clayton 1929 (pl. 1) have knights wearing chainmail, with shields, and with feet resting on lions. They are Sir J. D'Aubernoun (Stoke d'Abernon, Surrey), 1277; Sir R. de Trumpington (Trumpington, Cambs.), 1289; Sir R. de Bures (Acton, Suffolk), 1302; Sir R. de Setvans (Chartham, Kent), 1306. Even closer to the Norton tiles is the brass of Sir J. de Creke (Westley Waterless, Cambs.), *c*. 1325, which has a knight in chainmail with a full shield and a lion (*ibid.*, pl 2). The brass of Sir J. D'Aubernoun (Stoke d'Abernon, Surrey), 1327, has all these features

Fig. 91. Lion's face, reconstructed from fragments of tiles from the north east chapel.

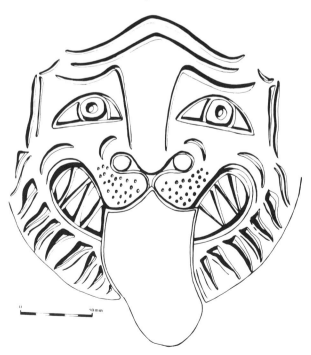

Fig. 92. Stamped decoration on the mosaic tiles, plus
(top left) a pair of inlaid tiles of birds and vine, and
alongside a similar design using differential glazing.

with the addition of a crocketted canopy (*ibid.*, pl. 5). A similar date for the Norton floor would therefore seem to be likely (see below). A simple triangular crocketted canopy of the type found on the Norton tile would be expected on a brass of this date (later they are usually ogival). An example is the brass of Joan, Lady de Cobham (Cobham, Kent), which dates from 1320 (illustrated Boutell 1847, 82).

Affinities of the Norton Priory mosaic tile floor

An outstanding characteristic of the Norton Priory mosaic tile floor is the wide range of techniques used by the tile makers, and their willingness to experiment to achieve their decorative effects. To assess the relationship of the Norton floor to other line impressed mosaic floors it is necessary to examine how the whole range of techniques employed at Norton compares with other floors of a similar type elsewhere.

The nearest similar floor to Norton covered the choir of the Augustinian friary church at Warrington. The two sites are just 8 km apart. The floor was discovered in 1887; a reassessment and comparison with the Norton floor has been published (Greene, Keen and Noake 1976). Points of similarity between the floors were identified, but there were also notable differences. In view of these it is unlikely that the same tile makers were responsible for both. The floors may represent the work of two groups of tile makers, using the same tile stamp and perhaps with some personnel in common (*ibid.*, 58). One possibility is that a locally recruited member of the team that created the Norton floor remained in the area after other members had moved on to another commission; he retained tile stamps and sufficient knowledge to make the Warrington tiles but he lacked the expertise and flair of the itinerant craftsmen.

The Warrington floor is therefore likely to have been made within a few years of the Norton floor. There is no evidence that it led to any more commissions for its maker.

Floors with *opus sectile* mosaic designs – Ely and Warden

Two outstanding mosaic tile floors share characteristics with the Norton Priory floor. The floor in Prior Crauden's chapel at Ely survives *in situ* in a standing building, with published illustrations appearing from as early as 1792 (Eames 1980, 84). The floor at Old Warden Abbey in Bedfordshire on the other hand was discovered as recently as 1974 (Webster and Cherry 1975, 233 and pl. XVIIB). The writer has been able to examine the Ely floor, and also had the opportunity of visiting Warden to see that tile floor *in situ*; Evelyn Baker has subsequently shown the writer the loose tiles recovered in her excavation.

The Ely floor has a number of features that are closely associated with the Norton floor. The most striking is the presence of various kinds of *opus sectile* lions. There

are fourteen panels of such lions, plus a gryphon and a dragon. The lions occur in two sizes. All the lions were glazed yellow using a light clay slip as at Norton. The most striking affinity with the Norton tiles is the manner of representing the mane and other hair with identical flame-like incisions. The treatment of the jaws and teeth is also identical in the few Ely examples where sufficient detail has survived. It appears that the eyes were filled with a dark clay – the only difference from Norton, but, given the use of darker inlay clay in for example the calendar tiles (9), not a particularly significant difference. The Norton eyes are cut deeply into the darker base clay (fig. 91).

The major panel at Ely is placed in front of the altar. It measures 1.15 m by 0.65 m and is occupied by a representation of the Temptation. Eve, Adam, the Serpent and the tree are depicted in four colours. The Norton *opus sectile* tiles (11 above) include one that is apparently the back of a head, and the others that represent tree leaves. It is possible that these were part of a picture mosaic – indeed they would not be out of place in a Temptation panel. That a panel of picture mosaic was placed in front of the altar of the Norton lady chapel in a similar manner to the Ely panel is certainly a possibility.

The Ely panel provides a direct link with Warden Abbey, where elements of an identical Temptation panel have been found – for example the head of the serpent (which is given a woman's face). Another link with both Ely and Norton is the discovery in the Warden floor of a lion's head. Its treatment has similarities, particularly in the representation of the mane, with the other two floors. The glazing on the Warden floor has survived virtually unworn. The eye of the lion was glazed black (using iron) whereas the rest is yellow through the use of a surface slip. The use of differential glazing at Warden is another strong link with Norton (the wear on the Ely floor makes judgements about its glaze difficult).

A strong affinity between the Warden and Norton floors is life size tomb covers. The Norton knight tomb has been described; at Warden elements of the tomb of an abbot have been found. At Warden tiles which constituted an *opus sectile* panel have 'labels' on the sides – words in Latin describing the parts of a body that the tiles represent. None of the Norton tiles have this, although the 'wing' like tile appears to have a keying symbol on the underside. However, the use of writing not only on the tomb marginal inscription (fig. 11) but also on the background tiles (category 7 above) gives the Norton floor an atmosphere of literacy that is striking and which provides another link with the Warden floor where the implication of literacy of at least one tile maker is unexpected but inescapable.

A further field of similarity between Norton and Warden is the execution of pictures on some tiles. At Warden elements of a 'rose window' design have been found embellished with subjects such as a knight, an angel and a lion. The use of inlay to provide a two colour effect on an individual basis is reminiscent of the use of the technique at Norton. The quality of the design and execution at both places is of a high order.

At all three sites most of the floor consisted of geometric designs. Although reproduction of specific arrangements at more than one site is limited, the overall approach to composition and the arrangement of elements is broadly similar. Common to all is the use of rosette stamps to embellish the tiles – as at Norton, the Ely and Warden floors employ single and double rosettes. The six-pointed star and small hexagon border are also common to all three. All share the use of pseudo-mosaic (including substitution of centres of tiles) by impressed divisions on square and lozenge shaped tiles. Pseudo-mosaic inlaid tiles are found at both Norton and Ely.

The Norton, Ely and Warden line impressed mosaic tile floors have so many characteristics in common, particularly with regard to the composition and execution of *opus sectile* panels and the overall technical excellence of the floors, that there is every likelihood that they were produced by a group of itinerant tile makers led by an accomplished individual who was responsible for design at all three sites.

The dates of the Norton, Ely and Warden floors

Documentary evidence suggests that the floor in Prior Crauden's chapel at Ely dates from 1324 (Eames 1980, 91). It has been argued (Keen 1979) that the panels of the floor (the lions and the Temptation) were intended for the lady chapel and were adapted for Prior Crauden's chapel following the collapse of the central tower in 1322. The argument is based on amendments to some of the panels, the view that the Temptation panel is out of scale, and a supposed iconographical scheme with lions on the steps of the throne of Solomon being the original intention for the lady chapel. I am not convinced by this argument. The existing pavement works well as a composition, the representation of Original Sin in front of a chapel altar at which the Eucharist was celebrated was appropriate, and the heraldic associations of the lions account for their widespread popularity. In addition, lions' heads are an architectural motif which can be found on the masonry decoration of Prior Crauden's chapel. A date for the Ely floor of 1324 is therefore accepted here.

The relationship of the Warden floor to that at Ely is difficult to assess. The presence of an identical Temptation panel at both sites suggests that their date is close, relying as it does on the existence of the same template. The Warden floor is the finest of the three. All the techniques, whether the placing of rosettes, the representation of the lion's mane or the detail of the inlaid slip figures, are assured and developed. The sense of confidence behind the Warden floor suggests that it was probably made after the Ely floor, but not long after, due to the use of the same template – sometime between 1324 and 1330?

A striking aspect of the Norton floor is the sense of experimentation – a wide range of techniques used to produce a variety of effects. This is most notable in the treatment of the cusping, but it also can be seen in the other uses of differential glazing, inlay and individually inscribed decoration. The Norton floor therefore gives the impression of being the earliest in the series, predating both Ely and Warden, produced by a team still developing their art but already capable of creating a floor of superb quality. The Norton floor therefore probably dates from before 1324. On the basis of stratigraphic and coin evidence, a date of 1312 ± 10 has been suggested for the Norton floor. Is there any historical evidence which correlates with this date range?

One clue is provided by the tomb cover, which must have related to the burial of a Dutton of the rank of knight. There are only two possible candidates, Hugh Dutton who died in 1294 and his son, another Hugh, who was born in 1276 and who died in 1326. The first date seems too early to be related to the floor, the second may be too late. However, it is possible that the floor was commissioned between those two dates by the younger Hugh who took the opportunity to provide a splendid cover for his father's grave. It need not therefore be related closely to either year of decease. Another factor was Norton Priory's relations with the Duttons, which periodically became strained. One such dispute reached the bishop's offices in 1315, when Sir Hugh de Dutton complained that the prior and convent had not provided a chaplain and a lamp at Poolsey Chapel (Beamont 1873, 170). The complaint was probably lodged after a period of antagonism during which the Duttons are unlikely to have felt particularly sympathetic towards the expense of donating a new floor to the priory church. The canons themselves were probably in a poor financial shape and were unlikely to have been able to afford it – in 1310 the prior had been accused of wasting the goods of the priory (*VCH Chester* 3, 166) so available finance was probably in short supply.

It can probably be assumed that after the problems with Poolsey chapel had been resolved in 1315 relations between the Norton brethren and their benefactors returned to normal. The Duttons might then have provided a floor (in which particular emphasis was placed on their burial chapel). Thus the most likely date for the Norton floor on historical grounds falls within the range 1315 to 1324, the latter date being that of the Ely floor. The Norton floor would have taken two years to complete under optimum conditions (it may have taken three or even four years however), and can therefore be assigned most probably to the period 1315 to 1324, with a start date of 1322 at the very latest. This accords with the latter part of the span suggested on stratigraphic and coin evidence (1312 ± 10). It is also consistent with the probable date provided by analogy with the memorial brasses discussed previously.

Other line impressed mosaic floors

If the Norton floor falls into a sequence Norton–Ely–Warden with a date range of possibly 1315 to 1330 (perhaps shorter), where did the tile makers come from to Norton, and are there other floors in the sequence between these three or later? These questions cannot be answered easily. There are probably other floors of this type still to be discovered, for in 1970 neither Norton nor Warden were known. Others must have been completely destroyed.

The Norton floor is not the only line impressed mosaic floor in western England and Wales. Eleven sites were mapped in 1972 (Eames and Keen 1972, fig. 2) to which the Norton and Warrington floors can be added, and a floor at Holme Cultram in Cumbria (Hodgson 1907); most recently mosaic tiles have been recovered from Lancaster (examined by the writer and published in Penney 1982). Of these floors only the Warrington floor can be closely related to that at Norton. None of the others has the appearance of being the product of the Norton craftsmen, although the expertise and standard of design of tile stamps of several is undoubtedly high (e.g. the Buildwas series, the Chester floor and the Bangor floor – described in Eames and Keen 1972). The tile arrangements of the Chester floor and the Buildwas series can be paralleled at Norton.

In eastern England many sites have produced evidence of line impressed mosaic (twenty-eight are shown on the map in Keen and Thackray 1974, fig. 50). Those which have closest affinity with the Norton–Ely–Warden series are Icklingham (*ibid.*); Higham Ferrers (Eames 1975); Meesden (Keen 1970) and Cambridge. Dating of the series has been discussed in Eames 1980, 91–2.

The fourteenth century – inactivity

After the substantial building operations in the late thirteenth and early fourteenth centuries there seems to have been inactivity for the remainder of the fourteenth century. No evidence has been found for any construction work during that century, after the laying of the tile floor. This is consistent with the impression of financial mismanagement given by documentary sources. To summarise:

> 1310 – prior accused of wasting the goods of the priory
> 1315 – dispute with the Duttons
> 1329 – election of prior declared invalid
> 1331 – high tides and flooding diminished Norton's finances
> 1349 – the Black Death
> 1354 – complaints of taxation of the spiritualites
> 1354 – disputes with the Duttons and the Astons

> 1357 – admonition to the prior for his 'illegal and rash contracts'
> 1358 – sale of Radcliffe on Soar to raise funds

The turning of the tide came in the 1360s with the election of Richard Wyche. There is no evidence that he engaged in building activities in his long tenure of office, which lasted until 1400. Instead he concentrated on reviving the priory's financial standing, and on enhancing the prestige of both Norton and himself. This culminated in the elevation of Norton to the status of a mitred abbey in 1391.

Fifteenth-century buildings

The elevation to abbey status was followed in the fifteenth century by the erection of a building adjoining the west range on its west side, projecting into the outer courtyard. The building appears to be a tower house which would have extended the abbot's accommodation beyond the upper floor of the west range, which had hitherto served the priors of Norton. The tower house is shown on the 1727 Buck engraving (fig. 18) and the late seventeenth-century Randle Holme sketch plan (fig. 17). The northernmost part of the structure's foundations was found in excavation in 1977. Restoration of the undercroft in 1974 revealed the junction with the main northern wall of the tower, with moulded vault ribs terminating in a corbel in the form of an angel with outstretched wings. The construction of the porch to the Georgian house in 1868 had removed all other traces of the tower house.

Together these different sources of information can be used to describe the tower house (fig. 29). It consisted of a large central block flanked on the north and south by two smaller blocks. That on the north may have served as a staircase tower. Its foundations were found to have a diagonal angle buttress which is also shown on the Randle Holme sketch. The latter also indicates a doorway on the north side. The engraving has a staircase turret emerging above the roof on the main tower; the turret is apparently hexagonal and has a door opening which gives access to the roof. On the south side was a second smaller tower. It was of two storeys, each with a three-light traceried window.

The main tower was approximately square in plan, measuring about 6.3 m north–south by 5.7 m east–west externally. Internally it was 5.1 m square. The engraving shows it to be twice the height of the walls of the undercroft, which would make it about 11.4 m high. The square headed door in the centre of the west face will have given access to the vaulted ground floor, from which the west range undercroft could also have been reached. The principal feature of the west elevation of the tower was a pair of tall oriel windows of half octagonal plan. They rose through most of the height of the building above the door. Two bands of glazing with a blank band between suggest that two separate storeys were illuminated by them. The building had a crenellated parapet.

The excavation produced no datable material in association with the foundations, so it is the mouldings and corbel which can alone provide an indication of the date of construction. The angel corbel has the upper torso and head missing; the remainder is carved to a good standard but is unhelpful as regards dating. The vault ribs consist of straight sides with convex surfaces in the angles. Their date is likely to be within the fifteenth century, probably in the latter half, which is consistent with the external appearance of the tower (comments by John Maddison, personal communication).

The accommodation of prelates in the late medieval period

The expansion of the abbot's quarters is by no means unique. Similar developments can be observed at many other religious houses of a similar size to Norton. By the fifteenth century the expectations of many prelates demanded enhanced accommodation – a phenomenon which transcends the differences between orders of monks and canons. At Lanercost a tower was added to the south

Fig. 93. Entrance track, leading to the site of the gatehouse. Successive remetallings of the part in the foreground had been necessitated by subsidence into a large twelfth-century drain. A wheel rut (filled with water) can be seen.

side of the refectory at its west end. Here the prior's concern may have been more with security in this turbulent part of Cumbria than with aggrandisement. At Haughmond the abbot was provided with a magnificent range of buildings. These comprised a large fourteenth-century hall, to which in the late fifteenth or early sixteenth century chambers of more than one storey with an elaborate bay window were added (Hope and Brakspear 1909, in which the hall is identified as the infirmary). At Cluniac Castle Acre Priory in the second half of the fourteenth century the prior occupied the whole of the west range, with added buildings on the west, for his own and his guests' use; they formed 'a fairly substantial secular mansion' (Raby and Reynolds 1952, 15–19). In the fifteenth century at Cistercian Valle Crucis, Clwyd, much of the monks' dormitory was converted into a hall for the abbot, with a chamber alongside it (Radford 1953, 17). It was the south range that became the abbot's house at Benedictine Muchelney Abbey in Somerset. At Gilbertine Watton Priory in Yorkshire an architecturally elaborate abbot's lodging was added in the late medieval period.

The expansion of the abbot's quarters at Norton was therefore part of a general trend. It is a measure of the degree of comfort and the extent of the facilities provided by the buildings cited above that all were utilised with little modification as post-Dissolution secular mansions.

The gatehouse

A gatehouse is shown on the left hand (northern) side of the Buck brothers' 1727 engraving (fig. 18). The excavation proved that all trace of it had been removed when the area to the west of the Georgian house was levelled in 1868, although part of the wall which ran to the undercroft did survive. The engraving shows it as a typical monastic gatehouse with a large opening for carts and carriages and a smaller one for pedestrians. It has a room above, and a lodge building on the western side. The Randle Holme sketch (fig. 17) confirms this plan. The gatehouse governed access to the outer courtyard, but the west door of the church could be reached without needing to enter the courtyard. The design of the windows on the engraving suggests a fifteenth-century date. A track, resurfaced on a number of occasions, was found in the 1976 excavations leading to the site of the gatehouse (fig. 93). It was still standing when the J.E. 1757 estate map (fig. 13) was drawn but it had been demolished when the perspective drawing (RIBA Library – Paul Mellon collection) was made for the Brookes as part of their battle with the duke of Bridgewater in about 1770 (fig. 21).

The north aisle of the church

In the fifteenth century an aisle was added to the nave on its north side. The only evidence for date is provided by a small amount of pottery found in the rubble and mortar makeup of the aisle. Only the foundations survived, without any associated mouldings. They were substantial, consisting of blocks of sandstone bonded with clay. Some of the sandstone was re-used. It included fragments of

Fig. 94. Model of the church, with the north aisle in the foreground; above it clerestory lights are assumed. To the right is the early thirteenth-century extension of the nave. All that remains visible of the twelfth-century core is the north transept and lower part of the tower.

sandstone grave slabs. The west end of the aisle did not extend as far west as the nave. It had a diagonal buttress at its north west corner, and four projecting buttresses along the north wall. It is likely that the wall separating the nave from the aisle was pierced by arches but no direct evidence for this survived. It also seems likely that the roof of the aisle was built lean-to against the north wall of the nave; the latter would presumably have been provided with clerestory windows (fig. 94). No floor surfaces survived in the aisle but many of the graves contained fragments of the second tile floor (see below), so it may once have had such a floor. At the eastern end an altar base was found, behind which were the foundations of a screen wall. Further east was a second wall. The significance of the latter may be that the dog-leg passage around the north west pier was enlarged by taking down the twelfth-century wall and incorporating the same principle in the new structure.

The aisle is unlikely to have been needed for extra accommodation for the living in the nave of the church. The floor area of the nave following its extension westwards in the late twelfth- to early thirteenth-century expansion was about 210 square metres. The aisle added about 82 square metres. As there is no evidence of worship by lay people in the nave at Norton it is unlikely that the extra space would have been needed for an enlarged congregation – which would be unexpected in the fifteenth century anyway. Instead, as with the transept chapels, the aisle seems more likely to have been built to accommodate the dead. Within the aisle were numerous burials, particularly in front of the altar.

Many Augustinian churches were aisle-less in their original plan. If circumstances for expansion of the nave occurred, the presence of the cloister on the south prevented the construction of an aisle there. A number of Augustinian churches share with Norton the characteristic of a nave with one aisle on its northern side. Examples

Fig. 95. Mosaic tile floor, showing variations in wear between tiles near the wall, and those where movement of the canons has been more intensive – particularly on the left which is close to the processional door to the east cloister walk.

Fig. 96. The fifteenth-century tile floor which replaced the worn mosaic floor (fig. 95). There is marked variation in wear – indicating for example that there was an opening in the pulpitum screen between its southern end and the nave altar base (represented by the fragmentary stone blocks on the right). The slate and brick drain is nineteenth-century in date.

are Bolton, Brinkburn, Burscough, Canons Ashby, Haughmond, Lanercost, Lilleshall and Newstead.

The fifteenth-century tile floor

The lack of precision with dating applies not only to the Abbot's tower and the north aisle, but also to a tile floor. Even 'fifteenth-century' is based on likelihood rather than hard evidence as far as the floor is concerned. As it post-dates the mosaic floor it was nearer to the ground surface and was therefore more susceptible to gardening and the other destructive activities. Despite damage, its constituents can be described and its extent can be estimated. In the choir it was laid to replace the mosaic floor, the central panel of which had become very worn as a result of processions and other traffic up the centre of the church. In many places the tiles had been reduced to half their original thickness (fig. 95). A layer of mortar was spread over the existing floor and the new tiles were set on it (fig. 96).

The floor consisted mainly of counter relief tiles of a limited repertoire of geometric designs (fig. 97). They were square, and were laid in east–west bands but arranged to run diagonally within the bands. Each band was separated from its neighbour by a single line of tiles of the same type. Petrological analysis (D. Williams, Southampton University) has shown that the tiles were similar in their constituents to the mosaic tiles, but this only proves that they were made of boulder clay. This is so widespread in Cheshire as to be without value for defining kiln sites.

One building, possibly of fifteenth-century date, remains a mystery. It had seven sides, and was situated south of the warming room in the east range. It was badly damaged by a cistern and culverts in the eighteenth century.

Building operations in the decades preceding the Dissolution

Two pieces of building work took place in the period prior to the Dissolution. One was a contraction of the southern part of the dormitory range, where a building was erected which made use of the east and south walls but required a new wall for its west and north sides. This narrowed the building to 3.66 m internally; its length was 15.28 m. The foundations incorporated re-used masonry. Pottery (particularly fragments of urine jugs – jordans) testified to its pre-Dissolution date. Its function is unknown. It is possible that further north the dormitory continued to function as previously; a degree of retrenchment at its southern end would still have left plentiful room for the small number of canons at this date.

The second building operation to be carried out in the early sixteenth century was, by contrast, an ambitious architectural scheme. It involved the demolition of the mid-thirteenth-century arcade, fragments of which were used as rubble in the foundations. The new cloister had a very unusual plan (fig. 4). It was symmetrical about both the east-west and north-south axes. Each side consisted of a central projecting bay flanked by a pair of regularly placed buttresses (fig. 98). On the cloister garth side was a facing consisting of foundation blocks, a second course of rectangular ashlar blocks 0.25 m high, and a capping

Fig. 97. A geometric, continuously repeating pattern, part of the fifteenth-century floor (0.5 m scale).

Fig. 98. Foundations of the sixteenth-century wall on
the south side of the cloister. The central rectangular
projecting bay can be seen, and the pair of buttresses
either side. Between them and the angled facing were
found all the fragments of the thirteenth-century cloister
arcade (figs. 58–63).

course of 0.15 m blocks projecting 0.04 m. The angles on each side of the projecting bays were faced diagonally; the facing then ran straight to the corners of the garth.

The structure within the garth was difficult to resolve. The most likely arrangement consisted of a central grassed area retained by a small wall following the line of the cloister facing or simply square in plan. In places the existence of such a wall, subsequently completely robbed, was suggested by the configuration of the underlying boulder clay. Water stood in the area between the cloister wall facing and the putative retaining wall. In the centre of the west face of the cloister wall was a drain with an invert above the level of the cloister drain invert through which water flowed out from the garth. This was a re-use of a drain which had been inserted when the mid-thirteenth-century cloister arcade was built. Thus water was held in the cloister garth by design; it would have been fed by roof water from the inner sides of the four claustral ranges. The western drain acted as an overflow. The second possibility is that water covered the entire area of the garth. For this to be the case it has to be assumed that all the soil within the garth was placed there after its abandonment. This may indeed be the case, for it contained a great deal of 'rubbish' (pottery, organic objects and some animal bone) and a number of fragments of demolished buildings. Their presence however could be explained by objects sinking into a marshy cloister if the drainage had ceased to function in the years of abandonment following the Dissolution. What cannot be in doubt however is that the level of the cloister garth was deliberately reduced as part of the new scheme. This had the objective of creating a situation in which water would accumulate. Thus, whether the existence of a broad decorative drain or the entire flooding of the cloister garth is the correct interpretation, what cannot be doubted is that expanses of water formed part of a remarkable architectural scheme.

The date of the new cloister

The context which provided the most useful source of datable artifacts which could be directly associated with the construction of the new cloister was the infill between the foundations and the facing. Here rubble (mainly fragments of the demolished cloister arcade) and boulder clay were packed. Pieces of black or dark brown iron glazed pottery were found within this fill. Elsewhere at Norton iron glazed pottery is found only in the very latest medieval layers and in post-Dissolution layers. Thus the new cloister wall must have been constructed in the decades prior to the Dissolution (or soon afterwards).

It might be argued that the elaborate cloister was not monastic, but part of the post-Dissolution mansion. This can be rejected on several grounds. A rebuilding of the cloister after the Dissolution would imply an adaption of the claustral ranges as a residence on a pattern similar to that at Newstead Abbey, Nottingham, or Lacock Abbey, Wiltshire. However, there is no evidence that any of the ranges except the west range were utilised as part of the Tudor house. There is no doubt that the Brookes, who purchased Norton in 1545, did not have the capital resources to engage in expensive building operations. Richard Brooke had taken out mortgages totalling £1,500 (*inquisition post mortem* of 1569, Cheshire Record Office CR 63/1/226 [7]) – a sum approximating to Norton's purchase price. He had experienced difficulty in paying the £1512 1s 9d purchase price to the Crown (*Cal. Patent Rolls*, Mary, 24, Dec. 1553). Brooke had little option but to adapt the most suitable part of the abbey – the west range – as his residence. The cloister became an enormous rubbish dump. It is highly unlikely that the expensive work on the cloister was put in hand by the Brookes who then allowed it to be filled with rubbish. In the south west corner of the cloister the structure incorporated a small stone drain which emptied into the cloister drain. The stone drain carried water across the south cloister walk from a block with a square dished surface set in the north face of the refectory wall at floor level. This must have been where the downspout from the lavatorium emptied. The lavatorium, where the canons washed their hands before meals, was an essential part of monastic life but had no significance following the Dissolution. The incorporation of the drain in the new cloister wall must imply that it was constructed when monastic life was still taking place at Norton.

The cloister must therefore have been constructed prior to 1536, during the period in which iron glazed pottery was in use (1500 to 1536 seems most likely).

The form of the cloister

There can be little doubt that the rebuilt cloister was designed to be roofed by a masonry vault, unlike its predecessor which would have had a timber lean-to roof. The size and depth of the foundations, as well as the presence of the buttresses, are consistent with the extra support required by a vaulted structure. The spacing of the buttresses would have permitted a window between each pair. One motive for building the new cloister walk must have been the desire for more shelter in comparison with the draughty open arcade.

The major puzzle is the presence of the projecting bays in the centre of each side. They are a unique feature, although several sites have a single projecting bay. At Croxden Abbey, Staffordshire, there is one such feature opposite the entrance to the chapter house. At Strata Florida (Dyfed), a shallow half octagon bay projects from the centre of the north side. Byland, Yorkshire, has a rectangular bay in this position. The early arrangement at Jerpoint, Co. Kilkenney, had a similar projecting bay on the north side in the twelfth century – an arrangement which was repeated in the successor cloister alley of the fifteenth century. Tintern had a rectangular projection into the cloister garth on the north. The Croxden bay has been interpreted as a porch, but the suggested function of the bays at Strata Florida, Byland, Jerpoint and Tintern is to provide light for the collation reader's lectern (Gilyard-Beer 1981, 130).

The presence of four bays at Norton is difficult to explain. They could have been used for a variety of purposes, for example as carrels (i.e. places for the canons to study), bookstores, or porches leading to the cloister. In terms of their architectural appearance the last suggestion may be the most appropriate. The construction of each side of the cloister in the form of a porch, flanked by walls pierced with windows and strengthened by buttresses, would have been impressive in appearance. This accords with Gilyard-Beer's view that the Norton bays 'are more likely to have been an architectural embellishment than to have served any practical purpose' (*ibid.*).

The form of the cloister with its projecting bays and use of water was therefore essentially decorative. It can be seen as partly in the spirit of formal Tudor gardens and partly in the tradition of the monastic cloister. It demonstrates that right to the end of its days Norton was capable of architectural design and embellishment embodying quality and innovation.

It is conceivable that the cloister supported an upper floor as at Newstead and part of Lacock, but it is unlikely. With the diminished number of brethren there was no shortage of space at Norton at this date. Such a major building operation in the decades which preceded the Dissolution need cause no surprise. Although with hindsight the early sixteenth century appears to be the twilight of monasticism in England, there is no evidence that there was any sense of impending doom at the time. To engage in a construction programme at a religious house which had already existed for over three and a half centuries was merely to continue a lengthy tradition. There are numerous instances of religious houses engaging in building works at this time. At St Werburgh's Abbey, Chester, the monks constructed a new vaulted cloister between 1525 and 1530 (Pevsner and Hubbard 1971, 147). The structure of the cloister pays little heed to the existing masonry on the west and north sides, cutting across the lavatorium etc. Possibly further building work was intended to follow the remodelling of the cloister but was prevented by the Dissolution.

Fire repairs

Some of the last building works to be carried out at Norton before the Dissolution are those referred to in the request by Abbot William Merton (1510–17) endorsed by Henry VIII (Cheshire Record Office DAR/G/50/1). The warrant enabled the abbot to receive thirty oaks from Delamere Forest to make boards and shingles to repair buildings damaged by fire. Nothing else is known of this accident and no archaeological traces of it were found. During Merton's abbacy Norton was in debt to the Crown in 1511, 1512 and 1515 (*Letters and Papers Henry VIII*, 2, 1484; 1, 1493 and 2, 1364). It is possible that the grant of the oaks was not without charge – if it occurred in 1510 it would explain the unpaid debt.

In 1525 the episcopal visitation had to be held in the abbot's oratory as the chapter house was dilapidated. Repairs were ordered within the resources of the house (Heath 1973, 126–7). The location of the oratory is not specified – it may have been above the passage at the north end of the west range, or more likely it was a feature of the abbot's tower house.

The Dissolution

On 10 October 1536 the King's commissioners Combes and Bolles arrived to dissolve the abbey of Norton. A mêlée ensued during which they were forced to take refuge in a tower, according to Sir Piers Dutton's account of the night's events (*Letters and Papers Henry VIII*, 11, 681, p. 265). It seems likely that the tower referred to was not the church tower but the abbot's tower house. When Sir Piers eventually arrived the rioters disappeared, fleeing into the 'pools and waters'. This must refer to the moat system which surrounded the priory (fig. 13).

Once the abbot and canons had been removed religious life ceased. The church was probably made uninhabitable by removing the roof. It is likely that the other buildings simply stood empty, slowly deteriorating, until the purchase by Sir Richard Brooke almost nine years later.

The Brooke purchase (Beamont 1873, 200–2) specified that it included lead gutters and windows but excluded all other lead and bell metal, which was reserved by the Crown. When they took up residence the Brookes concentrated on the buildings of the outer courtyard. The cloister became a rubbish dump. After four centuries as a religious house, a new era had begun for Norton.

8
Conclusions

Augustinian foundations were more numerous than those of any other order in England (fig. 5). They were also close to the mainstream of English monasticism. Information derived from Norton Priory is therefore often of general relevance – the priory can be regarded as representative of medium sized English monasteries.

Foundation and endowment

The single most important factor in determining the future success of the priory, apart from the act of foundation itself, was the decision to move from Runcorn to Norton. The possible reasons for the move have been discussed and placed in the context of changes of site of other houses (usually involving shorter distances in the case of Augustinian houses than of Cistercian houses). The Norton canons moved away from the settlement and river crossing point of Runcorn to a peaceful location where demands of hospitality would have been lighter. Birkenhead Priory, established beside another ferry crossing nearer the mouth of the Mersey, suffered a financial drain as a result of its convenience for travellers (*VCH Chester* 3, 129). Of much greater importance however was the possession by the canons of a large, compact land holding in the form of the manor of Norton (comprising the townships of Norton and Stockham) to which Eanley was later added. Aggregation of scattered properties was a problem that faced many monasteries; it often took generations to achieve a rationalised pattern of ownership. The canons of Norton were fortunate to achieve an efficient ownership structure at an early date.

The manor was valuable both in its Domesday assessment and in its economic potential. The Domesday survey listed its value as sixteen shillings in 1086 – one of only six manors in Bucklow hundred to exceed ten shillings (Higham 1982, 17). Ploughlands surrounded

the two nucleated settlements of Norton and Stockham. The priory was located in previously unexploited land, as pollen analysis proved. The canons must therefore have initiated a programme of utilising the land around them. They must also have been the driving force behind the draining and embanking of the low lying marshland alongside the Mersey at the northern end of the manor. In this activity they shared in a widespread reclamation movement carried out by religious houses. Other examples are the clearance of marsh in the Lincolnshire fens by Ramsey, Peterborough, Spalding and Crowland abbeys, and drainage of the Somerset Levels by Glastonbury Abbey (Platt 1984, 73). The digging of the moats around Norton Priory, as part of an integrated water management scheme, was another heavy investment in improvement – involving at least the equivalent of forty labourers for three years.

The manor of Norton was a valuable asset at the time of the Dissolution – £78 10s 5¼d according to the Augmentation Office Ministers' Accounts. Norton's total of six manors or granges in 1536 corresponds closely to the average for Augustinian houses (6.5).

Resources

The Dissolution assessment expresses Norton's monetary value in the sixteenth century, but the examination of the resources of the manor gives a better idea of its true worth to the canons over the period of four centuries. There can be little doubt that a considerable range of their requirements could be produced from within its boundaries.

Some of the materials which would have been bought in from outside include lead for a wide range of plumbing activities, iron ore for smelting on site, glass for windows and lime for mortar. Cloth for garments and leather footwear were probably bought at local markets. Wine and pepper are two commodities that the canons used which must have been imported. However, unless the canons developed a taste for the exotic and expensive of the kind that cost the monks of Whalley more than half their annual income (Ashmore 1962), the great majority of their requirements could be met from their own resources. The cellarer could have obtained most of his needs at the markets of Halton and Frodsham. Goods produced further afield (such as wine) would have been bought at Chester, the principal port of north west England. The extent of self-sufficiency is underlined by the pottery found at Norton. The great bulk of it is locally produced; there are small quantities of Stamford ware (brought from the priory's Lincolnshire properties?) as well as a little Saintonge polychrome pottery and German stoneware (both associated with wine imports).

Economic management

By the sixteenth century Norton's land was managed in two ways. The demesne in Norton manor was largely kept in hand, and the lands owned elsewhere, in Cheshire and beyond, were let out to rent. This pattern is clear from the Augmentation Office Commissioners' Accounts. Elsewhere there had been large scale abandonment of demesne farming by the late fourteenth century (Platt 1984, 188). There was nothing inherently superior about demesne farming, and the pattern adopted by Norton seems a rational solution to management problems associated with widely scattered holdings. Directly farmed demesne could provide the bulk of the canons' needs. Rent and lease income from the other holdings and from tithes would have been paid in cash – easy to collect using the system of stewards and bailiffs, and at a pre-determined level which would have facilitated accounting and budgeting. Norton's mix of demesne and leased farming can be regarded as an eminently sensible use of resources. In the late fifteenth century the rise in demand and commodity prices enabled monastic houses that had retained control of some of their land to profit from it – an increase in income that might be reflected in renewed building activity (*ibid.*, 209). Norton's rebuilding of its cloister at this period accords with the general pattern. In 1536 29.5% of Norton's temporal income was derived from its demesne compared to 17.7% in a sample of thirty-one other Augustinian houses based on their *Valor* assessments (Robinson 1980) – an indication of the large size of Norton's home farm.

The varying quality of financial management at Norton has been described. The explanation of the repeated crises which affected so many religious houses is simple. The system of election of abbot or prior often brought to the fore a person whose qualities, whatever their positive aspects, did not include financial prudence and husbandry. Despite the responsibilities of the cellarer and sacrist in some areas of management, the concentration of power in the hands of the near autocratic superior might lead to over-ambitious building schemes, corrupt practices or sheer incompetence. Thus 1310 'wasting the goods', 1354 'indiscreet undertakings' and 1357 'illegal and rash contracts' are phrases used about priors of Norton, but which could be applied to the actions of certain superiors at almost all religious houses. The system itself was bound to lead to such results. In contrast, the emergence of a good manager could restore the economic (and spiritual) well-being of a house. The example of Richard Wyche is prominent in the history of Norton. From the problems of the first half of the fourteenth century, Richard restored Norton's fortunes to the extent that it was possible to obtain abbey status in 1391.

Accidents and natural disasters

The effects of accidents and natural disasters on a religious house could be traumatic both for the morale of its inmates and its economy. A blow could be so serious that a house might never fully recover. The example of Creake, an Augustinian abbey in Norfolk is extreme. In 1483 a fire destroyed a considerable portion of the buildings; in 1506 an outbreak of disease killed all the canons. The twin disasters led to the closure of the abbey. However, it is the resilience of most religious houses in the face of catastrophe that is generally impressive. The certainty of continuity in a permanent corporation meant that, whatever the setback, restoration had to begin. It is the speed and quality of response that is a guide to the spirit and economic strength of a religious house at a particular date. Five disasters of various kinds are known to have struck Norton. Others must undoubtedly have occurred but have not left any record.

The fire of 1236 is an event which is mentioned in a document (the Whalley Abbey annals) and which also left extensive traces in the archaeological record. It is an excellent example of how archaeological and historical sources can be complementary, the former providing different categories of information to the latter. In particular the rebuilding of the cloister as a highly elaborate structure is a vivid demonstration of Norton's self-confidence and financial health in the mid-thirteenth century.

Flooding of Norton's lands, leading to an application to fully appropriate Castle Donnington church to compensate for the resulting loss of income, came in a half century in which the priory suffered a variety of problems. Flooding however was not of its own making. Climatic deterioration affected many religious houses at this time, cutting crop yields and livestock numbers as well as rental income (Platt 1984, 127). Appropriation of churches was frequently the response of houses whose income had been reduced.

The direct effect of the Black Death in 1349 and subsequent years upon Norton Priory is not known. The election of a new prior in that year might be coincidence. The indirect consequences will however have been felt by the canons thereafter: difficulties of recruitment of brethren, shortage of tenants for rented lands, problems with labour on demesne land. No religious house could escape completely from such a misfortune.

In 1429 floods and ruined buildings are recorded. No further information is available about them, or of the response by the canons. The fifth disaster is the fire in the early sixteenth century which resulted in the grant of oaks from Delamere Forest for repairs. Nothing else is known about the fire but again the canons repaired the damage. The fact that the visitation of 1529 had to take place in the abbot's oratory rather than the ruined chapter house may be connected with the fire. However, 'ruined' can be interpreted as 'in disrepair' so lack of maintenance may be the explanation.

Spiritualities

Norton's original endowment included seven churches. Of these Runcorn and Budworth were local, whereas Pirton in Oxfordshire, Kneesall and Ratcliffe upon Soar in Nottinghamshire, Castle Donnington in Leicestershire and Burton on Stather in Lincolnshire were located in more distant parts of England where the baron of Halton held properties. St Michael's, Chester, and Grappenhall were local churches which were subsequently given to Norton and were eventually disposed of. Grants of tithes completed Norton's ownership of spiritualities. Spiritualities were therefore a very important part of Norton's endowment. Their value is clearly demonstrated when expressed as a percentage of total income in 1536 (based on the *Valor*). When all orders are considered, spiritualities account for 20% of monastic income. The Augustinian order was more dependent, relying on spiritualities for 36% of income. In the case of Norton no less than 56% of income in 1536 was provided by spiritualities. By this date Norton retained only five churches. As well as St Michael's, Chester, the date of disposal of which is unknown, Radcliffe had been sold in 1357, Kneesall in 1459 and Grappenhall in 1460 – all in response to severe economic difficulties. The remaining five were all fully appropriated, with Norton having the right to provide canons as priests. They were therefore the most valuable to retain, with an average value £28 per annum – considerably greater than the average for Augustinian owned churches of £11 14s 0d.

Patrons and benefactors

As with many other aspects of Norton's existence, its circle of patrons and benefactors was very local. Barons of Halton were active in support of the canons in the period 1115 to 1200 when the barony was based at Halton Castle. Thereafter until the endowment was complete in about 1330 the Duttons assumed a dominant role through the two branches of the family. The restricted nature of the circle of support is further emphasised when benefaction from further afield is examined. Gifts by William de Warenne, Roger fitz Alured and their like result from marriage by their relatives to patrons or benefactors. Small gifts came from the bishop of Chester and the earl of Chester, but these were a tiny part of the total endowment.

Members of the barons' families were buried at Norton, but none of the barons themselves. Instead, the dominant mortuary role was assumed in relation to the Duttons. From foundation to dissolution Duttons were buried in the church, with the north east chapel, the lady chapel, becoming the family mausoleum. A striking link between documentary evidence and that from excavation is provided by the memorial tiles. Periodic disputes about the provision of chaplains at the Duttons' chapels did not permanently damage the mutual dependence between the lay protectors and donors on one hand and their spiritual advisers on the other.

Building activities

The close correlation between evidence produced by the excavation and historical information is at its most impressive when the expansion of buildings in the late twelfth and early thirteenth centuries is compared to the growth in the endowment and the indications from later poll tax assessments of a doubling of the number of canons. The impact of the fire of 1236, leaving not only the debris of the disaster but also the evidence of repair and recovery, is another instance. The diminution of building activities throughout the bulk of the fourteenth century accords with the troubled state of the priory's finances at that time. Recovery in the latter part of the century culminated in abbey status, which in turn demanded new building work – a tower house for the abbot built in the fifteenth century. The erection of the remarkable new cloister in the decades preceding the Dissolution testifies to a spirit of confidence at a late stage in Norton's history.

The most impressive feature of building operations at Norton is however the quality of workmanship that is demonstrated throughout its history. It is evident from the excavated remains that masons of very high quality worked on different building schemes. This is all the more remarkable given the lack of an indigenous building industry in the north west until the late medieval period.

The evidence of quality is apparent from the beginnings of work at Norton. The timber buildings were impressive structures, built of carefully shaped and positioned timbers. The paucity of comparative material elsewhere makes it impossible to assess the buildings in terms of the generality of temporary monastic quarters. The twelfth century church however can be compared with contemporary buildings for similarly sized communities. The adoption of a simple cruciform church for a community of thirteen brethren is not restricted to the Augustinian order – Cistercian, Benedictine and Premonstratensian examples exist. The church was laid out utilising simple ratios with a likely foot of 0.295 m. The quality of workmanship was high. The beak-heads, the probable source of the canons in Bridlington Priory, the Yorkshire connections of the founder and Eustace fitz John, and the name of the master mason (Hugh de Cathewic) all indicate that at this date Norton's architectural links crossed the Pennines.

When the expansion of the buildings began towards the end of the century it involved most of the priory. The south and west ranges, the west and east ends of the church, the rere-dorter, the transept chapels, the chapter house – all were either extended or rebuilt on a larger scale. The evidence of the west range undercroft, particularly of the passage, is of workmanship of a very high standard, truly Transitional in design and experimental in detail. The date of the passage (and of the undercroft) is within the decades either side of 1190. The mason appears to have been attracted, not from Yorkshire, but from the West Country. The Romanesque doorway cannot be attributed to any particular regional source, but it is part of the late twelfth-century expansion campaign. As the finest surviving Romanesque doorway in Cheshire it is another example of the canons' demand for high quality embellishment of their buildings as part of the rebuilding of the priory. This demand can also be seen in the erection of the new west front; although fragmentary even at foundation level, sufficient survived to demonstrate that it was intended to dominate the outer courtyard.

The significance of the spirited response to the fire of 1236 has been discussed above. Architecturally its result was a masterpiece – a most elaborate and accomplished cloister arcade wall. The mix of secular subjects – animals, heads, grotesques and foliage – with apparently religious themes in the spandrel sculpture is found in contemporary schemes in some major ecclesiastical buildings. The West Country may have been the home area of the mason.

Travelling bell makers were brought to Norton in the twelfth and thirteenth centuries, on each occasion to cast a large bell for the church. Their home bases are not known, but the casting operations are two further examples of the need to import specialist craft skills for

tasks associated with building operations. A further example is provided by the fourteenth-century tile makers who created the fine mosaic tile floor. Their origins remain a tantalising mystery. After leaving Norton, they may have gone to Ely and later Warden Abbey. Once again, the canons had employed craftsmen of the highest calibre – possibly financed by the Duttons, whose family chapel received an ornate new floor.

It is suggested that the finance for the construction of the eastern chapel may have resulted from actual or anticipated donations by pilgrims to the 'holy cross' that the chapel was probably designed to house. The tracery of the east window is of an unusual design, the closest parallels being in St Albans Abbey and Merton College Chapel, Oxford.

Insufficient is known about the buildings of the fifteenth century – the abbot's tower, the gatehouse, and the north aisle – to make any judgements about the origins of the masons who built them. However, in contrast to previous centuries this was a period of intensive building in Cheshire, the reasons for which are obscure – a sudden burst of ambitious church architecture in the fifteenth century and the first half of the sixteenth century (Pevsner and Hubbard 1971, 12). Whatever the source of prosperity may have been, it resulted in activity which could sustain a home-grown Cheshire building industry. Thus the mason who designed and built the remarkable new cloister in the years before the Dissolution was probably recruited locally. A man such as Thomas Hunter, who built the fine tower at St Helen, Witton (Northwich), the rich chapel of ease of Great Budworth – where it is probable that he also built a tower (*ibid.*, 227)

Fig. 99. The eighteenth-century country house. The medieval undercroft was hidden behind the ground floor facade at the left hand end. The external steps were removed and replaced by an entrance porch incorporating the Norman doorway (fig. 54) in 1868. The sheep were highly effective lawn mowers for the parkland.

– would be an obvious choice to carry out work at the abbey that owned both churches.

Post-Dissolution history

The continuing impact of the four centuries of monastic ownership is apparent from the study of the landscape and the products and resources of the manor. In the case of the buildings the utilisation of the outer courtyard as the Brooke mansion (fig.18) has demonstrated the suitability of the abbot's quarters as the basis of a gentry house (cf. Dickinson 1968). Its surroundings continued to be dominated by the moats, millpond and drainage systems established centuries earlier. Even when a thorough break with the past was made by the erection of the Georgian country house (fig. 99) the west range of the priory was retained as the basement. Ultimately the house was

demolished, the west range undercroft was left standing, and this became the focus for the efforts to preserve and excavate the site in the 1970s. Its new role as part of a museum devoted to monastic life is the latest chapter in a story of eight centuries' duration.

Further research

Until the reawakening of interest in monastic archaeology in the 1970s it was widely assumed that there was little to be learnt from excavation that had not been already revealed by excavators such as St John Hope and Brakspear half a century and more earlier. In their different ways, excavations at Norton Priory and Bordesley Abbey have shown – on very different sites – how classes of information previously unrecognised can complement and extend the historical record. Further research at other monastic sites can therefore be of considerable value, provided that they are selected on the basis of their potential for answering some of the many questions that remain. Research topics range from the nature and purpose of early temporary buildings to the

Fig. 100. Norton Priory in 1974, from the air. The layout of the claustral ranges can clearly be seen. Excavation, consolidation of the foundations, landscaping and restoration of the undercroft are all in progress.

large scale investigation of a Gilbertine house – the field is very extensive indeed. Five principles however should govern such work:

1. It should be carried out on a large scale. Piecemeal excavation may be appropriate to solve specific problems at a previously excavated site, but to understand a particular monastery it is necessary to study the complete range of buildings from the church to the kitchens and the mill. Each will provide different classes of information.

2. It should be carried out over a number of years. This is an inevitable consequence of 1, but it has virtue in its own right. The very complexity of a monastic site requires considerable thought, the testing of hypotheses, and the input of 3 and 4. With the need to correlate disparate sources of information a rush to judgement would be mistaken.

3. The full range of scientific research should be available as part of the exercise. The value of such research will be apparent from this study – analysis of tile glazes, bell metal, pollen; identification of animal bones; radiocarbon dating; petrological studies, etc.

4. Historical research should parallel excavation and other archaeological work. The value of such research, even in the case of Norton where surviving information was slight, is clear from this study.

5. Any study should be made in the context of an investigation into surrounding earthwork and water management features, and the landscape in general.

Further research at Norton will continue on the classes of excavated material – publications on medieval tiles and the human remains are planned for the near future, with pottery, glass and other topics to follow. The potential for further excavation remains. The guest quarters and associated buildings have been studied most recently, but it is clear from excavation in 1984 that extensive remains of buildings exist still further to the south and west. The infirmary is still to be excavated. The extended chapter house, at present largely covered by trees, deserves detailed study. There is much to be learnt about the water management system. The 'early church' requires full investigation. As Norton has already been the subject of such an extensive investigation there is considerable virtue in renewed campaigns. The results of each particular part of the exercise are multiplied in value by the opportunities of correlation and comparison with information obtained since the large scale investigation began in April 1971 (fig. 100).

Bibliography

D'Ancona and Aeschlimann 1969
P. D'Ancona and E. Aeschlimann, *The Art of Illumination*, London
Anon. 1901
Duttons of Dutton, privately printed and published
Ashmore 1962
O. Ashmore, 'The Whalley Abbey bursar's account for 1540', *Trans Hist. Soc. Lancashire and Cheshire* 114, 51–2
Baker 1970
D. Baker, 'Excavations at Elstow Abbey, Bedfordshire, 1966–68', *Bedfordshire Archaeol. J.* 7, 27–41
Baker and Butlin 1973
A. R. H. Baker and R. A. Butlin, *Studies of Field Systems in the British Isles*, (includes G. Elliott 'Field systems of north west England', 41–92)
Barraclough 1957
G. Barraclough, *Early Cheshire Charters*, Oxford
Barraclough 1962
G. Barraclough, 'Some charters of the earls of Chester' in P. M. Barnes and C. F. Slade, *A Medieval Miscellany for Doris Mary Stenton*, Pipe Roll Soc., London
Beamont 1849
W. Beamont, *Warrington in 1465*, Chetham Soc.
Beamont 1873
W. Beamont, *A History of the Castle of Halton, and the Priory or Abbey of Norton*, Warrington
Beamont 1879
W. Beamont, *An Account of the Rolls of the Honour of Halton*, Warrington
Bennett 1972
M. J. Bennett, 'The Lancashire and Cheshire clergy 1379', *Trans. Hist. Soc. Lancashire and Cheshire* 124, 1–30
Beresford and Hurst 1971
M. W. Beresford and J. G. Hurst, *Deserted Medieval Villages*, Guildford and London
Beresford and St Joseph 1979
M. W. Beresford and J. K. St Joseph, *Medieval England: an aerial survey*, second edition, Cambridge

Binding 1977
G. Binding, 'Helzankerbalken im Mauerwerk mitterlalterlicher Burgen und Kirchen', *Château Gaillard* 8, 69–77
Binns 1934
L. E. Binns, *The Decline and Fall of the Medieval Papacy*
Blair, Lankester and West 1980
J. Blair, P. Lankester and J. West, 'A transitional cloister arcade at Haughmond Abbey, Shropshire', *Med. Archaeol.* 24, 210–13
Bond 1906
F. Bond, *Gothic Architecture in England*, London
Booth 1976
P. H. W. Booth, 'Taxation and public order: Cheshire 1353', *Nothern History* 12, 16–31
Booth and Dodd 1979
P. H. W. Booth and J. P. Dodd, 'The manor and fields of Frodsham', *Trans. Hist. Soc. Lancashire and Cheshire* 128, 27–57
Boutell 1847
C. Boutell, *Monumental Brasses and Slabs*, Oxford
Brakspear 1905
H. Brakspear, *Waverley Abbey*, Surrey Archaeological Society, Guildford
Brooke 1974
C. Brooke, *Monasteries of the World*, London
Brownbill 1914
J. Brownbill, *The Ledger Book of Vale Royal Abbey*, Lancs. and Cheshire Rec. Soc. 68
Bryant 1831
A. Bryant, *Map of the County Palatine of Chester*
Burdett 1777
P. P. Burdett, *A Survey of the County Palatine of Chester*, reprinted Hist. Soc. Lancashire and Cheshire Occ. Ser. 1, 1974
Burne 1962
R. V. H. Burne, *The Monks of Chester*, London
Butler 1982
L. A. S. Butler, 'The Cistercians in England and Wales: a survey of recent archaeological work 1960–1980' in M. P. Lillich, *Studies in Cistercian Art and Architecture*, Michigan, 88–101
Chambers 1966
D. S. Chambers, *Faculty Office Registers*, Oxford
Chesters 1962
G. Chesters, 'Power politics and roguery in Tudor Cheshire', *Cheshire Round* 1, no. 2
Clark 1897
J. W. Clark, *The Observances in Use at the Augustinian Priory of Barnwell, Cambridgeshire*, Cambridge
Clay 1949
C. T. Clay (ed.), *Early Yorkshire Charters* 8
Clayton 1929
M. Clayton, *Catalogue of Rubbings of Brasses and Incised Slabs*, Victoria and Albert Museum – HMSO, London reissued 1968
Coad 1969
J. G. Coad, *Hailes Abbey* guidebook, HMSO
Cook 1965
G. H. Cook, *Letters to Cromwell on the Suppression of the Monasteries*, London

Craster 1956
  O. E. Craster, *Tintern Abbey* guide book, HMSO
Craster 1963
  O. E. Craster, *Llanthony Priory* guidebook, HMSO
Crossley 1938
  F. H. Crossley, ' Cheshire churches in the twelfth century', *J. Chester Archaeol. Soc.* 32
Crossley 1949
  F. H. Crossley, *The English Abbey*, London (3rd edition)
Crossley 1976a
  P. Crossley, *Medieval and Early Renaissance Treasures in the North West* exhibition catalogue, Whitworth Art Gallery Manchester
Crossley 1976b
  P. Crossley, *Medieval Architecture and Sculpture in the North West*, Whitworth Art Gallery Manchester
Cunliffe 1977
  B. W. Cunliffe, *Portchester Castle 3, Medieval*, Soc. of Antiq. Res. Rep. 34: Augustinian priory, by A. Borg and D. Baker, 96–120
Darby 1973
  H. C. Darby, *A New Historical Geography of England*, Cambridge
Darby and Maxwell 1962
  H. C. Darby and L. S. Maxwell, *A Domesday Geography of Northern England*, Cambridge
Davey 1977
  P. J. Davey, *Medieval Pottery from Excavations in the North West*, Liverpool
Dickinson 1950
  J. C. Dickinson, *The Origins of the Austin Canons and their Introduction into England*, London
Dickinson 1956
  J. C. Dickinson, *The Shrine of Our Lady of Walsingham*, Cambridge
Dickinson 1965
  J. C. Dickinson, *Furness Abbey* guidebook, HMSO
Dickinson 1967
  J. C. Dickinson, 'Furness Abbey – an archaeological reconsideration', *Trans. Cumberland and Westmorland Archaeol. Soc.* 67, 51–80
Dickinson 1968
  J. C. Dickinson, 'The buildings of the English Austin canons after the Dissolution of the Monasteries', *J. British Archaeol. Assoc.* 3rd ser. 31, 60–75
Dimier 1962
  A. Dimier, *L'Art Cistercien*, Zodiaque, France
Dodgson 1970
  J. McNeil Dodgson, *The Place Names of Cheshire 2, Nantwich and Bucklow Hundreds*, English Place Name Society 45, Cambridge
Driver 1971
  J. T. Driver, *Cheshire in the Latter Middle Ages*, Chester
Drury and Pratt 1975
  P. J. Drury and G. D. Pratt, 'A late thirteenth- and early fourteenth-century tile factory at Danbury, Essex', *Med. Archaeol.* 19, 92–164
Dunn 1811
  J. Dunn, surveyor, 'Maps of sundry estates belonging to Sir Richard Brooke, Bart, surveyed in the years 1806–1811', MS book, Cheshire Record Office, DPB (part) 1443 Potts collection
Eames 1975
  E. S. Eames, 'The fourteenth-century tile paving at Higham Ferrers', *Northants. Past and Present* 5 no. 3, 199–209
Eames 1980
  E. S. Eames, *Catalogue of Medieval Lead Glazed Earthenware Tiles*, London
Eames and Keen 1972
  E. S. Eames and L. Keen, 'Some line impressed tile mosaics from western England and Wales', *J. British Archaeol. Assoc.* 3rd ser 35, 65–70
Ekwall 1960
  E. Ekwall, *Concise Oxford Dictionary of English Place Names* 4th ed. Oxford
Farrer, 1914, 1915, 1916
  W. Farrer, *Early Yorkshire Charters* 1, 1914; 2, 1915; 3, 1916
Farrer 1924
  W. Farrer, *Honors and Knights' Fees 2*
Fergusson 1983
  P. Fergusson 'The first architecture of the Cistercians in England and the work of Abbot Adam of Meaux', *J. British Archaeol. Assoc.* 136, 74–86
Fernie 1985
  E. C. Fernie 'Anglo-Saxon lengths: the "Northern" System, the perch and the foot', *Archaeol J.* 142, 246–54
Fishwick 1896
  H. Fishwick, 'Pleadings and dispositions at the Duchy Court of Lancaster', *Lancs. and Cheshire Rec. Soc.* 32, i, 64
Franklin 1983
  J. Franklin, 'The Romanesque cloister sculpture at Norwich Cathedral Priory' in Thompson 1983, 56–70
Gardner 1951
  A. Gardner, *English Medieval Sculpture*, Cambridge
Gasquet 1902
  F. A. Gasquet, *Henry VIII and the English Monasteries*, London
Geddes 1983
  J. Geddes, 'Recently discovered Romanesque sculpture in south east England' in Thompson 1983, 90–7
Gilyard-Beer 1959
  R. Gilyard-Beer, *Abbeys, an Introduction*, London
Gilyard-Beer 1960
  R. Gilyard-Beer, *Cleeve Abbey* guidebook, HMSO
Gilyard-Beer 1981
  R. Gilyard-Beer, 'Boxley Abbey and the *pulpitum collationis*' in A. Detsicas (ed.), *Collectanea Historica*, Kent Archaeol. Soc., Maidstone, 123–31
Gilyard-Beer and Coppack 1986
  R. Gilyard-Beer and G. Coppack, 'Excavations at Fountains Abbey, North Yorkshire, 1979–80: the early development of the monastery', *Archaeologia* 108, 147–88
Greene 1975
  J. P. Greene, 'Norton Priory, history for a New Town', *Museums J.* 75, Sept., 75–7

Greene 1979
J. P. Greene, 'The elevation of Norton Priory, Cheshire, to the status of mitred abbey', *Trans. Hist. Soc. Lancashire and Cheshire* 128, 97–112

Greene 1980
J. P. Greene, 'Tile making at Norton Priory', *Popular Archaeology* June, 41–4

Greene 1981
J. P. Greene, 'Experimental archaeology in England', *Archaeology* 34 No. 6, Archaeological Institute of America, Nov.–Dec., 24–31

Greene 1983
J. P. Greene 'The new museum at Norton Priory, Cheshire', *Museums J.* 82, 4, March, 219–22

Greene and Hough 1977
J. P. Greene and P. R. Hough 'Excavation in the medieval village of Norton 1974–1976', *J. Chester Archaeol. Soc.* 60, 61–93

Greene and Johnson 1978
J. P. Greene and B. Johnson, 'An experimental tile kiln at Norton Priory, Cheshire', *Med. Ceramics* 2, 30–41

Greene, Keen and Noake 1976
J. P. Greene, L. Keen and B. Noake, 'The decorated mosaic tile floor from Warrington Friary: a reassessment', *J. Chester Archaeol. Soc.* 59, 52–9

Greene and Noake 1977
J. P. Greene and B. Noake, 'Norton Priory' in P. J. Davey (ed.), *Medieval Pottery from Excavations in the North West*, Liverpool, 54–9

Hartley and Elliot 1925
D. Hartley and M. M. Elliot, *Life and Work of the People of England*, published in several parts in two volumes, London, from 1925

Heath 1973
P. Heath, *Bishop Blythe's Visitations*, Staffordshire Record Society 4th ser. 7

Henry and Zarnecki 1958
F. Henry and G. Zarnecki, 'Romanesque arches decorated with human and animal heads', *J. British Archaeol. Assoc.* 3rd ser. 21, 1–34

Hewitt 1967
H. J. Hewitt, *Cheshire under the Three Edwards*, Chester

Hibbert 1910
F. A. Hibbert, *The Dissolution of the Monasteries of Staffordshire*

Higham 1982
N. J. Higham, 'Bucklow Hundred: the Domesday Survey and the rural community', *Cheshire Archaeol. Bull.* 8, 15–21

Hirst, Walsh and Wright 1983
S. M. Hirst, D. A. Walsh and S. M. Wright, *Bordesley Abbey* 2, Oxford, B.A.R. British Series 111

Hobhouse 1880
Bishop Hobhouse, *Bishop Norbury's Registers 1322–1358*, Staffordshire Collections 1, 241–88

Hodgson 1907
T. H. Hodgson, 'Excavations at Holm Cultram', *Trans. Cumberland and Westmorland Antiq. and Archaeol. Soc.* new ser. 7, 262–8

Hope and Brakspear 1909
W. H. Hope and H. Brakspear, 'Haughmond Abbey', *Archaeol. J.* 66, 281–310

Hough 1978
P. R. Hough, 'Excavations at Beeston Castle 1975–1977', *J. Chester Archaeol. Soc.* 61, 1–23

Husain 1973
B. M. C. Husain, *Cheshire under the Norman Earls 1066–1237*, Chester

Hutton 1847
W. A. Hutton, *Whalley Abbey Coucher Book*, Chetham Society 10 and 11, 1847; 16, 1848; 20, 1849

J. E. 1757
J. E. (initials only), surveyor, 'A map of the Manor and Lordship of Norton' surveyed 1757. Warrington Public Library local history collection, loaned and displayed at Norton Priory Museum

Jones 1957
D. Jones, *The Church in Chester 1300–1540*, Chetham Society 3rd ser. 7

Kahn 1983
D. Kahn, 'Recent discoveries in Romanesque sculpture at St Albans' in Thompson 1983, 71–89

Keen 1969
L. Keen, 'A series of seventeenth- and eighteenth-century lead-glazed relief tiles from North Devon', *J. British Archaeol. Assoc.* 32, 144–78

Keen 1970
L. Keen, 'A fourteenth-century tile pavement at Meesden, Herts.', *Hertfordshire Archaeol.* 2

Keen 1979
L. Keen, 'The fourteenth-century tile pavements in Prior Crauden's chapel and in the south transept', *Medieval Art and Architecture at Ely Cathedral*, British Archaeological Association, 47–57

Keen and Thackray 1974
L. Keen and D. Thackray, 'A fourteenth-century mosaic tile pavement with line impressed decoration from Icklingham', *Proc. Suffolk Inst. Archaeol.* 33 pt 2, 153–67

King 1656
D. King, *Vale Royall of England*

Knowles 1948, 1955, 1959
D. Knowles, *The Religious Orders in England* 1, 2 and 3 Cambridge, 1948, 1955 and 1959

Knowles, Brooke and London 1972
D. Knowles, C. N. L. Brooke and V. London, *The Heads of Religious Houses, England and Wales 940–1216*

Knowles and Hadcock 1971
D. Knowles and R. N. Hadcock, *Religious Houses of England and Wales*, 2nd ed., London

Knowles and St Joseph 1952
D. Knowles and J. K. St. Joseph, *Religious Houses from the Air*, Cambridge

Leigh 1700
Leigh, *Natural History of Lancashire*

Leycester 1666
P. Leycester, *Cheshire Antiquities*

Losco-Bradley and Salisbury 1979
P. M. Losco-Bradley and C. R. Salisbury, 'A medieval fish

weir at Colwick, Nottinghamshire', *Transactions of the Thoroton Society* 83, 15–22

Lyons 1884
P. A. Lyons, *Two Compoti of Henry de Lacy*, Chetham Society 112

Lysons 1810
D. and S. Lysons, *Magna Britannia*, London, vol. 2

McCarthy 1971
M. McCarthy, 'The Naish Hill Kilns, an interim report', *Wiltshire Archaeol. Mag.* 66, 179–81

McNeil 1983
R. McNeil, 'Two twelfth-century Wich Houses in Nantwich, Cheshire', *Med. Archaeol*, 27, 40–88

Malet 1977
H. Malet, *Bridgewater, the Canal Duke, 1736–1803*, Manchester

Middleton 1880
J. H. Middleton, 'Stanley St. Leonards, the college of canons and the collegiate church', *Trans. Bristol and Gloucester Archaeol. Soc.* 5, 1–14

Moore, Hooper and Davis 1967
N. W. Moore, M. D. Hooper and B. N. K. Davis, 'Hedges: introduction and reconnaissance studies', *J. Applied Ecol.* 4, 210–20

Moorman 1945
J. R. H. Moorman, *Lanercost Priory* guidebook

Morris 1894
R. H. Morris, *Chester during the Plantagenet and Tudor Periods*, Chester

Nickson 1887
Nickson, *The History of Runcorn*, Runcorn

Ormerod 1882
G. Ormerod, *The History of the County Palatine and City of Chester*, 2 vols., 2nd ed. by T. Helsby

Parker 1845–6
J. H. Parker, *Glossary of Gothic Architecture*, 4th ed., Oxford, 1 and 2, 1845; 3, 1846

Parker 1874
J. H. Parker, *Introduction to Gothic Architecture*, 4th ed., Oxford

Peers 1952
C. Peers, *Byland Abbey* guidebook, HMSO

Peers 1967
C. Peers, *Rievaulx Abbey* guidebook, HMSO

Peers, no date a
C. Peers, *Finchale Priory* leaflet, HMSO

Peers, no date b
C. Peers, *Kirkham Priory* leaflet, HMSO

Penney 1982
S. H. Penney with J. P. Greene and B. Noake, 'Excavations at Lancaster Friary 1980–1', *Contrebis* 10, 1–13

Pevsner 1963
N. Pevsner, *The Buildings of England – Herefordshire*, Harmondsworth

Pevsner 1968
N. Pevsner, *The Buildings of England – Worcestershire*, Harmondsworth

Pevsner 1969
N. Pevsner, *The Buildings of England – North Lancashire*, Harmondsworth

Pevsner and Cherry 1977
N. Pevsner and B. Cherry, *The Buildings of England – Hertfordshire*, Harmondsworth

Pevsner and Hubbard 1971
N. Pevsner and E. Hubbard, *The Buildings of England – Cheshire*, Harmondsworth

Phillimore 1912
W. P. W. Phillimore, *The Rolls of Hugh of Wells, Bishop of Lincoln, 1209–1235*, Lincoln Record Society 3

Platt 1969
C. Platt, *The Monastic Grange in Medieval England*, London

Platt 1984
C. Platt, *The Abbeys and Priories of Medieval England*, London

Raby and Reynolds 1952
F. J. E. Raby and P. K. B. Reynolds, *Castle Acre Priory* guidebook, HMSO

Raby and Reynolds 1970
F. J. E. Raby and P. K. B. Reynolds, *Thetford Priory* guidebook, HMSO, reprinted 1970

Rackham 1976
O. Rackham, *Trees and Woodland in the British Landscape*, London

Radford 1952
C. A. R. Radford, *Ewenny Priory* guidebook, HMSO

Radford 1953
C. A. R. Radford, *Valle Crucis* guidebook, HMSO

Randle Holme Sketch
Randle Holme, sketch plan of Norton Abbey, B.L. Harleian MSS 2073. A family tree of the Brooke family on the reverse indicates that the sketch must date from the time of the second baronet, *i.e* between 1664 and 1678

Reynolds 1946
P. K. B. Reynolds, *Croxden Abbey* leaflet, HMSO

Richards 1973
R. Richards, *Old Cheshire Churches*, 2nd ed., Manchester

Rickman 1862
T. Rickman, *Gothic Architecture*, 6th ed. enlarged by J. H. Parker, Oxford

Rigold 1969
S. E. Rigold, *Lilleshall Abbey, Shropshire* guidebook, HMSO

Roberts 1972
B. K. Roberts, 'Village plans in County Durham: a preliminary statement', *Med. Archaeol* 16, 33–56

Roberts 1977
B. K. Roberts, *Rural Settlement in Britain*, London

Robinson 1980
D. M. Robinson, *The Geography of Augustinian Settlement*, B.A.R. British Series 80

Ryder 1959
M. L. Ryder, 'Report on the animal remains, Kirkstall Abbey', *Pub. Thoresby Soc.* 48

Ryder 1965
M. L. Ryder, ''Report on the animal remains'' (appendix H) in C. V. Bellamy 'Pontefract Priory Excavations', *Pub. Thoresby Soc.* 49

Salisbury 1980
  C. R. Salisbury, 'The Trent, the story of a river', *Current Archaeology* 8 no.3, 88–91
Salter 1922
  H. E. Salter, *Chapters of the Augustinian Canons*, Oxford Hist. Soc. Pub. 74
Sawyer 1976
  P. H. Sawyer (ed.), *Medieval Settlement – Continuity and Change*, London
Sawyer 1978
  P. H. Sawyer, *From Roman Britain to Norman England*, London
Selby 1882
  W. D. Selby, 'Lancashire and Cheshire records in the Public Record Office', *Lancs. and Cheshire Rec. Soc. 7*
Sherwood and Pevsner 1974
  J. Sherwood and N. Pevsner, *The Buildings of England – Oxfordshire*, Harmondsworth
Singleton 1978
  B. Singleton, 'The remodelling of the east end of Worcester Cathedral in the earlier part of the thirteenth century', *Medieval Art and Architecture at Worcester Cathedral*, British Archaeological Association, 105–15
Smith 1956
  A. H. Smith, *English Place-Name Elements*, English Place-Name Society 26, Cambridge
Speed 1610
  J. Speed, *Map of the County Palatine of Chester*
Stalley 1971
  R. A. Stalley, *Architecture and Sculpture in Ireland 1150–1350*, Dublin
Starkey 1980
  H. F. Starkey, *Runcorn in Times Past 1980*
Stewart-Brown 1911
  R. Stewart-Brown, 'Maps and plans of Liverpool by the Eyes family', *Trans. Hist. Soc. Lancashire and Cheshire* new ser. 26, 143–74
Stewart-Brown 1934
  R. Stewart-Brown, *Cheshire Inquisitions Post-Mortem 1603–1660*, Lancs. and Cheshire Rec. Soc.
Stone 1955
  L. Stone, *Sculpture in Britain in the Middle Ages*, Harmondsworth
Swynnerton 1921
  C. Swynnerton, 'The Priory of St Leonard of Stanley, Co. Gloucester . . .', *Archaeologia* 51, 199–226
Swynnerton 1929
  C. Swynnerton, 'The Priory of St Leonard of Stanley, Gloucestershire, a continuation', *Antiq. J.* 9, 12–28
Sylvester 1958
  D. Sylvester, 'A note on the medieval three-course arable system in Cheshire', *Trans. Hist. Soc. Lancashire and Cheshire* 110, 183–6
Tait 1916
  J. Tait, *The Domesday Survey of Cheshire*, Chetham Society 75
Tait 1920
  J. Tait, *Chartulary of the Abbey of St Werburgh, Chester*, Chetham Society 79 and 82

Tait 1939
  J. Tait, 'The Foundation Charter of Runcorn (later Norton) Priory', *Chetham Society Miscellany* new ser. 100, 1–26
Tanner 1787
  Tanner, *Notitia Monastica*
Taylor 1912
  M. V. Taylor 'Chester: some notes relating to the abbey and other religious houses of Cheshire', *J. Chester and N. Wales Archaeol. Soc.* 19 (2), 162–96
Taylor 1973
  W. T. Taylor, *Hexham Abbey 674–1973* guidebook, Hexham
Thompson 1939
  A. H. Thompson, 'Lanercost Priory', *Archaeol. J.* 96, 323
Thompson 1948
  A. H. Thompson, *Easby Abbey* guidebook, HMSO
Thompson 1967
  F. H. Thompson, 'Norton Priory, near Runcorn, Cheshire', *Archaeol. J.* 123, 62–8
Thompson 1983
  F. H. Thompson (ed.), *Studies in Medieval Sculpture*, Soc. of Antiq. Occ. Paper (new ser.) 3, London
Tithe Map 1843
  Henry White, surveyor, of Warrington, *Tithe Apportionment Map, Township of Norton*, Cheshire Record Office EDT 307/2
Watkin 1914
  T. Watkin 'The use of the Norse standard of measurement . . . at Torre Abbey', *Trans. Devonshire Assoc.* 46, 326–45
Webb 1956
  G. Webb, *Architecture in Britain – the Middle Ages*, Harmondsworth
Webb 1970
  A. N. Webb, *The Cartulary of Burscough Priory*, Chetham Society 3rd ser. 18
Webster and Cherry 1975
  L. E. Webster and J. Cherry, 'Medieval Britain in 1974', *Med. Archaeol.* 19, 220–60
Webster and Cherry 1980
  L. E. Webster and J. Cherry, 'Medieval Britain in 1979', *Med. Archaeol.* 24, 218–64
Whitelock 1965
  D. Whitelock, *The Anglo-Saxon Chronicle*, London
Wilcox 1982
  R. P. Wilcox, *Timber and Iron Reinforcement in Early Buildings*, Soc. of Antiq. Occ. Paper (new ser.) 2
Wilson 1983
  C. Wilson 'The original setting of the Apostle and Prophet figures from St Mary's Abbey, York' in Thompson, 1983, 100–21
Woodward 1894
  J. Woodward, *Ecclesiastical Heraldry*
Zarnecki 1951
  G. Zarnecki, *English Romanesque Sculpture 1066–1140*, London
Zarnecki 1953
  G. Zarnecki, *Later English Romanesque Sculpture 1140–1210*, London

Index

clerical poll tax, 65
Clifton, Cheshire, 29; land, 4, 5; manor, 38
cloister arcade, C13 rebuilding, 63, 110–18, 155, figs. 58–63; C16
    rebuilding, 148–51, fig. 98
coal, 92
Cobham, Kent, brass, 142
coffins, sandstone, figs. 7, 8, 11, 74–9; wooden, 56; in Runcorn
    church, 16; in Daresbury chapel, 16
Coggeshall, Cheshire, 17
Colchester, Essex, Aug. priory, 2
Combermere, Cheshire, Cist. abbey, 65
Conishead, Cumbria, Aug. priory, 66
corbel tables, C12, 90, 91, fig. 39
corrodies, 15, 53, 64
Coventry and Lichfield, diocese, 65
Creake, Norfolk, Aug. abbey, fire, 153
Cromwell, Thomas, 70–2
Crowland, Lincs., Ben. abbey, drainage, 152
Croxden, Staffs., Cist. abbey, 90, 122; cloister, 150, 151
Cuerdley, Lancs., rights of common, 3

dairying, 52
Danbury, Essex, tile kiln, 136
Danyers, William, of Daresbury, benefactor, 16
Daresbury, chapel of, 16, 31, 57; township, 30
Dee, river, 50
deer, 6, 53
Deerhurst, Glos., church, 91
Delamere Forest, grant of timber, 19, 57, 69, 151, 153; timber for
    Vale Royal, 73
Derby, house, 6
Dieulacres, Staffs., Cist. abbey, 53
Dissolution of Norton, 14, 69–72, 111, 145–51, 156
Diva, Ralph de, prior of Hospitallers, 16
dogs, 53, 54
Domesday book, 28, 29, 41, 46, 49, 152
Donnington, *see* Castle Donnington
Droitwich, Worcs., church, sculpture, 118
Dublin, Christ Church cathedral, sculpture, 118
Dutton family, benefactors of Norton Priory, 4, 6, 9–15, 63, 102, 154,
    155; burials, 10–14, 86, 128, 130, 140, figs. 9–11; coat of arms
    13, 14, 128, 140, fig. 11; disputes with canons, 64, 143, 144;
    pedigree, 15; tiles, 128, 140, 143, 144
Dutton, Adam de, benefactor, 9, 45, 47
Dutton, Lawrence de, burial at Norton Priory, 10, 128
Dutton, Sir Lawrence de, burial at Norton Priory, 10, 14, 53, 69, 128,
    130
Dutton, Sir Piers, Augmentations Office commissioner, 14, 17, 19, 71;
    suppression of Norton and dispute with Sir William Brereton, 35,
    69–72, 151
Dutton, Sir Thomas, founder of Warrington friary, 65
Dutton, Cheshire, manor house, 9; chapel, 10

Eanley, Cheshire, 15, 25, 29, 45–7, 72
Easby, Yorks., Premon. abbey, 105
Edward I, taxation, 17; commandeering transport, 53; Vale Royal,
    130, 131
Edward III, charter, 6
elevation of Norton to abbey, 65–8, 144, 145, 153, 154
Elstow, Beds., Ben. nunnery, 109
Ely, Cambs., Ben. cathedral priory, 103; sculpture, 116, 118; lady
    chapel, 124, 130; prior Crauden's chapel, tiles, 142–4, 155
enclosure, fields, 42–5
environmental evidence, 25, 38
Eugenius IV, pope, 69
Eustace fitz John, 4th baron of Halton, benefaction, 5, 89, 93, 154;
    burial, 7
Ewenny, Glam., Ben. abbey, 85, 86
Exeter, Devon, cathedral, lady chapel, 130

farms, established after Dissolution, 31
Felday, Piers, forger and perjuror, 70
field systems, 23, 41–6

Finchale, Co. Durham, Ben. cell, 78, 87
fish bones, 49, 50
fish ponds, 50
fisheries, 29, 49, 50, 55
flax, 61
flooding, 31, 64, 67, 153
Forde, Dorset, Cist. abbey, 116
forgery, 19, 70
Fountains, Yorks., Cist. abbey, foundation, 3, 5; plan, 73, 74, 81, 85,
    86, 107, 109; arcade, 116
fraterer, 61, 62
Fraunkevylle, Thopmas de, prior of Norton, 64
Frodsham, Cheshire, land, 10, 17; deanery, 14, 17, 19, 71; market,
    152; royal manor of, 31, 55
fulling mill, 51
Furness, Cumbria, Savignac abbey, 3, 62, 109

Gant, Walter de, 2
Gaunt, John of, duke of Lancaster, 9, 65, 66
Gernons, Randle, earl of Chester, 5
Glastonbury, Som., Ben. abbey, drainage, 153
glebe land, 20
Gloucester, Ben. cathedral abbey, 85; lady chapel, 130
Grand Junction Railway, 23, fig. 12
granges, 19–21, 152
Grappenhall, church, 16, 19, 68, 154
Great Budworth, Cheshire, church, 4, 10, 19, 66, 67, 72, 154; lady
    chapel, 130; land, 9, 19
Great Malvern, Worcs., priory, lady chapel, 130
Great Schism, 66
Gregorian reform movement, 2
Grosvenor, Sir Robert de, 65
Guilden Sutton, leases, 20; manor, tithes, 3, 5, 6, 17, 19; mill, 17

Hadstock, Essex, bell pit, 120
Hailes, Glos., Cist. abbey, shrine, 130
Halton, barony of, 1, 5; castle, 57, 72, 89; land, 10; manor, 51;
    market, 152; mill, 3; fisheries, 3; rights of common, 3; tithes, 6;
    name, 29; township, 45
Halton, barons of, relations with priory, 6–9, 63, 110, 154
Hatton, branch of Dutton family, 14
Haughmond, Salop., Aug. abbey, 145; plan, 85, 86, 89, 109, 148;
    cloister, 116, 117; doorway, 103
Hayton, Cumbria, 42
hedge dating, 45
hemp, 61
Henry I, founder of Aug. houses, 2
Henry II, charter, 5
Henry IV, confirmation of Norton's abbey status, 66; act, 67
Henry VIII, grant of timber, 14, 19, 57
Henry, prior of Norton, 63
herbs, 61
Hereford, cathedral, 100, 130
Hexham, Northumberland, Aug. priory, 2, 71
Higham Ferrers, Northants., tiles, 144
Home Cultram, Cumbria, Cist. abbey, tiles, 144
horses, 53
Hugh, son of Odard, founder benefactor, 4
hunting, 15, 47, 53

Icklingham, Cambs., tiles, 144
Iffley, Oxon., church, 91
Ilmington, Glos., 42
Ince, Cheshire, marshland, 31
infirmary orchard, 37, 61
Ireland, ship to, 64

James I, king, 53
Jerpoint, Co. Kilkenny, Ireland, Cist. abbey, 150, 151
John XXII, pope, 31, 64
John fitz Richard, 6th baron of Halton, 7

Keckwick, Cheshire, 9, 30; mill, 10, 57